To Mum + Dad
at Christmas 1990

lots of love
Tiftie
xx

The Story of Bowls

THE
STORY OF BOWLS

From Drake to Bryant

Edited by
Phil Pilley

STANLEY PAUL
London Melbourne Auckland Johannesburg

Stanley Paul & Co. Ltd

An imprint of Century Hutchinson Ltd

62–65 Chandos Place, London WC2N 4NW

Century Hutchinson Australia (Pty) Ltd
PO Box 496, 16–22 Church Street, Hawthorn, Melbourne, Victoria 3122

Century Hutchinson New Zealand Limited
PO Box 40-086, Glenfield, Auckland 10

Century Hutchinson South Africa (Pty) Ltd
PO Box 337, Bergvlei 2012, South Africa

First published 1987
© Phil Pilley 1987

Set in Sabon by Rowland Phototypesetting Ltd
Bury St Edmunds, Suffolk

Printed in Great Britain by Redwood Burn Ltd
Trowbridge and bound by
WBC Bookbinders Ltd
Maesteg

British Library Cataloguing in Publication Data

The story of bowls: from Drake to Bryant
1. Bowling on the green—History
I. Pilley, Phil
796.31   GV909

ISBN 0 09 166380 6

Contents

To Bob Farrall, who taught me the fun, though not all the skill, of cricket – and who now, I believe, derives even more enjoyment from bowls.

Acknowledgements

Every reasonable effort has been made to trace the ownership of copyrighted material and to make due acknowledgement. Any errors or omissions will be gladly rectified in future editions.

I must thank many authors and publishers for their kind permission to quote their material. Where modern newspapers and magazines are concerned I have given, where known, the sources alongside the name of the authors following the relevant passages. Additional acknowledgements are due to the following book publishers, etc.:

Godfrey R. Bolsover, OBE, TD. for the historical passage (p. 38), comment on Drake Legend (p. 68), 'One Magic Hour' (p. 30) and story of Ben Baker (p. 207) from his *Who's Who & Encyclopedia of Bowls* (1959); *Southern Newspapers* for the history of Southampton Old Green (p. 39); Liss Printers for 'Clear as Iron and Gravel' (p. 70) and passage about Boules (p. 174) from *The Game of Boules*; Prentice-Hall Inc for 'The Forgotten Bowl' (p. 193) and 'The Old Order Changeth' (p. 208) from *Bowls* by Douglas Lampshire; Ronnie Harper, *Belfast Telegraph*, for the passage re modern bowls (p. 22) from an Irish BA brochure; Allen & Unwin for 'A Countryman in Town' from *W. G. Grace – His Life and Times* (p. 103); The Normal Press for the introductory passage on p. 34, legend of the origin of bias (p. 50), passage re Drake (p. 67) and 'Hong Kong – Wartime Struggle' (p. 170) from *World Bowls*; Robert Hale Ltd for the passage re history (p. 38) from *Encyclopedia of Bowls*; John D. Vose for sundry writings on crown green from *Corner to Corner*; Century Hutchinson Ltd for 'Tough for Pirrett' (p. 195) and 'Bosisto – Four Times Champion' (p. 210) from *Bowling Along*; 'Dignity Regained' (p. 28), 'The 99 to One Shot' (p. 197) and 'I looked a "Mug" – But We Won!' (p. 198) from *Tackle Bowls This Way* and passages by Algy Allen, C. M. Jones, Jack Jones and Percy Baker ('Great Players, Great Matches' and 'Miscellany' sections); Grafton Books and A. D. Peters & Co Ltd for the passage from Stephen Potter's *The Theory & Practice of Gamesmanship* (p. 269); Wm. Heinemann Ltd for 'Brimble – The Looker-Ahead' (p. 213), 'Bryant – Uncanny Mastery' (p. 220) and 'Indoors and Outdoors' (p. 276) from *Indoor Bowls*, and 'A King's Laws' (p. 77) and passages in 'Era of the Amateur' and 'A Gentle Game for Girls' from Felix Hotchkiss's *The Game of Bowls*; Faber and Faber Ltd for 'He's Got Me!' (p. 191) from *Bowls – How to Become a Champion* and passages on women's bowls, firing and temperament by John W. Fisher from *A New Way to Better Bowls*; A. P. Watt Ltd (for the Trustees of the Wodehouse Trust No. 3 and Century Hutchinson Ltd) for the passage from *The Man with Two Left Feet* (p. 278); Thomas Nelson & Sons Ltd for 'Snedden's Last Bowl' (p. 184) and the passage on temperament (p. 267) from *Bowls for All*; Ward and Foxlow Ltd for passages by Robert

Stanley, Peggy King, Jack Jones and Cecil Hall from *The Bowls News*; The Bodley Head for 'Imperial, Imperious England!' (p. 104), the passage re Australia (p. 159) and 'Their Presence Not Too Welcome' (p. 128) from *A History of the Game of Bowls*; Macmillan Publishing Co Inc for 'Toddler Fan to Champion' (p. 26), 'Concentration Lost, Gold Medal Won' (p. 201), and 'A Three-Minute Measure' (p. 199) from *Bryant on Bowls*; Golden Eagle Books, Dublin, for the passage re road bowling (p. 175) from *Come Day, Go Day*; Longman Group for the passages from *Gauvinier Takes to Bowls* (p. 23 and 176); Willie Wood and David Cutler for the descriptions of how they began playing (p. 33); Wilke and Co Ltd, Melbourne, for the passage re temperament (p. 265) by R. H. Harrison from *How to Become a Champion at Bowls*; Angus and Robertson Ltd for 'Mixed Reception' by Dorothy Honeybone (p. 134) from *Lawn Bowls – The Australian Way*; Howard Timmins Ltd, S. Africa, for 'Look Here, Young Man!' (p. 32) from *The Bowling Companion*; Wolfe Publishing Co, Australia, for 'Bumps in the Wrong Places' (p. 130), 'Matters of Dress' (p. 135) and 'The New Aggressive Look' (p. 209), from *The Modern Approach to Bowls*; *The Listener* for 'The Team's the Thing' (p. 120); Donald Newby, editor of the new *Bowler's Times*, for much help and reproduction of his own writings.

Photographic Acknowledgements

For permission to reproduce copyright photographs the author and publishers would like to thank Duncan Cubitt/*Bowls International*, Stephen Line, C. Mills, G. Webster, Photo Source, *Blackpool Gazette and Herald*, Illustrated London News Picture Library, The Mansell Collection, Mary Evans Picture Library, The National Library of Scotland and Towner Art Gallery, Eastbourne.

Foreword
by Tony Allcock

There is a story that I was born on the bowling green, but it isn't strictly true! What *is* true is that I was 'carried' on the green! My mother continued to play competitively during pregnancy and in fact won a competition. I gather I was born some time between the third round and the quarter-final, so I think I could call that my first tournament win!

My mother, Joan, played for England in the late 1970s and my father for Leicestershire for a number of years, including 1964 when his county won the Middleton Cup. Their club was Goodwood (Leicester), but my earliest years tended to be spent with other children across the fence from there in an open-air lido. A little later I got into show jumping, competing in gymkhanas and pony-club events, but occasionally I still went along to the club and gradually grew interested in the game watching and supporting Mother. I was far more nervous watching her than I have been in any of my championships.

I decided I wanted to play and soon grew desperately keen. Occasionally I would try my skill with some old lignums on rough pieces of ground, perhaps by the flower bed at the side of the green or on a cricket pitch. A boy of twelve was just not allowed to play on the green, let alone join the club, but at fourteen I joined the Fosseway club in Syston (Leicestershire) as a junior. It was a small club, with frequent opportunities to play in matches, and in my first season I won the four major club titles, going on from strength to strength.

An old gentleman in his seventies called Len Hardyman was in many ways an influence on my career. We used to catch the bus from the village where I lived and travel to the next village to play. We had some great fun, but he never coached me. I do not remember ever having a coaching lesson, but perhaps that reflects on my delivery! I think a lot of my delivery and quick 'snatching' derive from the number of bowls I used to deliver as a lad on my mother and father's long lawn beyond their bungalow which I used as a bowling green. I played many, many international matches there, playing everybody's bowls, my team's and the opposition's. I would play from dawn to dusk and even in frost and snow: indeed it was jolly good in the frost because the ground was so hard the green was a lot faster than normal. It was great experience, playing all the shots and learning how to build the head. My parents didn't push me, they adopted the correct attitude: if I was going to take up the game they knew I would do it my way.

Bowls has often been misunderstood and for many years its progress was inhibited by its 'old-man's-game' label. Until recently it was a participant, not a spectator sport, but fortunately it has now been shown on TV screens in most households and people are realizing there is more to the game than first meets the eye. It is now a sport for all: for all ages and for handicapped and able-bodied alike. Old habits die hard, but the stigma that seemed attached to it through being regarded as purely for old people is quickly vanishing. While the public image of the game has changed, the enjoyment, comradeship and respect among players remains as strong today as ever. A lot of people questioned whether this would change with the introduction of prize money and televised events, but . . . yes, bowls can be highly competitive but also it can be one of the friendliest and most enjoyable of games, still maintaining the etiquette for which it has always been renowned.

Now, as one of the 'new-breed' generation of bowlers, I am delighted to write a foreword to this anthology, which is unequalled among the bowls books I have on my shelf at home. How different this one is: refreshing and unique; a book that can be compulsive consecutive reading or be taken in the car and picked up and read 'in bits' while waiting for the wife to finish her shopping in Sainsbury's!

Many books have been written on technique, tactics and the general principles of play but this one gives us great depth and insight into our game, and certainly is complementary to those instructional publications. All too often in any sport we take things for granted: we do things *because* they have been done and don't really know *why* they've been done. This book helps remedy that. It isn't straightforward history; it is a collection of various writings that will make the bowls library complete.

The editor is obviously very enthusiastic and, really, I am amazed at the content within his anthology. What a delight it is for me to read information about fellow players and great friends such as David

Bryant and Willie Wood that perhaps I should already have known. I am also fascinated with the section which includes the quotations from Shakespeare; and being a member of the flat-green code, indoor and out, in England, I have found it absorbing to read writings on crown green and bowls elsewhere. I think sometimes I and others become very insular in looking at the game as though it were just played in Britain.

And this book, like bowls, is not just for males, and I am sure at least one passage in the section on 'A Graceful Game for Girls' will cause a laugh as well as interest for both women and men. Perhaps it's just as well that the publisher of Mr Frank Soars, who makes a comment about 'bumps in the wrong places,' lives Down Under, because were he over here I think a lot of angry British ladies would be on his trail!

I wholeheartedly recommend every bowler to read this anthology to get a complete picture of the game.

To cure the mind's wrong bias, spleen,
Some recommend the bowling-green;
Some hilly walks; all, exercise;
Fling but a stone, the giant dies.
Laugh and be well.

Matthew Green (1696–1737)

Introduction

In the boiler-room bowels and Victorian halls of the two best sports libraries in Britain lie sixty-two volumes on bowls. Twenty-six are essentially instructional, eleven generally historical and seven are official handbooks. Of the remainder, three concentrate on specific ancient periods, four are encyclopedic, three concern crown green, two are biographical and two fictional; and the rest are devoted to eccentric, albeit related, overseas pastimes.

This book fits into none of these categories. It is an anthology of writings about bowls – not only from the sixty-two library volumes but from countless other publications and documents, sporting and social. And it gives the reader an option: dip in and out, reading a few morsels at a time, or read the book from beginning to end. If the reader elects to play the latter hand he will, incidentally, get a good idea of the game's history because the contents are arranged in roughly chronological order. However, this is not an academic history, let alone a record book.

What I have done is combed the literature of sport and beyond, selected pieces of value about bowls and shuffled them into a logical sequence. Although the various writings, long and short, combine to *convey* history there are cracks in between, gaps in the story, questions unanswered and topics left in the air. At times I have interposed editorially, but only when I felt it essential; having ordained my order of play, I have preferred to let the authors, reporters, essayists and poets speak for themselves. At times it becomes almost a dialogue between them; at least it is unique.

How did I make my selection? I culled what interested, amused, entertained or surprised me. I looked first for good writing, irrespective of the importance of the subject; but I selected also pieces that told me interesting or significant things about bowls and bowlers, and if those pieces were sufficiently scholarly I lowered the literary standard in order to include them. Nobody can find literary merit in past laws of the game, but in a few cases they have been added because otherwise writings about them would have lolled in a vacuum.

Wherever possible I have chosen writings contemporary with the subjects, though sometimes it has been necessary to utilize the work of later authors where theirs seemed the best and most scholarly summing up of given situations. I have kept sub-editing to a minimum. At times my early background as a newspaperman sorely tempted me to scar the typescripts with black pencil and decrease the verbiage, particularly that of the earlier scribes. I resisted, and as far as possible have left their original styles, idiosyncracies and sometimes even their errors. This is partly out of respect; but I feel the manners, beliefs, actions and reactions of particular periods are conveyed and understood more vividly when expressed not by a latter-day author but by the people and phraseology of those times. Just as, in a few paragraphs' time, I shall allude to a character played so superbly by George Cole in a current TV series that will be long forgotten when people take *this* book from the library shelves in eighty years' time, so I have been pleased to retain George T. Burrows's reference to Wilkie Bard, a great name in Victorian and Edwardian music halls, in his dissertation on the nerves of non-Scottish bowlers!

Bowls so far cannot boast a literature to rival that of several other sports. The game has not yet developed its Cardus, Arlott, Darwin . . . nor any of those other writers who have proved able not merely to pen an evocative phrase but to view sport as part of life itself (and not as a phenomenon outside it) yet simultaneously lift it to planes far above the normal and obvious. Neither has the game attracted special attention from nor been the subject of occasional works by great literary outsiders as some other sports have done. And please don't disagree with me on the grounds of a few fragmentary allusions from Shakespeare!

Yet there exist scholarly, well-researched books; and when it comes to art as opposed to mere fact, there are half-hidden gems and hints of considerable talent. From among early bowls writers Burrows surges through as a giant. His little word-picture of the outstanding early champion Irvine Watson ('He never once raised his arm to strike viciously; his delivery was the most studied, most careful and sweetest of all men I knew') reveals insight into character and technique and the skill, in a phrase, to associate one with the other; and the unfulfilled potential of some latter-day journalists is glimpsed in the fragment of

C. M. 'Jimmy' Jones's portrait of Arthur Knowling ('One cannot say he bowls his woods; he decants them . . .'). The opportunities for writers should enlarge with the increase in space gradually afforded the modern game; and the literary potential of that game is vast because, as David Rhys-Jones has perceived, it has the slow-burning, deceptive somnolence that can ignite dramatically within seconds, plus the pace and protraction to promote conversation, character and anecdote. Cricket has the same virtues and its literature is considerable.

Some of the most readable recent pieces have been by sports journalists not specialized in the game, but they occasionally smack also of naivety and patronage. If the flat-green reporters can dismiss the shackles of intimacy, bring imagination as well as journalistic knack to their craft and shake off their inhibitions – and above all, if they are given the chance – they may yet bring us the colour and character that bursts out from the best reportage of the lusty crown-green game and its salty personalities. Perhaps it is mere geography and dialect that makes one think of Cardus when reading John D. Vose's 'The Panel Match' or Burrows's conversation piece with 'Owd Toss' the professional; or perhaps it is the game and those who populate it. Burrows, who played both codes, is often at his best on the subject of crown green, not least when contrasting its life with that of the cossetted private-green bowlers of the south ('Think of that, ye Bowlers of Suburbia, particularly ye who enclose yourselves inside four high walls and no man can gain admittance without having a special key . . . !'). Burrows was to change his mind on the merits of the codes. Perhaps, again, 'intimacy' was the problem: this one-time critic of the English Bowling Association became one of its councillors. An intriguing poacher turned gamekeeper!

But who am I to pontificate? Indeed, why should I, successively sports journalist, film and TV producer, edit a book on bowls at all? The game fascinates me. I see its potential as a major sport, and in a media context believe I was one of the first to do so after World War II.

In the 1950s, as a young Fleet Street sub-editor on the *Evening Standard*, I alighted on part-time bowls reporting as, to quote Arthur Daley of *Minder*, 'a nice little earner'. Divorced as I was from those in the sport I milked it dry of spicy news. I scooped the story of fifteen-year-old Roger Bird, the Hampshire schoolboy whose prospective schoolmaster opponent in a bowls final declined to play him, plus the follow-ups about the EBA meeting held to discuss what the word 'men' in their rules really meant and the decision to ban anyone under eighteen from entering their national championships. Those developments are quoted now in every reference book. Among other things, I ran the story of the great international Algy Allen refusing to play for England ever again after being dropped, exposed a TV match as a set-up, and reported the precocious first appearances in the English championships of the youthful David Bryant and his equally young-looking partner, Roger Harris.

In short, I cashed in on bowls without too many altruistic thoughts for its benefit. Indeed, I wrote anonymously, even secretively. The vanity of athletic youth dissuaded me from telling even close club-cricketing friends that in my spare time from sub-editing I associated with this game of mature years, waddling legs and absurd flat-heeled brown shoes.

But I opened a few eyes and minds. Reading my articles in the *Standard, News Chronicle, Sunday Express* (with Percy Baker, four times EBA singles champion) and other columns motivated others to contribute stories to London newspapers, and at least two writers represented in this book would confirm that fact. 'Jimmy' Jones (who, sadly, has died since I began this book) sought my advice before beginning *British Bowls*, later *World Bowls*, which jolted the bowls-periodical business out of its parish-magazine syndrome.

On leaving Fleet Street to join the BBC I gave it all up, though I fervently believed in the visual potential of bowls and arranged probably the first head-to-head singles match shown on British television. Later, when I ran an American-owned production company, I pushed that belief further to motivate more TV programmes (and, incidentally, to earn a little money therefrom for the associations of England, Scotland and Wales). But my judgement in a business sense was faulty. I favoured tradition and the outdoor game. Consciously I looked away from the indoor sport, regarding it as a bastard of the real thing and ignoring the attributes of accurate play, weatherproofing and enterprise that have made it an absorbing on-screen spectacle.

Today the champions are as young as I was when I was too embarrassed to admit I wrote about the sport. My hockey bag lies a crumpled corpse in a cupboard. My cricket bag, cobwebbed boots therein, lies inactive before its time, taken on a once-a-year outing to a Cotswolds village game or a boozy tour. My golf clubs are in my car boot, patiently waiting, frustrated by their master's work-load. The bowls greens, though not yet its carpets, call in increasingly seductive tones. At least, please regard me as an enthusiast and, from afar, an admirer of your game.

Phil Pilley
Shepperton, 1987

I

A Game to Play or Not to Play?

When the game is played, as it now is, in the open atmosphere of a green and by select, respectable individuals whose object is simply to pass a portion of their leisure time in a species of amusement fitted to promote their bodily and mental vigour, we think it may safely be affirmed of the game of bowls that it is likely to secure these advantages in as high a degree as any of the athletic exercises of modern times. Whilst it demands no violent exertion it calls into salutary action the muscular system in general, and while it exercises the body without unnecessary fatigue it also imparts a healthful and vigorous tone of mind by the interest which the procedure of the game invariably creates.

Albany Bowling Club (Glasgow) rules book, c.1860

No other game is so provocative of genial mirth, nor more conducive to sociality and good fellowship. It is not only a gentle and enlivening recreation, but in strategy and general interest is unsurpassed; and as it is only played in pleasant weather, in the open air and over a green lawn finer and more kindly to tread upon than the most luxurious and costly carpet, it can be and is resorted to by all, without regard to skill, sex, age, grade, class, craft or condition. Thus, beginners and adepts, ladies and gentlemen, the maid and the matron, youths in their teens and veterans of three score, the Earl and his tenantry, the lawyer and his client, the representative and his constituent, the baker and the brewer, the delicate and robust, all there meet and co-mingle in harmony.

Manual of Bowl Playing, 1864

Through the senses how delightful the game is! In the handling of the shapely polished spheres there is pleasure to the touch; the very poetry of motion is the course of the bowl to the jack; Nature is refreshing to the senses; and lastly there is the adjournment to the village hostelry, where, with 'church-warden' and a mug of 'home-brewed', battles are fought over again and the inner man regaled.

Chess and kindred games demand great mental activity and are more distractive than recreative; their 'dual solitude' also renders them less social. Robust athletic exercises as a means of training the body are almost second nature to the British youth and should be carefully fostered; but bowling, as an outdoor pastime, is the most truly recreative, combining the minimum of mental and physical effort with the maximum of recuperative energy.

Touchers and Rubs, 1893

Enjoyable intervals for chat occur during play, and undue or violent exercise is never necessary such as in some games have a dangerous tendency to result in severe chills or lung mischief.

Bowls, Bowling Greens and Bowl Playing, 1894

The game affords much scope for unselfishness, good temper and modesty as well as dexterity of hand and eye, and those are the things which, far more than a long face and sanctimonious manner, go to make up the Christian character. It is a matter for great thankfulness and congratulation that there is a good, wholesome moral tone about our sport.

The Rev. F. Byard, *Carlisle Lloyds Weekly*, 1908

Nought can rival it for sport save good ale and a comely wench.

Old book, quoted in *Corner to Corner*

Bowling is a sober game. The ruffianism of football, the effeminacy of tennis, the manliness of cricket and the buoyancy of baseball give way to a stateliness and gracefulness met in no other sport.

Bowling, 1908

Bowls is a quiet and philosophic amusement which depends for its success entirely on a thorough realization that nothing happens in it, any more than in real life, exactly according to scientific calculation.

Canadian handbook, 1902

Cricket teaches grimness of purpose; football is a bout of breathless, bustling, hurrying unquiet; tennis is a jerky business of white flannels and shorts, not forgetting eyeshades; even golf must have its uniform. But bowls has no limitations. You may wear your most comfortable old slacks; you may doff your coat and show your braces unashamed before the world; you can turn out in your easiest and greasiest old hat, your shabbiest rubber shoes and your rankest pipe and the crowd on the green will greet you with a brotherly smile.

The thirty-five to forty yards of slow trundle towards the jack is the soul of the game. That is why bowls should be the game of all those whose minds rarely rest or those haunted by the tax-gatherer or the Devil himself. There is no act in any sport so all-absorbing and of such concentrated interest as that deliberate trundle.

Perhaps bowls is the only perfect recreation and the only pure game so far invented by man! At what other sport do men persevere so resolutely to achieve just nothing?

George T. Burrows (sports journalist), 1915

We really are a wonderful people, we bowlers. We are such sociable human folk. Let a stranger show but a passing interest and what do we immediately do? We invite him to come along and take an end. Fancy a cricket team asking the onlookers to put down an over or two or have a turn at the wicket! But we bowlers get some shoes from the pavilion and say, 'Come along, sir, we're one short, come along now, please, and have a go.' Oh, yes, we trust him with an expensive wood and tell him about bias and all the rest of it and fill him full of technicalities – and he in return spoils the whole evening.

Robert Stanley, *The Bowls News*, 1927

Thank heavens for Mr Stanley! He has provided with his final shot the first drop of cynicism into the flood-tides of self-congratulation that wash incestuously through the game! Happily I have found a few others not so gullible as to accept bowls as a perfect panacea. They are, though, a precious few indeed – and the afficionados, affronted, invariably have an answer . . .

At the annual dinner of a well-known club, one of the members proposing a toast spoke of the advantages of the game and said, 'If a man is too thin it enables him to put on flesh; if a man has too much flesh it enables him to reduce it.' The game, we presume, is also good for all disorders of the liver; and for pains in the loins, loss of appetite, shortness of breath, nervous exhaustion, gout and toothache it is unsurpassed!

Anonymous letter, *Bowling,* 1908

What pastime is best when you have become just a stuffed shirt on the cricket field? The most obvious choice is golf. Bowls? An admirable, sociable and dignified game, but severe on the kidneys. Orthodoxy demands a stooping posture, and no one who releases his wood from an upright position has yet become a champion. However, try it – you may be the first. Stranger things have happened.

   Again, there is a certain lack of light-heartedness about the player: often he seems to be sharing in some religious ceremony rather than a game. Nor is physical danger entirely absent. A player urging a wood to obey is apt to land you a back-hander on the nose.

R. C. Robertson-Glasgow (cricketer journalist), 1958

I would not reflect for a moment on any game other than bowls. Golf is often played in grim silence. There is a story told of two men who played the eighteen holes without a word being spoken until they reached the last green. Then one of them holed a six-yard putt. 'A fine putt, Alec,' remarked his friend. 'Chatterbox,' retorted Alec and, picking up his ball, walked away. In a friendly game of bowls such reticence is almost inconceivable.

Silas K. Hocking (novelist), 1932

It is an institution which has youngsters now pitting their wits against seasoned international campaigners. A game full of ifs . . . if you hadn't played that hand, if you hadn't driven when you should have been drawing things would have been different. A game of remorse and unpredictability; a game of skill and a game of chance; a game of joy and a game of frustration; a game of dry throats and sweaty palms.

Ronnie Harper (bowls journalist), 1979

. . . In other words, bowls today is pressurized sport and not only a friendly pastime. Let one of the few passages of fiction devoted to the game, chapter one of Hugh de Selincourt's Gauvinier Takes to Bowls, *written after World War II and before the sport really took off, serve as a final tribute at this stage to the gentler attractions of the pastime, and as our link to the first games and reactions of sundry non-fictional characters . . .*

It would not be quite true to say that the excitement of his first afternoon at bowls kept Gauvinier from sleep, though he lay some hours in bed with the light off and his eyes shut, fully and happily awake. The new game, the new surroundings, familiar faces in a new setting, certainly jogged his mind to activity. The English scene renewed its fascination. 'This happy breed of men,' this nation of shopkeepers who yet could produce ten poets for every other nation's one, this place of cold houses and warm beer, this England. His mind passed swiftly without jump or jolt from the jolly bunch of bowlers in whose company he had spent a good afternoon to the poets who voiced what was deepest in his heart. This communication between man and man, this devotion of one man to another. What shines out for ever against the black background of Hamlet's tragedy but his last words to Horatio as he dies, 'No, live on, man, please, live on to give my version of this mess;' or as we have been keyed by the play to the level of beauty to hear and understand great language:

> 'Absent thee from felicity awhile
> And in this harsh world draw thy breath in pain
> To tell my story.'

The last word of friendship, the complete trust of one man in another, the innermost longing, dim perhaps or not so dim, in every mother's son of us, for who goes a furlong without sympathy walks to his funeral dressed in his shroud.

No far cry from these great articulate spirits who proclaimed the need of human beings one for another to that jovial bunch of bowlers eyeing the jack, bending, delivering the wood with every imaginable form of delivery, casual, comic, earnest, fantastic, good, screwing, tense, taut, to watch its progress . . . he turned over in his bed, smiling in the dark, to realize what excruciating embarrassment would be caused by any direct expression of affection: the very thought of it made him cover his blushes in the bed-clothes. Gestures could be eloquent and the tone of voice. Eyes could speak. Good fellowship, that was it, to which each contributed in his own way with varying success and in which each rejoiced in his own way, in so far as he was able to rejoice in anything.

And what a rare chance the game offered not only of becoming better acquainted with other men but, what is perhaps even more important, of becoming better acquainted with oneself. For what Montaigne, most honest of men (whom Will S. loved so that he blank-versed whole passages of his essays into his plays), wrote of chess is even more applicable to the game of bowls:

'To what a degree does this ridiculous diversion molest the soul, when all her faculties are summoned together upon this trivial account; and how fair an opportunity she herein gives everyone to know and make a right judgment of herself . . . Every particle, every employment of man manifests him equally with any other.'

And he writes in another passage, the truth of which Gauvinier's heart had for many years acclaimed:

'I find the rough manners and language of country people commonly better suited to the rule and prescription of true philosophy than those of philosophers themselves.'

Queer how something drew you to one man, warned you off another. They nearly all felt it, though fortunately not with his own intensity, he had observed, and nearly all grappled with it so as not to mar the general good fellowship, the unwritten, unspoken law of the game. 'Oh yes, it's a good crowd,' he had heard a member explain to a spectator, 'No clicks much, or not so as you'd notice, and some are liked more than others. Free and easy, you know, most of us, though there are a few . . .' He had passed on out of hearing of all but a hearty laugh of agreement, and he betted himself a pint that one or other would modify any spicy stricture (and the quality of the laugh declared the stricture's spiciness) by remarking: 'Oh well, it takes all sorts to make a world!'

He went to sleep at length, thankful that he had been lured into membership of the bowls club, and quite decided, like a good little pupil, that practice, practice, practice was necessary and that he would turn up on Monday to see what was cooking. 'A lot I'm glad not to have missed,' he drowsed to think – Fent or Kenton, which was it –

> 'I have a journey, sirs, shortly to go
> My master calls me, I must not say no.'

Practise, practise, practise. Mustn't let down that triple, or ever, ever, ever talk about balls . . . Woods . . . not . . . balls! He slept.

Hugh de Selincourt, 1949

2

'How I Began'

From fiction to reality; to begin with, from Gauvinier's reaction to his first game, set by De Selincourt in a balmy, country-green atmosphere, to the recollections of David Bryant, champion of champions, whose image will haunt this book, synonymous as he is with the modern scene, competitive, international, professional . . .

Toddler Fan to Champion

My dad was a fine player. He represented England in the 1958 and 1959 international matches and led for the Clevedon (Somerset) four who won the EBA championship at Paddington in 1957. I almost lost count of the times he won the Clevedon club championship. His delivery remains one which anyone could copy profitably.

Even when I was a babe in arms, mother used to take me down to the club; and long before I began school at St Nicholas's, Clevedon, I used to toddle round to Princes Road, climb on a seat at the end of the green and watch the afternoon bowlers in action. Part of each summer holiday was a visit to Exmouth, where Dad competed regularly in the open tournament. Mother would take me to the beach in the morning and then we would go to the green to cheer on Dad.

What wonderful days they were, with the sun always shining – or so it seems now – and Mum and I sharing in every shot Dad delivered. If for no other reason, I shall always love bowls for the happy bonds it helped forge between us all.

Much as I enjoyed watching, the urge to go out and try for myself was ever present, and when I discovered a set of old bowls behind the Exmouth clubhouse Dad had no peace until he had asked the green-keeper if they were wanted. They were not, Dad handed over five shillings and I became the owner not only of a set of woods but of a jack to go with them. Soon they were augmented by a set of sixteen croquet balls, discards collected from a relative's house in Taunton. These, of course, were not biased, but as the family lawn slopes across its ten-yard length, this did not matter too much. Soon some of the most important fours in the English season were taking place on our lawn, with seven-year-old David Bryant filling all positions in both sides – but only in trust for the men I watched daily from the bank at the Clevedon club. School finished at 3.30 p.m. and within minutes I would be comfortably ensconced and deeply enthralled by the players on the green.

Dad was always telling me to master length bowling and the draw shot, and – often overlooked – the importance of being content with second wood when the head looks ominous. But at that stage of my life I was much more taken with the cannons, yard-on shots, jack-trailers and, above all, firing shots. How I loved the speed with which the bowl careered on to the target, slumping with disappointment when it sped through without touching. It was these cannons and drives which I tried out the most. I became very accurate with the firing shot – and I was seven years old.

I had my first game on the club green at eight, and later that year war broke out. For most of the next six years Mother was almost my only opponent and very good she was, too.

I have always been keen on billiards and snooker and there is still a fascination in playing one ball on to another to find out what happens. I am always experimenting, and that has carried over into bowls. In one way this has been an advantage, because to experiment one has to think, and by copying the bowlers at the club or anywhere else I was certainly forced to think a great deal. These continual experiments did not please Dad, whose great strength had always been length, and under his watchful eye the chances of my falling into damaging habits were considerably reduced.

It was not until October 1947 had come and gone that Dad asked me if I wanted to join Clevedon. I decided I would. At about this time my eyesight deteriorated badly, though I did not realize it right away, and I found that my performances on the cricket field, where I was opening bat for a school team, were not very satisfactory. My other love was tennis, but I began to play bowls in the evenings and, finding the games did not mix, decided to concentrate on bowls, though until recently I mixed this with table tennis in the winter.

Modern educational theory lays great stress on the importance of youngsters advancing through success, and this undoubtedly worked as far as my bowls was concerned for I won the Clevedon club handicap in my first summer and reached the semi-finals of the Somerset singles in my second year. In that same year Roger Harris and I reached the semi-finals of the pairs in the Clevedon open tournament where we lost to my great-uncle and his partner; but I beat Great-Uncle in the singles.

It was about then I realized I possessed some flair for the game and decided to try seriously to improve.

David Bryant, 1966

A Scarcity of Sixpences

In my schooldays I passed several times daily a green enclosed with lofty and, to me, unclimbable walls. From the outside, though I could hear ejaculations of the players, nothing of the game was to be seen unless I mounted the palisades of the neighbouring residence of a crusty old gentleman, who owned as well a suspicious-looking dog not particularly well disposed towards boys of any kind and generally keeping a sharp lookout for all trespassers. Now and then, dog and master being conspicuous by their absence, I dared to ascend, and obtained a hurried, apprehensive and unsatisfying glimpse of a portion of the green and some of the players.

Of course there was a regular entrance to the green, but I noticed near it a board thus inscribed: 'Gentlemen are expected to spend sixpence each evening.' Apart from my not being a gentleman, other circumstances besides the chronic scarcity of sixpences I experienced about that period kept me 'without the walls' and many years passed before I was introduced upon a bowling green.

E. T. Ayers (author), 1894

Dignity Regained

When I was young I never gave the game a thought. Like most Wearsiders in the 1920s I was mad about football and the height of my ambition was to play regularly for a First Division League club. My chance came in an offer of a month's trial with Chelsea, but this I rejected because of a conceited belief that I was good enough to be signed without trial. Hull City followed with an offer and on a fateful Saturday afternoon I turned out with the reserves. The pitch was muddy, I twisted my knee and that was the end of football for two years.

It was also the end of my job so, like so many other people from north-east England, I moved to the south. Jobs were not easy to find, but football helped and I settled in Rochester in 1937. Football for the works team in winter and tennis in summer satisfied my sporting instincts, but by 1941 it was difficult to play either game. In the one case all my contemporaries were in the Army and it was almost impossible to raise twenty-two men; in the other, tennis balls were non-existent.

Consequently, during a holiday back in Durham, six of us scraped four woods each, hired a rink in the local park and settled down to while away an afternoon trundling the woods at a jack. Those twenty-four woods scattered around the green were a shocking sight: they were everywhere. My dignity was hurt by my inability to make my woods go anywhere near the spots I wished them to finish and I decided there and then that they would not master me.

The holiday over, I returned to London and before the end of that summer played half a dozen or so games at Parliament Hill, the club I joined the following year and of which I have been a member ever since. My father, a keen bowler himself, bought me a pair of woods as a present and every possible afternoon that summer I took myself and the woods to the greenside, there to wait hopefully until someone needed a fourth and asked me to make up. Not until that season had gone by did I realize that one of my two precious woods carried more bias than the other. Eventually I bought a set of four matched woods and they made a tremendous difference to my accuracy and consistency.

Many afternoons I sat without playing. Parliament Hill, like most clubs, had its own little cliques and sets and it was not easy to find acceptance in them. The second year of my membership was much happier, for I won a place in the club team as a number two and secured promotion to number three; but, hard as I tried, improvement seemed impossible. Despite my keenness, no one volunteered to help or advise me, so in the winter of 1942–3 I joined the local library and obtained every book on bowls on which they could lay their hands.

Of all the things I learned from these books nothing was to play a more vital part in my career than the decision to change my mode of delivery. Until then I used a crouch delivery and many bowlers have

reached great heights with such a style. However, in view of my build
and a certain suppleness which came from football and tennis I
reasoned that the crouch was not best for me and decided to change to
the upright delivery, sometimes called the athletic. It was to be the
turning point in my career.

Norman King (winner of World, Commonwealth Games and EBA
Championships), 1959

One Magic Hour

My introduction to the game was at the age of eleven. I was not
allowed to play on the public greens in the Ormeau Park, Belfast, until
I was fourteen but I could place the mat for my brother, nine years
older, in practice matches. The game fascinated me.

Like most boys my real passion was cricket or football, but whenever there was a needle match between top-class bowlers at the greens
300 yards from my home, a diminutive youngster in short trousers
attentively followed every move. I had mastered most of the theory of
the game by the time I was fourteen and eligible to play in the public
parks – but men were not too keen to play with an infant prodigy
and I was not encouraged by the banter I had to endure from my
pals.

In the next few years my interest was mainly confined to watching
and occasionally reporting league matches for the local paper, but one
incident stands out vividly. I was practising by myself when a well-
known Irish bowler came on to the green and spent an hour giving me
tips on correct delivery, use of the mat and how to judge the correct
land. This gesture to a little lad in his teens laid the foundations of any
future success I had.

Paddy Orr (twice Surrey singles champion), 1959

'I Can't Do This to My Dad'

I was playing long before I had any burning interest in the game,
enjoying the more lively pastimes of Australian Rules football, tennis
and golf. The youngest of four sons and four daughters, I succumbed
to my dad's 'Come on over for some practice, son!' – a frequent
after-dinner request at our home.

It was the cue for a stroll across the street to the Prospect club green to roll them down in the beautifully mild Adelaide evening air. We would stay there until it became too dark to see. Then, together, we would walk back to the house, pleasantly tired. Only today do I realize that it was a good time in my life.

My father won seven club titles playing singles on South Australian greens; his name is in the records as club champion at Prospect, Gawler, South Park and Parkside. But I had no thoughts about taking up his game seriously. I was too obsessed with the vigour and action of faster-moving games to read in his mind an obvious desire for one of his sons to succeed him as a bowler. Looking back, one sees it so clearly. I would act so differently were it possible to live that particular period of my life over again knowing what I know now.

My dad said to me one day, 'I will teach you bowls so that when you start playing regularly you won't have to spend six years learning.' He followed this up with his relaxed tuition. When he thought there was evidence of progress in my game, he said, 'Come on now, we'll play 21-up and you go your hardest.'

I remember to this day leading 18–15 and feeling I could win. Dad was now sixty-five and I happened to look across at him just as he was picking up his bowl. Whether it was because I was convinced he was facing defeat I do not know, but he suddenly appeared before me in such a manner that I said to myself, 'I can't do this to my dad.' I pulled my punches and he won 21–19.

Walking home, he put his arm round my shoulder and said, 'Look here, son, I played as hard as I could tonight and I'm proud of what I've taught you. One of these days you'll be a good bowler.' It is the only time in my life that I have felt overjoyed at losing.

Today, I know what a marvellous man I had as a father. One of my greatest regrets was that in 1949, as I accepted the first of my Australian singles trophies, he was not alive to share the elation of victory.

Glyn Bosisto (four times Australian singles champion), 1963

Young Boy's Luck, Old Man's Prize

I was fourteen and went with a friend to a works sports day. The usual sports, sideshows and refreshment tent were the main attractions, but on an adjacent bowling green a competition was being held: the aim was to place a wood inside a circle roughly two feet across on the crown of the green. I tried my hand and with my first wood placed the bowl in the circle: a fluke, maybe, but from 3 p.m. until 8 p.m. efforts were made to do the same and no one succeeded. The prize was mine; but what a dilemma the committee were in! The prize was a fob watch on a chain – an old man's prize. They had never dreamed a youngster would enter, let alone win. I got ten bob instead!

John D. Vose (crown green author), 1969

'Look Here, Young Man!'

From marbles to hockey, from hockey to tennis, from tennis to golf: that was the sequence. Then after ten years or so of golf, during which time I managed to reduce my handicap from 24 to 18 (and proud of it), fate dealt me a foul blow in the commissariat department necessitating a major operation. From then, the golf course looked and was much too long, and footling around a few holes did not please me at all. I gave up golf and devoted my time to work, reading, gardening and pottering about: not at all exciting. Then, when forced into early retirement due to my physical handicap, I had nothing to do but *more* reading, gardening and pottering about.

While on holiday in a Fair City that shall be nameless I was sitting in the hotel lounge reading a newspaper after breakfast when a resident came up and said bluntly: 'Look here, young man, you shouldn't be sitting in an armchair on a fine morning like this doing the damn' crossword puzzle!' I asked him cautiously what I should be doing. He immediately replied: 'You should be out playing bowls!'

Well, that shook me somewhat, for I had never thought of bowls as a real game: one doesn't, you know, after golf. Golf can be a religion, a science; thrilling and enthralling, heart-breaking and harrowing, depending on the state of your game at the moment; you become obsessed by it. Could bowls, 'glorified marbles', compensate for the seven years I had wasted pottering about?

I hedged. I explained that I had never played and that I hadn't any bowls to play with, anyway. He countered this by saying, 'If you will get out of that damn' chair and come with me now I will lend you some woods and shoes and show you what to do!' I did and he did. I was taken along to a lovely green on the seafront. Fascinating? Of course it was. My health improved; I said goodbye to boredom.

P. G. Goodwin (South Africa)

Wood on Target

Bowls is in my blood. My late father became Scottish singles champion in 1967 and my grandfathers and uncles were all good bowlers, too.

In my home village in Scotland when I was a boy the members used to mark out the bowling green with six targets. They played what was called a 'points' tournament: the man or woman with the highest points in any one round was the winner. Six schoolboys were required to mark the scores and I started doing so in 1949, when I was eleven. When I was not busy keeping scores at my allotted target I would grab the chance to try my own skill. I thought to myself, 'I'm doing better than some of the competitors!'

It was 1951 before I could join the club. A year later, I won a club singles event and four years after that, when I was about eighteen, was club champion.

Willie Wood (former Commonwealth Games singles champion and world championship silver medallist), 1987

Coincidences

At the end of summer in 1968, when I was fourteen, I was walking home from school through Poltair Park, St Austell, when I happened to spot a distant cousin playing bowls. He explained that he was not a regular player but merely having a casual game for relaxation on the advice of his doctor.

He invited me to try my hand. I did so and immediately became hooked. I was a keen footballer at the time, but bowls gradually took over.

The coincidences were astonishing. I have never seen that cousin since; and as far as I know, he never played the game any more.

David Cutler (youngest winner, at eighteen, of an English title), 1987

3
The Grandaddy of Them All!

Such records as are available establish bowls as the grandparent of all English sports, with the solitary possible exception of archery. Bowls, however, is purely and solely a game; it makes no claim to being also a technique or training for combat as in the case of archery or even hunting. Bearing this fact in mind, it can be said that it has a past – and a tradition – unsurpassed by any of its rivals.

Dr John W. Fisher (England international and author), 1956

When Did It Begin?

The pastime of bowling, whether practised upon open greens or in bowling alleys, was probably an invention of the Middle Ages. I cannot by any means ascertain the time of its introduction but have traced it back to the thirteenth century.

The earliest representation of a game played with bowls occurs on a manuscript of that century. Here, two small cones are placed upright at a distance from each other and the business of the players is evidently to bowl at them alternately, the successful candidate being he who could lay his bowl nearest to the mark. The French, according to Cotgrave, had a similar kind of game, called *carreau*, from a square stone which, says he, 'is laid in level with and at the end of a bowling-alley and in the midst thereof an upright point set as the mark whereat they bowl'.

At the top of the same plate is a fourteenth-century drawing from a beautiful MS Book of Prayers. It represents two other bowlers; but they have no apparent object to play at, unless the bowl cast by the first may be considered as such by the second and the game require him to strike it from its place.

Below these we see three persons engaged in the pastime of bowling; and they have a small bowl, or jack according to the modern practice, which serves them as a mark for the direction of their bowls. The action of the middle figure, whose bowl is supposed to be running towards the jack, will not appear by any means extravagant to such as are accustomed to visit bowling greens.

In the three delineations just mentioned we may observe that the players have only one bowl for each person; the modern bowlers have usually three or four.

Joseph Strutt (social historian), 1801

However doubtful may be the origin of the game, lexicographers agree that the words *bowle* (Old English) and *bowl* (present day) are derived from *bulla*, Latin for bubble. The following all have a bearing on the subject: in French *boule* (bowl), *balle* (ball), *billes* (billiard balls and marbles; Scotch for marbles, *bools*); in Icelandic, *böllr*; Old High German, *balla* and *pall*; Spanish, *bala*; Italian, *balla*; Greek σφαῖρα, *pila* . . . all meaning ball. *To bow* has been defined as to bend sideways (with a bias); *bowlder*, a round mass of rock; *bowl*, a round mass rolled along the ground; and *ball*, anything made in a round form.

Conning over the derivations, it is curious to note how closely allied are the words 'ball' and 'bowl'; and how easy is the transition of the game of ball to that of bowls: the one more or less in the air, the other on the ground.

Strutt, an authority at the beginning of the present century on all games, says that bowling was an invention of the Middle Ages and he had traced it back to the thirteenth century. This is no doubt true regarding the forms of the game as he knew it, but sculptured and painted antiquities of Ancient Greece and Egypt establish that games consisting of throwing and rolling balls and other circular objects were quite common thousands of years ago. Meagre is the information regarding their methods of play and laws; it is also difficult to reconcile the diverse opinions of early writers and their translators. But certainly Strutt was not infallible.

The remains at Thebes and Beni-Hassan (commemorating incidents in the life of Thotemes III, the Pharaoh of the Exodus, 1490 BC) are prolific in interesting records, and the game of ball as practised by the ancient Egyptians is depicted in various ways. Balls about three inches in diameter, made of leather or skins, sewed with string and stuffed with bran or husks of corn, have been found in tombs. Some in the British Museum are made of rush stalks, plaited together into a ball and covered with leather; others of more immediate interest to a bowler are a little smaller and made of porcelain gaily painted. These earthenware balls, it is reasonable to suppose, were played on the ground: to play with them in the same manner as the stuffed ball would render the amusement to say the least risky when their weight is considered. It is quite possible they were indoor toys of the young Egyptians, like our carpet-balls, and if this supposition is anywhere near the truth our outdoor game of bowls is only a variation of the same form of pastime.

For the game of ball we have incontestable evidence in the mural decorations of the tombs and palaces. In these delineations women principally figure as the players, though men and children also played ball – and *ball* and *bowl* were almost synonymous terms in early times. There can be little doubt that the ball is the most naturally perfect primitive plaything. It is not a very wild stretch of the imagination to picture Cain and Abel toying with such luscious and attractive spheres as oranges, pomegranates and apples and accept as a fact that the partiality for ball-toys is inherent and our first-parents to blame therefore.

From mother Eve down the apple has always had special attractions for the gentler sex, and is often conspicuous in ancient mythology and history. In an article on the Tanagra Figurines of the fourth and fifth centuries BC mention is made of female figures seated, with red balls or apples in their hands: doubtless ball-players, for on some antique vases ball-players, seated, are shown. The transition from play with an apple to ball-play seems quite natural. In comparatively modern times the ball had some deep significance in religious ceremonies, which, if still in force, would be no less startling than the demonstrations of the Salvation Army or the Ghost-Dancers.

Ball games were played under a variety of names under the Roman Empire. *Pila* was the small ball played with the hand, *follis* the large air-ball played with both hand and foot: these seem to have been the most common. The *paganica* was, in size, between the *pila* and *follis* and was solid; how the game was played with it is not known but from its size and weight we may suppose it was played on the ground.

With the ancients, quoits seems to have been the most popular of games for exhibiting the great strength of the competitors, while javelin-throwing and archery took foremost places as games of skill. However, it would appear that the quoit or discus was sometimes *rolled* away – or when thrown would strike the ground on its edge and roll some distance further. The game thus played might have suggested skittles. There is every reason for believing that the quoit was not always a discus. Dr Johnson makes a distinction between them: the former, he says, was a game of skill and the latter a game of strength. The early Greeks sometimes hurled the quoit 'in the manner of a bowl', and the quoits, according to Potter's *Grecian Antiquities* were of different sizes and figures, including the sphaeristic. Hone, in noticing the 'parish game of curling', says the 'stones used are called coits, quoits, coiting or quoiting-stones'. In Smith's *Antiquities* it is stated that the discus was sometimes a sphere.

In these ground games and their simple elements (i.e., rolling, bowling and throwing circular and spherical objects with skill and judgment) may be recognized the leading features of our game of bowls; and notwithstanding the ambiguity among early writers regarding the quoit and discus, the opinion may be advanced that the spherical quoit was the immediate progenitor of the bowle.

Humphrey J. Dingley (author), 1893

The game was played long before Britain came into notoriety. Herodotus, the 'father of history', mentions it as an invention of the Lydians, a celebrated people of Asia Minor; but how they played, or with what kind of bowls, I do not know. Herodotus says (I quote from Beloe's translation) that the Lydians, during a great scarcity of corn which lasted eighteen years, invented bowls and dice, with many other games, devoting themselves on alternate days to diversions and their necessary repasts. Perhaps, however, they took some 'light refreshment' on bowling days, for we can hardly believe games of any kind would for any long period assuage hungry feelings.

E. T. Ayers, 1894

All statements about the beginnings of bowls need qualification: first, its early history is difficult to trace with certainty; second, it is impossible in early references to distinguish between bowls and skittles. For example, implements found buried with an Egyptian child who died about 5000 BC resemble tenpins and Stone Age men probably bowled pebbles at larger pointed stones or sheep joints.

Much later, even when bowling games had taken root in Britain, it is impossible to be certain whether 'casting of stones' and similar descriptions suggest bowling or throwing, accuracy or distance. However, the various games are closely related, and rolling stones at stationary objects obviously was one of the first available forms of sporting competition.

Sculptured vases and ancient relics suggest that a form of bowls was played by distinguished people in Egypt 4000 years ago. Later it was played in Greece and Rome, from where it was introduced – almost certainly by the tenth century – to southern France and the rest of Europe.

Nobody has established who introduced bowling games to Britain, nor when. It was probably the Romans, although some people believe the Normans did so in the twelfth century. Anyway, it is generally accepted that bowling had begun to take root in England at that time.

Encyclopedia of Bowls, 1974

Attempts to trace the origin of bowls are as elusive and unprofitable as research into the now extinct Brontosauri. There is a theory that the pioneers were from Asia Minor in the pre-Christian era and played a variation of the game with knucklebones. A less appealing and more macabre beginning is attributed to an ancient and barbaric Pictish chieftain or Scottish king who celebrated victories on the battlefield by collecting the heads of his enemies and throwing them along the ground at a peg. There is no evidence of his method of scoring or whether he had any opponents.

Less steeped in the lore of antiquity and more concerned with a basis which could logically provide for the growth of the game as we know it today, we are more inclined to take our stand or, if you will, bend our knee on the premise that bowling began to take shape around the early twelfth and later eleventh centuries.

Who's Who and Encyclopedia of Bowls, 1959

The Oldest Green

Proof that bowls is an ancient pastime is not solely documentary, for the green of the Southampton Town Bowling Club was laid down towards the end of the reign of Edward I, before 1299, and tradition avows that it has been bowled over continuously ever since. In virtue of its claims of long descent, the club has adopted an agreeably old-fashioned custom. The members dub their president 'Master' and their chief medallist 'Knight'. The struggle for this latter honour provokes keen rivalry. At the close of play the winner kneels before the

Master, who performs the accolade by hanging the medal bedecked with ribbons around the victor's neck, then exclaiming, 'Rise, Sir —, Knight of the Southampton Bowling Green.' Thereupon the new Knight invites the company to drink champagne with him. At the annual dinner every Knight who has omitted to bring his medal is fined a bottle of wine. During play on the green the Knights are always addressed as such.

A match is held annually between Knights and non-Knights, which the former, as their prowess would lead us to expect, generally win. On September 2nd, 1870, however, the fates were against them as they were also against Napoleon III, and Mr Edward Lanham, who helped to beat the beknighted Bowlers, tells me that, for several years, the mnemonic ran: 'Fall of Sedan, Fall of the Knights.'

J. A. Manson (journalist), 1912

Southampton Old Green is the oldest in the world. Its antiquity cannot be challenged although its history is one of tradition rather than documentary record. There is no reason to doubt the tradition that the green was established prior to 1299, for while there is no direct evidence that bowls was played here at so early a period, there is no question that it was then known as 'The Master's Close', that the site had been used for recreational purposes for a considerable time and that bowls was then an established game. The origin of the Old Green cannot be traced, but it has sturdily weathered the vicissitudes of many centuries.

The green is in the oldest part of the ancient town, on a site which was originally part of what was termed in medieval times the Salt-marsh. This comprised the land bounded on the south and east by the sea, on the north by Marsh Lane and on the west by some gardens which were known as 'Three Fields' and belonged to the Warden of the Hospital of St Julian, or 'God's House', an institution established for the poor by Gervoise le Riche, a burgess of Hampton, in 1185. There were many attempts at enclosures, and these led to frequent disputes until finally, in 1503, when the authorities of 'God's House' laid claim to Saltmarsh and several lands adjoining, the matter was referred to arbitration and Saltmarsh was declared to be common land.

The green was unenclosed at this time and there is no mention as to when the site was hedged. It does not seem to have been specifically mentioned in these controversial matters and may have formed part of the land to which the town seems to have prescribed a right, but there is a suggestion, and it appears well founded, that in 1299 it was a part of the appurtenances of 'God's House'.

The probable first reference to the green itself as a place of recreation occurs under 1550. At that time 'inferior people' were prohibited from playing bowls, and it is recorded that a townsman, the lessee of the King's Orchard close to the site, was 'presented for keeping common playinge with bowles, tabylles and other unlawful games against the King's statute'. His fate is not recorded – and truly, here in the matter of the prohibition of bowling, is full and sound reason why the history of the Old Green was never recorded! On a plan of Southampton dated 1611 the green is shown with figures of men playing bowls, and in 1637 it was described as a ground 'where many gentlemen with the gentile merchants of this town take their recreation'.

In 1894, it would appear, the question of the Southampton Bowling Club's rights in the green were questioned in Council. The Town Clerk made report, and concluded: 'It appears probable that the ground was set apart for recreation and bowling from the earliest period of the history of the town, that a "Master of the Green" was elected so far back as 1299, when it was called "The Master's Close", and that, although the ground itself no doubt belongs to the town, the present club or association who occupy and manage the green would appear to have obtained prescriptive rights thereon from length of usure for the purpose of playing the game of bowls.' The Southampton Bowling Club has been in existence for upwards of 160 years and, while the premises are rated and taxed, the club pays no rent.

Many of the customs of the Old Green have disappeared with the years, but one faithfully observed annually since it was inaugurated on August 1st, 1776, is the unique Knighthood Tournament. It was inspired by one Mr Miller when he was eighty-two and president of the Green, and for 172 years the game has been played under conditions as identical as possible with those first laid down. Now it is a quaint and exceedingly picturesque combination of ancient and modern.

Tradition compels the Knights of the Green, who supervise the tournament, to appear in ceremonial attire: top hats, frock coats and the medal of their rank suspended on the chest. A Knight may return after any period of absence from the town to enjoy the privileges of membership. The medal, which is the insignia of office, is of silver.

Every medal awarded has borne the inscription, 'Win It and Wear It', while on the reverse side of many of the medals some outstanding incident of national importance which happened in the preceding year was recorded. The earliest medal belonging to the club is dated 1784.

The Knights determine both the length and position of the jack, and many a good player has been confounded by having to bowl across the green at an unaccustomed angle. Each competitor bowls two woods; each bowl is measured and removed; at the conclusion of the end the Knights award a point to the player who bowls the nearest wood; he who first obtains seven points wins the Knighthood. On the green and beneath the jack is placed a penny, so that if the jack is displaced the coin remains to mark the position. A wood which displaces the jack and rests on the coin is called a 'lodger'. The rules are strictly enforced and the tournaments are seldom completed under three days.

World War II left its scars on the Old Green. A bomb dropped on the top left-hand corner on August 13th, 1940: the crater was six feet deep and eighteen feet across. Another bomb dropped in the rear of the pavilion, blowing out a portion of the boundary wall, wrecking the dressing-room and uprooting a tree which landed on the roof. Every year, despite air raids and air-raid warnings, the Knighthood contest was played with the usual ceremonial dignity.

Time has wrought wondrous changes in the marshlands of medieval Southampton. What more striking contrast than this ancient green and the great docks, the 'Gateway of the Empire', so short a distance beyond. Often while playing within this sheltered, old-world spot one may glance up to see, towering above the walls, the great hull of one of the largest ships in the world cradled high and dry in the world's largest floating dock. Yet, despite these great developments, unimagined by the bowlers of even less than a century ago, the spirit of the past still lingers over the Old Green.

R. L. Andrew (editor, *Southern Daily Echo*), 1948

The first edition of the *Encyclopaedia Britannica* was compiled, in three volumes, by three Scotsmen who all lived in Edinburgh. The first volume was completed and bound in 1769 and the third by 1771. The first 'Bowling' entry read:

'Bowling, the art of playing bowls. The first thing to be observed in bowling is, the right chusing your bowl, which must be suitable to the ground you design to run on. Thus, for close alleys the flat bowl is the best; for open grounds of advantage, the round biassed bowl; and for plain and level swards, the bowl that is round as a ball. The next is to chuse your ground; and, lastly, to distinguish the risings, fallings, and advantages of the places where you bowl.' *

The entry was progressively enlarged and extended over the years, and yet until the 11th edition of 1910 there is still no mention of the club said to have been established in Southampton in or prior to 1299.

In the years between the middle of the 16th and 18th centuries, the bowling games in Southampton, as in London, were various forms of skittles. Southampton's Court Leet Records, going back to the middle of the 16th century, inform us that the bowling games played between 1550 and 1750 were, in chronological order: Closhe, Halffe-Bowle, Nine Holes, Kittles, Keetill Pinns, Nine-Pins and Roly Poly. Joseph Strutt tells us that these were games in which the number of upright pins you had to try and knock down varied from six (Closhe) to fifteen (Half-Bowl and Roly Poly).

Thus, we reach the second half of the 18th century and still no mention, in Southampton's records, of a game in which the purpose, as outlined for the first time in the 1788 edition of the *Encycl Brit* was to try to roll a large ball or bowl as close as possible to a smaller one. How, then, did the story get around that such a game could be traced back to the 13th century?

Sadly, Strutt must take some of the blame, for in spite of giving us detailed descriptions and drawings of some ten early bowling games, all related to knocking down skittles, the three illustrations** he included under the heading 'Bowling' are quoted as evidence that our game of bowls dates back to the 13th century. The Bodleian Library, however, now believes that the first two illustrations are the work of artists resident in France and that the third was drawn in Flanders. Strutt offered the opinion that one of the games he had illustrated was known as *carreau*, and there can be little doubt that the third drawing depicted the Continental game of *boules*.

Strutt's contribution to the seemingly exaggerated antiquity of the game now called bowls was, however, minimal when compared with that of the Town Clerk of Southampton, Mr Nalder, whose 1894

---

* See similar 17th century quotes on pages 72 and 83.
** See first photographic section.

report gave rise to the story that a bowling green had been in existence in the town since 1299. He added that 'the ground is and has been for the past 100 years upwards occupied by the Club called the Southampton Bowling Green Club', and the story soon got around in bowling handbooks and editions of the *Encyclo. Brit.* that the club itself dated back to the 13th century.

It is a relatively simple task to produce a mass of documentary evidence which tells us that there were no members' clubs in England and Wales before the middle of the 18th century in connection with any sport or pastime. This was partly because of the series of royal statutes issued between 1388 and 1745 which listed and made unlawful all known games of the period.

So when and where did any of today's three games of bowls – flat-green, crown green and Federation – first see the light of day? All the evidence I have been able to find suggests that the answers probably lie somewhere in the North of England or in Scotland; and at some time in the second half of the 18th century.

Donald Foulis (*World Bowls* magazine), 1986

We are too prone to treat the Old Green as something that does not matter very much. We do not grasp the fact that we have in our midst a priceless treasure that cannot be matched in any other country in the world.

Herbert Collings (bowls journalist)

4
Outlawed!

Mr Andrew, in his essay on Southampton Old Green, and Donald Foulis have drawn attention to a prohibition of bowls. Indeed, six kings and a queen of England were to impose bans on bowling games – even though some of them played themselves.

Whereas the people of our realm, gentle and simple alike, were wont formerly in their games to practise skill in archery and that now the said skill in archery having fallen almost wholly into disrepute, our people give themselves up to the throwing of stones and of wood and of iron and some even to other unseemly sports that be less useful and manly, whereby our realm will soon, as it appeareth, be stripped of archers. We, wishing that a fitting remedy be found in this matter . . . require that every man in the county, sobeit he be able-bodied, shall, upon holidays, make use, in his games, of bows and arrows and learn and practise archery. Moreover, that you prohibit all and sundry in our name from such stone, wood and iron throwing under penalty of imprisonment.

Edward III (to his Lord Lieutenant of Kent), 1363

. . . So began an early ban on bowling games. The game was not yet specifically 'bowls', though. Edward's phraseology makes it clear that bowling was still (and for a long time it would remain) a confusing, multiplying, developing mélange: implements of various shapes and sizes, stone, iron and wood, thrown and rolled, in sundry styles and on sundry surfaces.

The reason for prohibition was clear: young men were neglecting their archery, then a crucial technique in the tactics of war. But bowling and other games were to grow too popular for their own good, and subsequent statutes over the next 300 years would be motivated additionally by other reasons: notably betting, breaches of the peace and villainy. The penalties could be fines and imprisonment.

History books enumerate the finer details, reign by reign, statute by statute, but the whole protracted period seems now one of confusion, contradiction and chaos. In 1455 bans on playing within the walls of London were lifted . . . writers commended 'casting a bowle' as a healthy pursuit . . . then came more prohibitions. Judgements according to people's standing and the company they kept – religion, politics, trade, war and class all factors in the maelstrom. And the games would go on through the centuries, keeping half-paces ahead of the law, fiddling their various rules to fit it. There was nothing singular about bowls. There were games of differing veins and differing settings: public and private, on country greens and in alleys, on church lands and in monasteries, by roistering inns and taverns. There were elegant alleys of hedged-in grass, exclusive alleys in posh spas for the gentry, alleys fit for a lady, indoor alleys to cheat the weather, alleys unhealthy and unwholesome, riddled with greedy promoters and crooked gamblers. You had your rich men's gardens, charmingly private, out of sight and immune; bowling centres where conspirators might meet; and the whole unhappy situation underpinned by the morals of the times.

But we jump ahead of ourselves. In 1509 Henry VIII, prince of culture, athlete, despot, came to the throne. He built bowling places in palaces, he played and he gambled. He both loved and played bowls with Anne Boleyn; so, perhaps, did Sir Thomas Wyatt, the poet . . .

Whose Shot? Whose Lady?

About this time it is said that the knight, entertaining talk with her as she was earnest at work, in sporting wise caught from her a certain small jewel, hanging by a lace out of her pocket or otherwise loose, which he thrust into his bosom; neither with any earnest request could she obtain it of him again. He kept it therefore and wore it after about his neck, under his cassock, promising himself either to have it with her favour or as an occasion to have talk with her wherein he had singular delight, and she after seemed not to make much reckoning of it, the thing not being much worth or not worth much striving for.

The noble Prince, having a watchful eye upon the knight, noted him more to hover about the lady and she the more to keep aloof of him; was whetted the more to discover her his affection, so as rather he liked first to try of what temper the regard of her honour was; which he finding not any way to be tainted with those things His Kingly Majesty and means could bring to the battery, he in the end fell to win her by treaty of marriage and in his talk took from her a ring and that wore upon his little finger; and yet all this with such secrecy was carried, and on her part so wisely, as none or very few esteemed this other than an ordinary course of dalliance.

Within a few days after, it happened that the King, sporting himself at bowls, had in his company (as it falls out) divers noblemen and courtiers of account, amongst whom might be the Duke of Suffolk, Sir F. Brian and Sir T. Wyatt, himself being more than ordinarily pleasantly disposed. In his game he took an occasion to affirm a cast to be his that plainly appeared to be otherwise. Those on the other side said, with His Grace's leave, they thought not; and yet, still he, pointing with his finger whereon he wore her ring, replied often it was his, and specially to the knight he said, 'Wyatt, I tell thee it is *mine*', smiling upon him withal. Sir Thomas, at the length, casting his eye upon the King's finger, perceived that the King meant the lady whose ring that was, which he well knew; and pausing a little, and finding the King bent to pleasure after the words repeated again by the King, the knight replied, 'And if it may like Your Majesty to give me leave to measure it, I hope it will be *mine*'; and withal took from his neck the lace whereat hung the tablet, (and therewith stooped to measure the cast), which the king, espying, knew and had seen her wear; and therewithal spurned away the bowl, and said, 'It may be so but then am I deceived'; and so broke up the game.

Now the King, resorting to his chamber showing some discontent in his countenance, found means to break this matter to the lady, who, with good and evident proof how the knight came by the jewel, satisfied the King so effectually that this more confirmed the King's opinion of her truth than himself at the first could have expected.

George Wyatt (grandson of Sir Thomas Wyatt)

For all his love of Anne, Henry had her beheaded; for all his liking for bowls, he suppressed it. With the dissolution of the monasteries, rowdy inns and genteel estates remained the extreme focal points of the games. The rich were to play on, but the lower classes and those who played and gambled in and around the taverns, alleys and gaming houses were banned.

'Inventative and Crafty Persons'

Of all the threatening Acts the most interesting is the 33rd of Henry VIII in 1541. In Henry's reign occurs the first statutory mention of the word 'bowls', and from the 1541 edict we learn that the conditions of 'bowyers, fletchers (arrow-makers), stringers and arrowheadmakers' had grown desperate from the 'customable usage' of bowls and other games devised by 'many subtil inventative and crafty Persons'. It was accordingly enacted that no person was to keep an alley or place of bowling for 'gain, lucre or living', nor suffer the game to be played, subject to a penalty of forty shillings for every day on which the law was broken. Section 12 declared that everyone who played was 'to forfeit for every time so doing 6s.8d.'. Moreover, magistrates and other competent persons were enjoined to visit places and alleys to ascertain whether forbidden games were secretly pursued and, if so, to arrest and imprison players and keepers alike until they found bail.

To render playing even more difficult and more irksome, section 16 of this ruthless Act stipulated that 'no manner of artificer or craftsman of any handicraft or occupation, husbandman, apprentice, labourer, servant at husbandry, journeyman, or servant of artificer, mariners, fishermen, watermen or any serving-man' should play bowls or other inhibited games 'out of Christmas, under the pain of twenty shillings to be forfeit for every time: and in Christmas to play only at any of the said games in their masters' houses or in their masters' presence; and also that no manner of persons shall at any time play at any bowl or bowls in open places out of his garden or orchard.'

As a concession to folk of title and the gentry, however, section 23 provided that, under licence, 'every nobleman and other having manors, lands, tenements or other yearly profits for term of life in his own right or in his wife's right to the yearly value of an hundred pounds or above' was free to play bowls, without penalty, 'within the precinct of his or their houses, gardens or orchards.'

Henry's fatuous attempt at repression remained on the statute book for more than three centuries, so until 1845 bowls was illegal!

J. A. Manson, 1912

5

Bias in an Unbiased Age

When Mary came to the throne in 1553 even the well-to-do's bowling licences were scrapped. The games had caused, obviously among Protestants, 'unlawful assemblies, seditions and conspiracies', plus other breaches of the peace. Now, enter the Elizabethan era . . .

Benefits and Evils

Before you go to your reflection moderately exercise your body with some labour, or playing at the tennis, or casting a bowl . . . to open your pores and to augment natural heat.

Andrew Borde (writing on health), 1557, a year before
Elizabeth's accession

Although I will not discommend altogether the nature of bowling if the time, place, person and such necessary circumstances be observed; yet as it is now used, practised and suffered it groweth altogether to the maintenance of unthrifts that idley and disorderly make that recreation a cosenage.

Robert Greene (dramatist, poet and pamphleteer, 1560–92)

Common bowling alleys are privy mothes, that eate uppe the credite of many idle citizens, whose gains at home are not able to weigh downe their losses abroade; whose shoppes are so farre from maintaining their play that their wives and children cry out for bread, and goe to bedde supperlesse ofte in the yeere . . . Oh, what a wonderful change is this! Our wrestling at armies is turned to wallowing in ladies' laps, our courage to cowardice, our running to ryot, our bowes to bowls and our darts to dishes.

Stephen Gossom (poet and dramatist turned clergyman), 1579

What should I speak of the ancient daily exercises in the long bow by citizens of this city, now almost clean left off and forsaken? I overpass it, for, by the means of closing in the common grounds, our archers, for want of room to shoot abroad, creep into bowling alleys and ordinary dining-houses nearer home, where they have room enough to hazard their money at unlawful games, and there I leave them to take their pleasure.

John Stow (chronicler and antiquary), 1598

When your husband comes from his rubbers in a false alley thou wilt not believe that his woods ran with a wrong bias.

Thomas Middleton (poet and dramatist, 1570–1627)

I live, like those that keep bowling alleys, by the sins of the people.

Thomas Dekker (dramatist, 1572–1632)

The apparent confusions and contradictions endemic in the judgement of bowls continued; so did the worst evils as well as the best benefits of the game. Beware the thought that the 'golden era' of Elizabeth, who herself made some attempt to keep down so-called unlawful games, was untarnished. Nonetheless the lady was, if nothing else, pragmatic.

'Oh, Well Bowlde!'

For the first time for many a decade a spirit of freedom was in the air, and in this atmosphere sporting activities were, if not actively encouraged, tolerated. In the later years of Elizabeth's reign there were to be the whisperings of a Puritanical reaction, but for the moment if anybody chose to ignore the laws banning illegal games little notice would be taken. Mary's statute of 1555 might still be in force (indeed, following Henry's, it was not repealed until Victoria's reign) but who cared anyway? And was not skill at archery now a thing of the past? No wonder Shakespeare felt free to make such frequent references to bowls.

We thus find in the middle years of Elizabeth's reign a spread of greens in London and the provinces. In the Chamberlain's account book for the Cinque Ports town of New Romney is an entry dated 1587: 'Paid to Andrew Vynall for enclosing ye bowling green – 12*d*.' And so it was in places all over the country. In many towns and villages the ghosts of medieval bowlers silently pace up and down 'Bowling

Green Lanes', 'Bowling Green Streets' and 'Bowling Green Alleys' – so named because of their old open spaces, where once was heard the shouted exclamation of 1588: 'O, well bowlde! When John o' London throwes his bowle, he will run after it and crie rub, rub, rub!'

The game as played in the days of Merrie England differed vastly from the well-regulated game of today. Games were organized on a 'rubbers' basis: the best two out of three, the first game being known as the 'foregame'. Play was normally on a singles basis, the object being to try to get one's wood to rest on the jack or 'mistress', often later referred to as the 'block'. Although the greens were specially constructed the grass was coarse, the surface bumpy and there was no division into rinks. The game was so simple in its conception that it needed no set of complicated rules. Bowls were hand-turned from a variety of different woods and crude by modern standards.

Alfred H. Haynes (author), 1974

In the confused medley of games of 'casting', throwing and bowling, the bowls themselves, which had developed from stone, now became iron for some and wood for others . . . but the distinctive, crucial factor in the skilful sport we know today had arrived in at least some forms of the game: bias. At first it had been obtained not through shaping but by the insertion or 'clapping-on' of brass, pewter, lead or iron.

A little altering of the one side maketh the bowl to run biasse waies.

Robert Recorde (mathematician), 1556

Bias – Who Began It?

The story goes that the game which decided bias was played in 1522 at Goole, Yorkshire – from which place the hero of this game, Charles Brandon, also known as Duke of Suffolk, had planned to elope with Princess Mary (sister of Henry VIII) to Spain.

A rink comprising George Thomas, lead, William Elliott, second, Clement Balfour, No. 3, and Brandon, skip, was opposed to a rink skipped by John Richard. Up to the 15th end the game stood about even, first one rink up two or three points, then the other. At the 16th end John Richard's team had one bowl about six inches in front of the jack, and when it was Brandon's turn to bowl he made a vigorous running shot. When this bowl hit the opponent's bowl which was in the way, Brandon's bowl split in half.

Brandon was not easily defeated. He ran to the nearest house and with a borrowed handsaw amputated the nearly round top from a post at the foot of the banister. Then, with a few easy touches from his sword he quickly had the rough spot where the disc should be smoothed out and was ready for his second shot. Bowled in his usual way, it went off several feet to one side.

At the next end he allowed for this bias, and his wood went out and around all the other bowls on the green and came in for shot. This was repeated on the 18th, 19th, 20th and 21st ends, thus bringing victory to Brandon by four shots. After this, it was not long before all bowlers had their bowls turned a little smaller on one side.

At the end of the game, Brandon visited the house of the widow Mrs Mary Woodhall, from whose house he had, without permission, sawn off the banister post, and rewarded her with £5, besides having a local carpenter instal a new post.

Whatever effect this game may have had on the evolution of bias it is known that still earlier bowls were, in fact, biased. There have been discoveries of primitive balls, discs and bowls in all the continents. Apart from Egyptian discoveries, relics have been discovered among the Red Indian, South American, Polynesian, Pacific and Maori tribes. These, however, were no doubt used in ancient games having a ritualistic or ceremonial basis which had usually become extinct long before they could have made any useful contribution to the development of our modern game. The Maori and Red Indian discoveries suggest that the natives recognized the effect of bias, but whether this was by design or accident our data is as yet too incomplete to allow us to do more than guess.

Dr John W. Fisher, 1956

I have no faith in the chestnut about Charles Brandon, Duke of Suffolk, which I first saw attributed to *The Bowls News*. Frankly, I don't believe a word of it and my doubts are borne out by the reference to Princess Mary planning to elope with the Duke. In 1522 the couple were already married. Princess Mary became Suffolk's wife in 1515. At that time she was the widowed queen of King Louis XII of France, whom she had married at the age of eighteen. Why, then, should she 'elope' with her own husband seven years later?

Nor is there any evidence that the game of fours as at present played was in vogue in 1522: all the evidence from the many books I have read is to the contrary. Yet the legend quoted refers to 21 ends being played and names leads, and 2's and 3's.

As for bias, there is evidence that this was operative even before Charles Brandon, Duke of Suffolk, was born. The game of half-bowl is described by a writer called Fitzstevens in 1477–8. This game was played with the aid of fifteen conical pins. Twelve pins were arranged in an axle, with another pin in the centre and two at the back. The object was to send the half-bowl round the two pins and then, because of the bias pulling the bowl, knock over the pins forming the circle.

Most books quote Shakespeare on bias – and his quotations in plays about English monarchs are set in the late twelfth (King John) and fourteenth (Richard II) centuries. A genius like Shakespeare is no more likely to have used bowling bias as a metaphor in the mouths of characters of earlier centuries if bias had not existed than we would expect a modern playwright to refer to Gladstone talking about microchips when writing a play about Victorian England.

I am convinced that bias has been with us a long time and existed well before the sixteenth century. In his *Bowls Encyclopaedia*, Australia's J. P. Monroe, BA, says that stone bowls (known as chunka) used by the Red Indians of Canada and the United States and by ancient Maoris in New Zealand were biased. To prove it, specimens of the Indian bowls, he writes, are in the Museum at Vancouver, British Columbia, in the collection of the late Mr Jones of Brooklyn (USA), and one of the Maori bowls is in the National Museum in New Zealand.

Donald Newby (*World Bowls* magazine), 1981

Bias the Philosopher was the first bowler and, ever since, the most part of bowles do in memory of their originall weare his badge of remembrance and very dutifully hold bias.

John Taylor ('The Water Poet'), 1630

I was privileged to examine nine bowls unearthed in the course of excavations for an extension of a brewery in the ancient London borough of Southwark. They are made of yew or box and bear no trace of lead. On the contrary, the bias-bulge is very pronounced and was no doubt effected by the lathe.

They are of the size of the archaic English bowl and, all things considered, in excellent preservation. They have, of course, lost their outward beauty. The varnish has gone; the eyes have vanished though the sockets remain; and the wood has cast a few flakes. Whether they are of Tudor age, as has been alleged, is a matter for conjecture, but it was not without emotion that a bowler of the twentieth century sat in Dr Johnson's easy chair and handled bowls that might have swept a Southwark green what time Shakespeare was acting hard by at The Globe.

J. A. Manson, 1912

Did Shakespeare Play?

William Shakespeare was not only a frequenter of greens and alleys but a keen and capable player. Leigh Hunt surmises, in his genially gossipy way, that Shakespeare divided his declining years between his books, his bowling green and his daughter Susanna. But he must have had an intimate acquaintance with the game long before he finally retired to Stratford-on-Avon in 1609, the year in which – so Dr Furnivall conjectures – he withdrew from active connection with the theatre.

The Commodity speech of the Bastard, Philip Falconbridge, in *King John* (Act II, scene i), considered to have been composed in 1596, makes particularly elaborate use of bias by way of metaphor:

> Commodity, the bias of the world;
> The world, who of itself is peised well,
> Made to run even upon even ground,
> Till this advantage, this vile-drawing bias,
> This sway of motion, this commodity
> Makes it take head from all indifferency,
> From all direction, purpose, course, intent:
> And this same bias, this commodity,
> This bawd, this broker, this all-changing word,
> Clapp'd on the outward eye of fickle France,
> Hath drawn him from his own determin'd aid,
> From a resolv'd and honourable war,
> To a most base and vile-concluded peace.

We derive no similar information about bowls from any other poet, ancient or modern, and the conclusion from that speech and allusions in other of his plays is irresistible that Shakespeare knew the game and played it as though he loved it.

J. A. Manson, 1912

Because of the absorbing interest he displayed in all that was going on around him it was typical of Shakespeare that he should introduce into his writings a number of references to bowls, but this does not necessarily mean, as some have asserted, that the Bard of Avon was himself a bowler. Shakespeare wrote knowledgeably on herbs and wild flowers but this does not prove that botany was among his hobbies; he wrote of treasures lying on the bed of the ocean but this does not mean he was ever a deep-sea diver. The most we can say with any certainty is that Shakespeare had more than a casual knowledge of the game. Whether this was acquired as a player, as a spectator or from associates we shall probably never know. Nor does it really matter. More important is that through the dramas and comedies he wrote during the period 1589–1613 some fragmentary knowledge concerning the game of bowls as it was played in the Elizabethan era has survived.

A piece of all-too-familiar bowls jargon in the matter of luck is 'the rub of the green'. The word 'rub' had become part of the bowler's vocabulary even in Shakespeare's time. In *Richard II* (Act III, scene iv) the Queen, obviously in an anxious and depressed state of mind, is found strolling in the Duke of York's garden at Langley:

Queen: What sport shall we devise here in this garden,
  To drive away the heavy thought of care?

1st Lady: Madam, we'll play at bowls.

Queen: 'Twill make me think.
  The world is full of rubs, and that my fortune
  Runs agains the bias.

Similarly in *Love's Labour's Lost* (Act IV, scene i) Lord Boyet's reply to the suggestion that he should challenge the Princess's lady-in-waiting, Maria, to bowls:

Costard: She's too hard for you at pricks*, sir;
Challenge her to bowl.

Boyet: I fear too much rubbing. Good night, my good owl.

The foregoing passages in *Richard II* and *Love's Labour's Lost* indicate that, difficult though it must have been to bend the knee in wasp-waisted and hooped dresses, unsuitability of attire did not keep the fair sex off the green. They, too, enjoyed bowls, and from Lord Boyet's comment in *Love's Labour's Lost* we may assume that the sexes played with and against each other. Whether or not we may also infer that the lady bowlers of Elizabeth's day relied more on rubs than on skill of delivery is a matter for delicate conjecture! The more positive inference is that the ladies were no less familiar with biased woods than the men.

Obviously Shakespeare had taken careful note of the manner in which woods deviated from a straight-line run towards the target object. A man who saw 'tongues in trees, books in running brooks, sermons in stones and good in everything', the ever-observant Shakespeare could not help but see in the curving path of a wood on the green a piece of metaphorical material which could well illustrate his thoughts. As a result he put the word 'bias' into the mouths of his characters on a number of occasions. How keenly observant he was of the property that gives to bowls their curving run came out to the full in that speech in *King John*.

Among Shakespeare's romantic dramas was *Cymbeline*, set in that period when Caesar Augustus was emperor of the Roman world. Full of historical importance to bowlers is Act II, scene i, in which Cloten, stepson of the King of Britain, complains about the bad luck he has had in a game:

Cloten: Was there ever man had such luck! When I kissed the jack, upon an up-cast to be hit away! I had a hundred pound on't; and then a whoreson jackanapes must take me up for swearing; as if I borrowed mine oaths of him, and might not spend them at my pleasure.

First Lord: What got he by that? You have broke his pate with your bowl.

---

* 'Pricks' is a reference to archery.

In later years the target-object was to have a variety of names, but here, in a Shakespearean play, is evidence that the word 'jack' used today was on the lips of bowlers 400 years ago.

I well remember one occasion when, by means of a firing or 'up-cast' wood, I whisked away a clubmate's bowl that was fondling or kissing the jack. 'Dirty trick!' yelled the annoyed opponent in tones so loud that play on the adjoining rinks was brought to a startled and temporary halt. Just as it happens today so it happened yesterday: Cloten was certainly not the first to express annoyance when he saw his 'sitter' being removed by an 'up-cast' shot. Nor, let it be said, will the indignant clubmate be the last! The language and emotions that go with the game span the centuries, and Cloten's outburst shows that in bowls as in everything else there is nothing new under the sun.

What intensified Cloten's anger was that the 'up-cast' wood had lost him a wager of £100. Even by today's monetary standards £100 would represent for most people a considerable stake; convert the money values of Shakespeare's time into present-day currency and the amount of Cloten's bet reaches a figure that none but the extremely wealthy would care to risk. Not only does the quotation give an indication of the very high stakes played for in Shakespeare's day; it also shows that betting (presumably on the shot wood) was indulged in by contestants as well as by spectators.

'And then a whoreson jackanapes must take me up for swearing,' explodes Cloten, 'as if I borrowed mine oaths of him, and might not spend them at my pleasure.' So it was not only gambling that was associated with the game, it was oaths and cursing as well. The picture that emerges is not very attractive. It is made all the less attractive by the glib and patronizing comment by Cloten's companion that at least his master had had the satisfaction of breaking with his bowl the head of the critic on the bank.

By introducing the game of bowls into *Cymbeline* Shakespeare posed an extremely puzzling question. Like every master of the dramatic art before and after him the great Bard had no hesitation when the occasion demanded in taking poetic licence. So long as they helped along the plot all sorts of artificial devices and unrelated characters and situations were introduced into the play. The three witches in *Macbeth* are an example. As has already been said, the period of *Cymbeline* is set in the days when Caesar Augustus sat on the emperor's throne. And yet Shakespeare goes out of his way to establish

Cloten as a bowls enthusiast and puts in his mouth the language of the green. Was Shakespeare taking advantage of poetic licence? Or did he, in fact, have available a long-lost source of knowledge to show that bowls was played in Britain in the days of early AD?

The game is referred to in a number of other Shakespearean plays. Thus in *Coriolanus* (Act V, scene ii) Menenius Agrippa to the Roman guard:

> Nay, sometimes,
> Like to a bowl upon a subtle ground,
> I have tumbled past the throw.

In *Love's Labour's Lost* (Act V, scene ii) Costard pays the curate, Sir Nathaniel, the compliment:

> He is a marvellous good neighbour, insooth; and a very good bowler.

The reference to clergy brings into focus John Aylmer (1521–94), Bishop of London, who thought it no sin to play at Fulham Palace on Sunday afternoons; the record has it that his language during play fell short of that expected of a dignitary of the cloth.

Exclaims Petruchio in *The Taming of the Shrew* (Act IV, scene v):

> Well, forward, forward! thus the bowl should run,
> And not unluckily against the bias.

Hamlet and *The Merry Wives of Windsor* –

> Alas! I had rather be set quick i' the earth,
> And bowl'd to death with turnips

– are but two of Shakespeare's other plays in which reference is made to the game.

Alfred H. Haynes

Hamlet (Act II, scene i) contains a very neat allusion: to my mind it is the prettiest of all the poet's references. Polonius directs his servant Reynaldo to find out how his son Laertes conducts himself in Paris. He is ordered to make very indirect enquiries, leading up to them by pretending but a slight acquaintance with Laertes, and to report what he can in that way learn from conversations with the Danskers in the city. Polonius, after giving many cunning suggestions, concludes:

> See you now;
> Your bait of falsehood takes this carp of truth:
> And thus do we of wisdom and of reach,
> With windlaces, and with assays of bias,
> By indirections find directions out:
> So, by my former lecture and advice,
> Shall you, my son.

From *The Winter's Tale* (Act IV, scene iii) the following extract must speak for itself:

Servant: Master, there is three carters, three shepherds, three neat herds, three swineherds, that have made themselves all men of hair; they call themselves saltiers: and they have a dance which the wenches say is a gallimaufry of gambols, because they are not in't; but they themselves are o' the mind, if it be not too rough for some that know little but bowling, it will please plentifully.

E. T. Ayers, 1894

In olden times bowls bulged on one side, hence:

> Blow, villain, till thy sphered bias cheek
> Outswell the colic of puff'd Acuilon.
> *Troilus and Cressida*

Dr John W. Fisher

The introduction of bowls in *Cymbeline* is included by Douce, in *Illustrations of Shakespeare*, in a critical list of Shakespearian anachronisms; but as the period of time is 43 AD (when quoiting, putting, football and cockfighting were familiar pastimes of the Romans) Douce may be wrong and Shakespeare right. The 'base football player' in *King Lear* and Cleopatra's invitation to 'billiards' in *Antony and Cleopatra* are unnoticed by the authority, so there is room for doubt.

The *Dictionnaire Universel des Sciences* says, 'The game of billiards appears to be derived from the game of bowls. It was known in England in old time and was perhaps invented there.' Strutt, writing of billiards, says: 'I cannot help thinking it originated from an ancient game played with small bowls upon the ground, and indeed that it was, when first instituted, the same game transferred from the ground to the table.' The thought occurs: might not the green lawn be the prototype of the green cloth? If billiards is derived from bowls it is quite probable that the Romans introduced some such games into this country and the allusion in *Cymbeline* may be quite appropriate.

Nothing authentic regarding the rules of the game of bowls, down to a comparatively recent period, seems to be available; nor whether the ground was specially prepared or not. In –

> Sometimes like to a bowl upon a subtle ground,
> I have tumbled past the throw

– from *Coriolanus* there is an indication of a peculiar character of the ground where a knowledge of the *surface* would be essential to success and that the early Romans played the game on greens (or grounds) that were not dead level. Ben Jonson uses the expression 'the subtlest bowling-green in all Tartary'. English greens are raised in the centre (in Scotland they are or should be level), which causes the bowl, having little or no bias, to run in a curved line. This peculiarity may be a perpetuation of the alluded-to subtlety.

The morris green was, in all probability, the bowling green about the time of Queen Elizabeth and earlier. It was certainly a green set apart for games and revelry. In *The Winter's Tale* –

> If it be not too rough for some that know little but bowling

– brings the morris dance and bowling in conjunction. The morris dancers were invariably masculine. The fool or clown in the morris dance (the Jack-on-the-Green) suggests the thought that the jack in bowls may owe its origin to the wide significance of the term as applied to individuals. We have the terms 'jack-ass' and 'jack-pudding', describing a merry-Andrew or clown; jack, a cunning fellow; jack-o'-lantern or Will-o'-the-wisp; and Jack-a-Lent, a puppet or butt thrown at for sport on Ash Wednesday. As the living 'Jack' was the butt or centre to which gravitated all the fooling, or was the main attraction of a convivial company in the Middle Ages, so the jack in bowls is the point round which all the interest of the game is centred. The analogy of the terms is both close and ancient.

Humphrey J. Dingley, 1893

On fine evenings there were morris dances on the elastic turf of the bowling green.

Thomas Macaulay (author, *History of England, c.*1850), describing Buxton in previous centuries

6

Drake: Did He or Didn't He?

Did Sir Francis Drake insist on finishing a game on Plymouth Hoe in 1588 despite the oncoming Spanish Armada? – a hoary but perennially seductive debate. The legend – legend? – has been perpetuated by a painting by John Seymour Lucas, RA (1849–1923) and Charles Kingsley's Westward Ho! *published in 1855 . . .*

What if the spectators who last summer gazed with just pride upon the noble port of Plymouth, its vast breakwater spanning the Sound, its arsenals and docks, its two estuaries filled with gallant ships, and watched the great screw-liners turning within their own length by force invisible, or threading the crowded fleets with the ease of the tiniest boat; what if, by some magic turn, the nineteenth century and all the magnificence of its wealth and science had vanished – as it may vanish hereafter – and they had found themselves thrown back 300 years into the pleasant summer days of 1588?

Kingsley proceeds to paint the scene that would have greeted a visitor – including the ships that would tomorrow 'begin the greatest sea-fight the world has ever seen'. Then –

But if, again, he had been a student of men rather than of machinery, he would have found few nobler companies on whom to exercise his discernment than he might have seen in the little terrace bowling-green behind the Pelican Inn on the afternoon of the 19th July. Chatting in groups, or lounging over the low wall which commanded a view of the Sound and the shipping far below, were gathered almost every notable man of the Plymouth fleet, the whole *passe comitatus* of 'England's forgotten worthies'.

The Armada has been scattered by a storm. Lord Howard has been out to look for it as far as the Spanish coast; but the wind has shifted to the south and, fearing lest the Dons should pass him, he has returned to

Plymouth uncertain whether the Armada will come after all or not. Slip on for awhile, like Prince Hal, the drawer's apron; come in through the rose-clad door which opens from the tavern, with a tray of long-necked Dutch glasses and a silver tankard of wine, and look round you at the gallant captains, who are waiting for the Spanish Armada as lions in their lair might wait for the passing herd of deer.

See those five talking earnestly in the centre of a ring which longs to overhear and yet is too respectful to approach close. Those soft, long eyes and pointed chin you recognize already, they are Walter Raleigh's. The fair young man in the flame-coloured doublet, whose arm is round Raleigh's neck, is Lord Sheffield; opposite them stands, by the side of Sir Richard Grenville, a man as stately even as he, Lord Sheffield's uncle, the Lord Charles Howard of Effingham, Lord High Admiral of England; next to him is his son-in-law, Sir Robert South-well, captain of the *Elizabeth Jonas*; but who is that short, sturdy, plainly dressed man who stands with legs a little apart and hands behind his back, looking up with keen, grey eyes into the face of each speaker? His cap is in his hands, so you can see the bullet head of crisp brown hair and the wrinkled forehead as well as the high cheekbones, the short, square face, the broad temples, the thick lips, which are yet firm as granite. A coarse, plebeian stamp of man; yet the whole fiture and attitude are that of boundless determination, self-possession, energy; and when at last he speaks a few blunt words all eyes are turned respectfully upon him – for his name is Francis Drake.

A burly, grizzled elder, in greasy, sea-stained garments contrasting oddly with the huge gold chain about his neck, waddles up, as if he had been born and had lived ever since in a gale of wind at sea. The upper half of his sharp, dogged visage seems of brick-red leather, the lower of badger's fur; and as he claps Drake on his back and with a broad Devon twang shouts, 'Be you a-coming to drink your wine, Francis Drake, or be you not? – saving your presence, my lord,' the Lord High Admiral only laughs, and bids Drake go and drink his wine; for John Hawkins, Admiral of the Port, is the patriarch of Plymouth seamen if Drake be their hero and says and does pretty much what he likes in any company on earth.

So they push through the crowd, wherein is many another man whom one would gladly have spoken with face to face on earth . . .

The author names the others and relates their conversation. During it, John Hawkins, the Admiral, says: 'I go play bowls with Drake.'

He 'waddles' off. Kingsley continues his account of the conversations. Hawkins joins in, then returns to Drake and bowls. Another man bursts in, the piratical Captain Thomas Fleming . . .

'Who com'th here now?'

'Captain Fleming, as I'm a sinner.'

'Fleming! Is he tired of life, that he com'th here to look for a halter? I've a warrant out against mun for robbin' of two Flushingers on the high seas now this very last year. Is the fellow mazed or dunk, then? Or has he seen a ghost? Look to mun!'

'I think so, truly,' said Drake. 'His eyes are near out of his head.'

The man was a rough-bearded old sea-dog who had just burst in from the tavern through the low hatch, upsetting a drawer with all its glasses, and now came panting and blowing straight up to the High Admiral –

'My lord, my lord! They'm coming! I saw them off the Lizard last night!'

'Who, my good sir, who seem to have left your manners behind you?'

'The Armada, your worship – the Spaniard; but as for my manners, 'tis no fault of mine for I never had none to leave behind me.'

'If he has not left his manners behind,' quoth Hawkins, 'look out for your purses, gentlemen all! He's manners enough, and very bad ones they be, when he com'th across a quiet Flushinger!'

'If I stole Flushingers' wines, I never stole negurs' souls, Jack Hawkins; so there's your answer. My lord, hang me if you will: life's short and death's easy, 'specially to seamen; but if I didn't see the Spanish fleet last sundown, coming along half-moon wise and full seven miles from wing to wing within a four mile of me, I'm a sinner.'

'Sirrah,' said Lord Howard, 'is this no fetch, to cheat us out of your pardon for these piracies of yours?'

'You'll find out for yourself before nightfall, my Lord High Admiral. All Jack Fleming says, is, that is a poor sort of an answer to a man who has put his own neck into the halter for the sake of his country.'

'Perhaps it is,' said Lord Howard. 'And after all, gentlemen, what can this man gain by a lie, which must be discovered ere a day is over, except a more certain hanging?'

'Very true, your lordship,' said Hawkins, mollified; 'come here, Jack Fleming – what wilt drain, man? Hippocras or alicant, sack or John Barleycorn, and a pledge to thy repentance and amendment of life.'

'Admiral Hawkins, Admiral Hawkins, this is no time for drinking.'

'Why not, then, my lord? Good news should be welcomed with good wine. Frank, send down to the sexton, and set the bells a-ringing to cheer up all honest hearts. Why, my lord, if it were not for the gravity of my office I could dance a galliard for joy!'

'Well, you may dance, Port Admiral: but I must go and plan: but God give to all captains such a heart as yours this day!'

'And God give all generals such a head as yours! Come, Frank Drake, we'll play the game out before we move. It will be two good days before we shall be fit to tackle them so an odd half-hour don't matter.'

'I must command the help of your counsel, Vice-admiral,' said Lord Charles, turning to Drake.

'And it's this, my good lord,' said Drake, looking up, as he aimed his bowl. 'They'll come soon enough for us to show them sport, and yet slow enough for us to be ready; so let no man hurry himself. And as example is better than precept, here goes.'

Lord Howard shrugged his shoulders and departed, knowing two things; first, that to move Drake was to move mountains; and next, that when the self-taught hero did bestir himself he would do more work in an hour than anyone else in a day. So he departed, followed hastily by most of the captains; and Drake said in a low voice to Hawkins:

'Does he think we are going to knock about on a lee-shore all the afternoon and run our noses at night – and dead up-wind, too – into the Dons' mouths? No, Jack, my friend. Let Orlando-Furioso-puntilio-fire-eaters go and get their knuckles rapped. The following game is the game, and not the meeting one. The dog goes after the sheep and not afore them, lad. Let them go by, and go by, and stick to them well to windward, and pick up stragglers, and pickings, too, Jack – the prizes, Jack!'

'Trust my old eyes for not being over-quick at seeing signals, if I be hanging in the skirts of a fat-looking Don. We'm the eagles, Drake; and where the carcass is, is our place, eh?'

And so the two old sea-dogs chatted on, while their companions dropped off one by one . . .

. . . 'There, Vice-admiral, you're beaten, and that is the rubber. Pay up three dollars, old high-flyer, and go and earn more, like an honest adventurer!'

'Well,' said Drake, as he pulled out his purse, 'we'll walk down now and see about these young hot-heads. As I live, they are setting to tow the ships out already! Breaking the men's backs overnight to make them fight the lustier in the morning! Well well, they haven't sailed round the world, Jack Hawkins.'

'Or had to run home from St Juan D'Ulloa with half a crew.'

'Well, if we haven't to run out with half-crews. I saw a sight of our lads drunk about this morning.'

'The more reason for waiting till they be sober. Besides, if everybody's caranting about at once, each after his own men, nobody'll find nothing in such a scrimmage as that . . . We'm going to blow the Dons up now in earnest.'

And now began that great sea-fight which was to determine whether Popery and despotism or Protestantism and freedom were the law which God had appointed for the half of Europe and the whole of future America.

Charles Kingsley, 1855

Oh, No, He Didn't . . .

Among the many legends that have sprung up round Drake, there is none that merits credence less than that which recounts his lunatic behaviour when this news arrived. Indeed, it would be quite as reasonable to accept the legend that he hewed his bowls to bits and threw the pieces into the sea and that from each chip there sprang a warship fully armed.

The odds which would have been so overwhelmingly against the Spanish if the north wind had not failed and Drake had succeeded in pinning them helplessly into the harbour of Corunna were now exactly reversed, and the English fleet was pinned in Plymouth Sound at the mercy of guns and fire-ships precisely as the Spanish would have been. The only thing that could possibly save England was that her Navy, in the teeth of the south-west wind which still blew, should regain the sea again before the Armada ruffling proudly along from the Lizard closed the entrance of the Sound. Every minute that elapsed brought utter and final disaster nearer and, since there is no real reason to suppose that the news sent Drake stark, staring mad, we must assume that he decided to postpone his game for less critical times and ran down to the quayside with the captains at his heels.

E. F. Benson, *Life of Drake*, 1927

Oh, Yes, He Did!

Most people regard the matter as a pure fiction, an invention of Charles Kingsley. But this is not so; and the writer has discovered evidence which may bring the narrative out of the region of tradition into the realm of fact. Creasy's *Fifteen Decisive Battles of the World* reports the incident; and, while other authorities might be cited to prove the authenticity of the old story, the following is sufficient:

In 1736 there appeared a *Life of Sir Walter Raleigh* prefixed to Raleigh's *History of the World* in which Oldys, the writer of the ill-fated courtier's biography, mentions the fact in detail and refers to another work, entitled *Phoenix Britannicus*, which appeared to carry the story back another hundred years. This work is *A Miscellaneous Collection of Scarce and Curious Tracts, Historical, Political, Biographical, Satirical, Characteristical, etc. in prose and verse, only to be found in the Cabinets of the Curious, Interspersed with Choice Pieces from Original MSS, Collected by J. Morgan, Gent.*, published in 1732. On pages 345–6 is the following statement, which occurs in a tract or pamphlet reprinted from the original printed in 1624. Says the Duke of Braganza, in a supposititious speech ascribed to that nobleman:

> Did we not in '88 carry our business for England so cunningly and secretly, as well as that well-dissembled Treaty with the English, near Ostend . . . as in bringing our navy to their shores while their commanders and captains were at bowls upon the Hoe at Plymouth; and had my Lord Alonzo Guzman, the Duke of Medina Sidonia, but the resolution (but, in truth, his commission was otherwise), he might have surprised them as they lay at anchor and the like.

This appears good evidence, for if the statement made as to the date of this pamphlet is reliable the story was currently known and believed less than forty years after the events were supposed to have taken place and while many persons were living who would remember the incidents and might have refuted them if incorrect.

W. H. K. Wright (Plymouth historian), 1888

Oh, No, He Didn't!

One prefers to support Mr Benson's view. Sir Walter Raleigh is included in the group assembled at the green; but Raleigh's great concern at the time as to the best methods of dealing with the Spaniards bears out Mr Benson's contention that a moment's delay would have been fatal. Before the invasion Raleigh wrote: 'A fleet of ships may be seen at sunset and after it at the Lizard, yet by the morning they may recover Portland, whereas any army of foot shall not be able to march it in six days.' With that in mind, Raleigh, who at that time was commissioned to raise and equip the land forces of Cornwall and was also Commander of Plymouth, would certainly not agree to the officers of the Navy, high as they were, who had put into port for a specific purpose, taking a national risk by playing a game of bowls.

George T. Burrows, 1948

Oh, Yes, He Did!

We do well to respect traditions long and generally held rather than follow the modern craze for discrediting every statement for which there is no certain documentary evidence. Unfortunately for such critics definite evidence does exist, in the *Vox Populi* of 1624. The game finished, the ships were duly warped out (since they could not at that time sail within six points of the wind) by the 'admirable industry of the seamen', as Oldys says. And in good time, too, since it was not till noon the next day that they 'ken'd the Spanish Fleet'.

C. W. Bracken, *History of Plymouth*, 1928

Well, *Did* He?

It seems fairly certain that a tide suitable for sailing was not running earlier than ten o'clock on the night of 19th July. When the news reached Drake at 4 p.m. the tide was low, so that Drake, undoubtedly aware of this, as would also be his officers, was not indulging in mock-heroics in refusing to be flustered and marking time until he could set sail on an out-going tide. Whether he was actually playing bowls cannot be substantiated. If he was, he was setting a bad example: bowls was illegal.

Dr John W. Fisher, 1956

Possibly the strongest shot in the locker of the 'it's-all-a-myth' school is that Drake, a vice-admiral, would hardly have had the authority to decide what steps to take when the Armada was reported. With him on Plymouth Hoe was Lord Charles Howard, the Lord High Admiral of England, and the decision to make ready to meet the Armada would rest with him.

Another reason given to discredit the story is that bowls was forbidden and senior Naval officers would have been unlikely to break the law in public. Against that one could put the twentieth-century betting laws, which are probably more honoured in the breach than the observance. In any case the legislation was enacted to safeguard archery, and the bow and arrow were obsolete as war weapons before Philip of Spain despatched his Armada.

Captain Fleming, it is generally accepted, first sighted the Armada . . . but could it not be that Drake on Plymouth Hoe, with a view over Plymouth Sound, saw the ships as quickly as anyone else and may have had the advantage of knowing that the Spaniards, possibly not sailing in battle order, were bound for the Netherlands? Drake, it may be argued, planned to let the Spaniards move up the Channel before beating against the wind to clear the harbour and then taking advantage of the westerly wind which would favour his lighter and more manoeuvrable craft against the heavier, clumsier Spanish ships. Obviously there was little to be gained by ordering – if he had power to do so – the English fleet to run out of harbour against an adverse wind. To have done so, with a treacherous shore behind them and lighter fire-power at close range, would have been as suicidal as General Lindsay's move from an impregnable hill at Dunbar down to the flat ground, where his army was virtually annihilated by Cromwell's cavalry. This theory is borne out by M. Lewis in his *History of the British Navy*, who says, 'In the days of sail, in waters where the westerlies prevail and when beating up-wind was a slow and chancy business, the defending fleet must keep the wind of any Channel invader – that is, remain to the west of it.'

However, Benson does not give much credence to the view that the Spaniards were Netherlands-bound: Plymouth and the English fleet were their objectives, he says. And while Oldys, in his *Life of Raleigh*, accepts that Drake was bowling, he insists he was persuaded to give up his game and take on a contest of a sterner nature.

Who's Who and Encyclopedia of Bowls, 1959

And Where?

There is no shred of local evidence as to the existence of a green on the Hoe in those days. Kingsley's Pelican Inn green is a literary invention.

George T. Burrows, 1948

The Hoe is a high hill standing between the town and the sea, a very delightful place whereon is an exceeding fair compass for prospect and recreation; and here the townsmen and sailors pass their leisure in walking, bowling and other pleasant pastimes.

Thomas Westcote, *A View of Devonshire*, **1930**

Though the Hoe may have been largely a furze-brake at that time, there is no reason why a green should not have existed on the slopes above Sutton Pool, near which Drake and his companions would certainly have lodged and congregated.

C. W. Bracken, 1928

The Hoe then extended from Lambhay to Millbay, the huge Citadel did not exist and there were inns in the locality of Lambhay either of which might answer to Kingsley's Pelican, a title adopted doubtless because of the name of one of Drake's ships. It is impossible now to locate inn or spot, and it would be equally futile to endeavour to prove that bowls now preserved in Torquay were the bowls with which Drake played.

W. H. K. Wright, 1888

All Bowls

In the Wellington club in New Zealand is an old wooden bowl, 6 inches by 4 inches thick. On it is inscribed, 'Said to be the identical bowl that was being handled by Sir Francis Drake when he was advised that the Spanish Armada was in sight. Dug from the ground when improvements were being made to Plymouth Hoe.' However, the bowl is not of lignum vitae – and as Drake knew the West Indies well and his men had played at Darien fifteen years before the Armada, it is believed that his bowls would be made of lignum vitae.

The Sir Francis Drake club in Plymouth has a set of bowls said to be those used by him, but they are studded all over with hobnails and are perfectly round. They are in all probability French bowls, which are unbiased, but we know that bowls were biased in Drake's day.

If the bowls exist at all, the most likely set are in the museum at the Bath Saloons in Torquay. They are coloured: one pair green, one pair yellow and one red. It is said they come from the tower of Trematon Castle, near Saltash, Cornwall, the residence of Drake's descendants.

Who's Who and Encyclopedia of Bowls, 1959

Clear as Iron and Gravel

It is strange what misunderstandings have persisted. To a player of iron bowls the affair seems clear.

In those days areas of bare sandy, stony soil abounded, as we can see from contemporary pictures, and bowls was widely played much in the manner in which it is played in France, Switzerland, Spain, Italy and South America today. It was not played, however, on the few delicate, spongy, camomile lawns or on the scythed rough grass of those times: it was not until 1832 that Budding invented the lawn-mower and the age of the shaven lawn really began. Gradually the big wooden bowls that were rolled slowly along the ground usurped the place of the fast-pitched bowls. The latter, however, have persisted to the present day as an even more popular game on the Continent, where grass lawns are less of a fetish than in this country.

The game of iron bowls was certainly played a long time ago by naval and military personnel on foreign stations. More often than not, looking out over the countryside or sea would be a level, gravelled terrace on which stood the primitive cannon of those days and, beside, a neat pyramidal pile of iron cannonballs. They were too heavy to hit with a bat or club or to catch safely when thrown, and the natural instinct would be to pitch or bowl them to a definite point, perhaps marked by a little coloured stone or other such object. Often more or less 'confined to barracks' through hostile inhabitants, the bored soldiers or sailors would become increasingly interested in the game, so that even in home ports they would want to go on with it. There is a picture of a sixteenth-century artilleryman playing *boules* with small cannonballs in *Les Fadas de la Petanque* by Francis Huger.

Drake and his fellows would certainly have been playing what is called in France *A la longue* or *Lyonnaise*: that is to say, with the jack about twenty yards from the throwing point. The short game, *Petanque*, is a comparatively recent invention.

So Plymouth Hoe at that time was an expanse of sandy gravel, and Sir Francis and his brother officers were playing there with these little iron cannonballs that, like cricket balls, fit so nicely into the human hand. The fateful messenger rushed up to Sir Francis who had his bowl already in his hand. As we know (Thomas Scott, *Vox Populi* or *News from Spain*, 1620) Navy morale was not high, and Drake's reply 'There is plenty of time to win the game and beat the Spaniards, too' (Tytler's *Life of Raleigh*, 1835) was a sensible morale-builder. Instantly Drake made his shot, but he failed to make the needed point to win the game and 'was soon prevailed on to go and play out the rubber with the Spaniards' (Morgan's *Life of Raleigh*, 1736).

Thus there should be no slur on this fine commander, who behaved throughout with typical good sense. In fact he would not have gone ashore to play bowls at all were it not that he was well aware that his ships, anchored in Plymouth Sound, could not in any event get to sea for six or seven hours due to on-shore winds and unfavourable tides.

Michael Haworth-Booth, *The Game of Boules*, 1973

And the Legend Bowls On . . .

'You've got your Sir Jack Hobbs, your Sir Leonard Hutton . . . last time a bowler got knighted it was Sir Francis bloody Drake.'

Attributed to F. S. Trueman

7

A Game Fit for Kings . . . and Knaves

A man shall find great art in chusing out his ground, and preventing the winding, hanging and many turning advantages of the same, whether it be in open wilde places or in close allies; and for his sport, the chusing of the bowle is the greatest cunning; your flat bowles being best for allies, your round biazed bowls for open grounds of advantage, and your round bowles like a ball for green swathes that are plain and level.

*Country Contentments, c.*1615

Preferment, like a game at boules,
   To feede our hope hath divers play:
Heere quick it runns, there soft it roules;
   The betters make and shew the way
On upper ground, so great allies
Doe many *cast* on their desire;
Some up are thrust and forc'd to rise,
   When those are stopt that would aspire.

Some, whose heate and zeal exceed,
   Thrive well by *rubbs* that curb their haste,
And some that languish in their speed
   Are cherished by some favour's blaste;
Some rest in other's *cutting out*
The fame by whom themselves are made;
Some fetch a *compass* farr about,
   And secretly the marke invade.

Some get by *knocks,* and so advance
   Their fortune by a boysterous aime:
And some, who have the sweetest chance,
   Their en'mies *hit,* and win the game.

> The fairest *casts* are those that owe
> No thanks to fortune's giddy sway;
> Such honest men good *bowlers* are
> Whose own true *bias cutts* the way.
> **William Stroud,** 1633

. . . Reminders from early in the Stuart period that bowling was popular but, besides, still a confusing brew of styles and venues. It has been suggested that the 'open grounds of advantage' may have been the forerunners of crown greens. James I had recommended a moderate indulgence in bowling to his son, Prince Henry; had himself licensed thirty-one alleys in London in 1617; then, next year, issued the Book of Sports, *officially sanctioning certain traditional pastimes on Sundays after divine service, the only time possible for most people. But there was a qualification . . .*

As for our good people's lawful recreation, our pleasure likewise is, that after the end of Divine service, our good people be not disturbed, letted or discouraged from any lawful recreation such as dancing and archery. But withal we do here account still as prohibited all unlawful games to be used upon Sunday only, as bear and bull-baitings, interludes and at all times to the meaner sort of people by law prohibited bowling.

Then, in 1625, Charles I came to the throne . . .

> Stop, traveller, stop! In yonder peaceful glade
> His favourite game the royal martyr played;
> Here, stripped of honours, children, freedom, rank,
> Drank from the bowl, and bowl'd for what he drank;
> Sought it in a cheerful glass his cares to drown,
> And changed his guinea ere he lost his Crown.
> **Old inn sign**
> at Collins End, near Goring Heath, Oxfordshire

Yes, Charles I; and after him, Charles II. The most concisely adequate summary of the times is perhaps J. M. Pretsell's, writing in 1908 with hindsight – and considerable help from Humphrey Dingley's Touchers and Rubs *of fifteen years earlier . . .*

In the reign of Charles I bowls attained its highest favour, as no royal patron was so enthusiastic. At Barking Hall, Essex, the seat of Richard Shute, MP for London, he was a frequent visitor, Shute having constructed one of the finest greens in the country. According to the custom of the day they frequently played for high stakes, and it is recorded that the losses were paid punctually. On one occasion, it has been said, Charles's losses amounted to £1000. Shute urged him to begin another game in the hope that his bad luck would turn, but the king refused, reminding Shute that he (Charles) must remember his wife and children.

During his enforced leisure at Holdenby, Northamptonshire, after he had been handed over to the Roundheads, Charles often rode over to Lord Spencer's place at Althorp or to Lord Vaux's at Harrowden, where the quality of the greens pleased him better: he is said to have been engaged in a game at Althorp when Cornet Joyce arrived at Holmby to take him to other quarters. Even during his confinement at Caversham Castle he is said to have indulged in his favourite game, and visited, under escort, the green at Collins End on the Oxfordshire side of the Thames. It is further recorded that while Charles was a prisoner at Carisbrook Castle the governor converted the barbican into 'a bowling green scarcely to be equalled, and built at one side a pretty summer house'. Among other places Charles played at Hardurdy House, near Caversham, and when still of royal authority had himself caused a green to be made at Spring Gardens, in St James's, London.

Royal patronage had stamped the game as the fashion, and up to the time of the Commonwealth it retained its position as an outdoor pastime among the privileged classes and was recommended and prescribed by physicians. There were those, however, who gave both game and players a poor recommendation, and John Earle, Bishop of Worcester and chaplain and tutor to Prince Charles, the future Charles II, said bowling was celebrated for three things wasted: 'Time, money and curses.'

Although betting was very common at this time, probably in no game was it found to such an extent. Many an estate was lost on the green, it is said, and Canon Jackson, in *Wilts Magazine*, states that Sir Edward Hungerford lost his in 1648, gambling his property on a match and remarking, as he threw his last bowl, 'Here goes Rowdon.' It is recorded that the sisters of Sir John Suckling, the courtier poet, were actually seen at the green in Piccadilly 'crying for fear he should lose all their possessions'.

It was perhaps natural that a game so strongly patronized by the sovereign should become so popular as to be seriously menaced and ultimately killed by the curse of betting, and this was undoubtedly the condition of the pastime towards the middle of the seventeenth century; and with the example of the nobility and gentry, it is little wonder the lower classes took advantage of the licence authorized by the *Book of Sports*.

James I's *Book of Sports* had been re-issued by Charles, and an edict renewed ordering the people to indulge in certain games on Sundays after public worship. This was met with strong opposition by the Puritans, who saw in the action a blow aimed at their cause by the High Church party, the leader and instigator of which was Laud, Archbishop of Canterbury. William Prinne, a barrister of Lincoln's Inn, was most severely treated for denouncing the pleasures and recreations of the day: he was fined heavily, put in the pillory and afterwards sentenced to imprisonment for life. Those of the clergy who refused to read the decree from their pulpits were punished by being deprived of their livings.

The game on the green, however, was quite different from, and should not be confounded with, the game in the alleys. These latter resorts, invariably attached to taverns or hostelries, must be blamed for most of the abuses which we find linked to the game during the seventeenth and eighteenth centuries. Let the reader imagine a skittle-alley – for preference attached to a tavern – with as little science and less skill necessary than is required for that amusement and he should have a pretty good idea of the ancient bowling alley of 'mine host'. It is unfortunate that in both forms the pastime received the same name, but that fact no doubt accounts for the odium which, through time, became attached also to the game on the green. It would be linked by the close of the seventeenth century, in Stow's *Survey of the Cities of*

London and Westminster, with 'recreations' like drinking and cock-fighting.

J. M. Pretsell

Kissing the Mistress

This wise game doth make the fathers surpasse their children in apish toyes and most delicate dog tricks . . . The mark that which they argue at hath sundry names and epithites, as a 'blocke', a 'jacke' and a 'mistresse' . . . but I hold 'mistresse' to be the fittest name for it, for there are some that are commonly termed mistresses which are not much better than mine aunts and a mistresse is oftentimes a marke for every knave to have a fling at. Everyone strives to come so neere her that hee would kisse her, and yet some are short, some wide and some over, and to whoso doth kisse it may perhaps sweeten his lips but I assure him it shall never fill his belly but rather empty his purse.

John Taylor, 1630

The Puritans

After the triumph of the Puritans during the Civil War the country fell under their drastic rule, and they forthwith laid their heavy hands on all popular amusements. In 1643 the *Book of Sports* was burned publicly, and the people were forbidden under severe penalties to practise bowls, wrestling and other pastimes on Sundays. Archbishop Laud was severely blamed by his Puritan opponents because he played bowls on Sundays; Laud gave a crushing reply and suggested that Calvin – a name held in the highest esteem by the Puritans – allowed and played bowls himself on Sundays.

James Hartley (bowls author), 1922

To the end of his life Cromwell remained the countryman, and his happiest hours were spent in the long weekends at Hampton Court, where he had constructed fish-ponds and enclosed a warren. That was the sole relaxation permitted him, for the times were too critical to go far from London. The only game he played was bowls, though in field sports he had a most catholic taste.

J. Buchan, *Life Story of Oliver Cromwell*

We need not blame the Puritans. They lived in times that tried men's souls and to err is human. Nor had sportsmen of the baser sort long to wait for relief. When the Merry Monarch 'came to his ain' (1660) the reins were speedily given to profligacy – and as a popular pastime bowls almost literally went to pot.

J. A. Manson, 1912

If Bishop Earle had tried to dissuade Prince Charles from bowling, he failed. When Charles acceded in 1660 he confirmed his love for playing, at decorous venues like Tunbridge Wells and Piccadilly Hall, London. The game, incidentally, had almost been fatal to him during his escape after the battle of Worcester . . .

A King's Escape

They came to Mr Norton's house through Bristol sooner than usual, and it being on a holiday they saw many people about a bowling green that was before the door; and the first man the King saw was a chaplain of his own, who was allied to the gentleman of the house and was sitting upon the rails to see how the bowlers played. William, by which name the King went, walked with his horse into the stable until his mistress could provide for his retreat.

Lord Clarendon, *History of the Rebellion*, 1609–74

A King's Laws

With the Restoration, bowls, in common with other things, came into its own again. Great care was taken both in the preparation of greens and the making of woods; the greens became really good, both to see and to play on, and some survive even today. The game became very fashionable and, receiving royal approbation, began to grow in popularity; greens and bowling centres increased in number in consequence. In 1670 twenty rules for the game – King Charles II's Rules* – were drawn up, a number of them closely resembling some of those which operate today.

Felix Hotchkiss (author), 1937

* Reproduced in modern language on p. 282.

A King's Green

	£.	s.	d.
To W. Herbert, for making ye bowling-green and walkes	10	0	0
For cutting turf for ye green	3	12	0
July 12-For 8 Pairs of Bowles and Carriage and Lamps	4	5	6
Sept. 26-Iron work for ye Bowling-green Door	1	17	11
April 18-Will Tonks, 4 days, and W. Herbert, 3 days, at 1/6 per day for making ye walke	0	10	6
Francis Goodall, for 2 days' work in ye walkes	0	2	0
	£20	7	11

Windsor Castle manuscript, 1663

Yet this is the king who enacted heavy penalties on bowlers, tennis players, card-players and others; and, as we have read, Cromwell, the great Puritan, also played bowls. These apparent hypocrisies can be explained only by saying that the repressive statutes were aimed not at the games themselves but at the betting and lawlessness they attracted. The two extremes still existed: the 'persons of quality', with their elegant greens and gardens, and the lowly rabble. Writings of the period, superficially contradictory, reveal the great divide . . .

The Good News . . .

The sports of England are becoming horse-racing, hunting, hawking and bowling. At Marebone and Putney we see persons of quality bowling two or three times a week.

John Locke (philosopher and writer), 1679

Handsome gravel walks with shades and an upper and lower bowling green whither very many of the nobility and gentry of the best quality resorted both for exercise and conversation.

Lord Clarendon (about Piccadilly Hall)

Farringdon: Within half a mile they have lately made a delicate bowling green, where in the summer time the gentry of these parts meet to divert themselves in this pleasant air.

Romford: Adjoining to the churchyard they have a fair bowling green, frequented by the gentry.

Thomas Baskerville (wealthy traveller)

May 1st, 1661: Up early, and bated at Petersfield, in the room which the King lay in lately at his being there. Here very merry, and played us and our wives at bowls.

June 5th, 1661: After dinner to the office, where we sat and did business, and Sir W. Pen and I went home with R. Slingsby (a naval chum) to bowls in his ally, and there had good sport and afterwards went in and drank and talked.

July 26th, 1662: White Hall garden and the bowling ally (where lords and ladies are now at bowles), in brave condition.

Samuel Pepys (diarist)

October 22nd, 1685: Accompanied my Lady Clarendon to her house at Swallowfield in Berks, where was a very fine bowling green.

August 14th, 1687: Went to Durdans to a challenged match at bowls for £10, which we won.

John Evelyn (diarist)

The game requires both art and address. It is only in use during the fair and dry part of the season, and the places where it is practised are charming, delicious walks called bowling greens, which are little square grass plots where the turf is almost as smooth and level as the cloth of a billiard table. As soon as the heat of the day is over, all the company assemble there; they play deep, and spectators are at liberty to make what bets they please.

Count Grammont (French wit at Court of Charles II, in his *Memoirs*)

. . . and the Bad News

Bowling would be much more commendable than it is were it not for those swarms of rooks which so pester greens, bares and alleys where any such places are to be found, some making so small a spot of ground yield them more annually than fifty acres of land shall do elsewhere about this City, and this done by cunning, betting, crafty matching and basely playing booty.

The Compleat Gamester (attributed to Charles Cotton), 1674

May 1st, 1683 (at Blackheath to see the new fair): This was the first day, pretended for the sale of cattle but I think in truth to enrich the new tavern at the bowling green.

John Evelyn (diarist)

June 16th, 1647: This morne I called on Captain Rich and went with him to Bolstertone to bowles. I stayed till 6-at-clock and then came by Hordrue home, in all nine myles. This day I spent for my dinner 6*d.* and lost 3 rubbers 7*s.* 6*d.*, and ale 4*d.*, total 8*s.* 4*d.*

June 23rd, 1647: This morne I went to Ballause and thence with Capt. Rich to Bolstertone to bowles, when I lost 6*s.* and spent 6*d.*, and so came home again at night, eight myles. This night my wife was worse in words than ever.

July 23rd, 1647: Borrowed Edward's colt and rid on him to Bolstertone to bowles, when I lost 2*s.* 10*d.*, spent 1*s.*, in all 3*s.* 10*d.*, and so came home again with Capt. Rich, in all eight myles.

July 30th, 1647: This day I stayed at home all day, by reason my wife was not willing to let me goe to bowles at Bolstertone.

Adam Eyre (Captain in Parliamentary Army)

A bowling green or bowling alley is a place where three things are thrown away besides the bowls: time, money and curses, and the last ten for one. The best sport in it is the Gamester's, and he enjoys it that looks on and betts nothing. It is a school of wrangling, and worse than the schools; for here men will wrangle for a hairsbreadth and make a stir where a straw would end the controversie.

Never did Mimmicke screw his body into half the forms these men to theirs; and it is an article of their creed that the bending back of their body or screwing in of their shoulders is sufficient to hinder the over-speed of the bowl, and that the running after it adds to the speed. Though they are skilful in ground, I know not what grounds they have for loud lying, crying sometimes the bowl is gone a mile, a mile, &c., when it comes short of the jack by six yards; and on the contrary, crying 'short, short' when he hath over-bowled as far.

How senseless these men appear when they are speaking sense to these bowls, putting confidence in their intreaties for a good cast. It is the best discovery of humours, especially in the losers, where you may observe fine variety of impatience, whilst some fret, rail, swear and cavel at everything, others rejoyce and laugh, as if that was the sole design of their creation.

To give you the moral of it, it is the emblem of the world, or the world's ambition, where most are short, over, wide, or wrong byassed, and some few justle in to the Mistress Fortune! And here it is as in the Court, where the nearest are the most spighted and all bowls aim at the other.

John Earle, *Micro-cosmographie,* 1628 (occasionally attributed to Charles Cotton, 1674)

Cupid v. Mammon

Seven years after Bishop Earle wrote his criticism, Francis Quarles, obviously borrowing from him, published a parable in verse beneath the text, 'Ye are of your father the devil, and the lusts of your father ye will do' (John, viii, 44). A bowls match: the players are Cupid and Mammon, the bowls sinful thoughts, the jack the world, Satan the 'director', Fortune the scorer, 'a crown for fools' the prize and (according to the Latin motto accompanying an illustration) 'a child's rattle' the reward for both.

> Here's your right ground: wag gently o'er this black;
> 'Tis a short cast; y'are quickly at the Jack.
> Rub, rub an inch or two; two crowns to one
> On this bowl's side: blow wind, 'tis fairly thrown:
> The next bowl's worse that comes; come, bowl away:
> Mammon, you know the ground, untutor'd play:
> Your last was gone, a yard of strength well spar'd,
> Had touch'd the block; your hand is still too hard.
> Brave pastimes, readers, to consume that day,
> Which, without pastime, flies too swift away!
> See how they labour; as if day and night
> Were both too short to serve their loose delight:
> See how their curved bodies wreath, and screw
> Such antic shapes as Proteus never knew:
> One raps an oath, another deals a curse;

He never better bowl'd; this never worse:
One rubs his itchless elbow, shrugs and laughs,
The other bends his beetle brows, and chafes:
Sometimes they whoop, sometimes their Stygian cries
Send their black Santo's to the blushing skies:
Thus mingling humours in a mad confusion,
They make bad premises, and worse conclusion:
But where's a palm that fortune's hand allows
To bless the victor's honourable brows?
Come, reader, come: I'll light thine eye the way
To view the prize, the while the gamesters play:
Close by the Jack, behold, Jill Fortune stands
To wave the game: see in her partial hands
The glorious garland's held in open show,
To cheer the lads and crown the conqu'ror's brow.
The world's the Jack; the gamesters that contend
Are Cupid, Mammon; that judicious fiend
That gives the ground is Satan; and the bowls
Are sinful thoughts; the prize, a crown for fools.
Who breathes that bowls not? What bold tongue can say
Without a blush he has not bowl'd today?
It is the trade of man, and ev'ry sinner
Has play'd his rubbers; every soul's a winner.
The vulgar proverb's crost, he hardly can
Be a good bowler and an honest man.
Good God! turn thou my Brazil thoughts anew;
New-sole my bowls and make their bias true.
I'll cease to game, till fairer ground be giv'n;
Nor wish to win, until the mark be Heav'n.

Emblems, Divine and Moral, 1635

In 1683 was published The Academy of Armory, *a book on heraldry and other subjects by Randle Holme, who eventually came from Chester to London to be Server to the Chamber in Extraordinary under Charles II. George T. Burrows acclaimed Holme more than 200 years later as a 'wonderful sporting journalist who lived a long time out of his time and generation'. To this the qualification must be made that a study of Holme's work suggests weighty borrowings from*

'Country Contentments', *Bishop Earle and probably Charles Cotton, all of whom have already been quoted. Pending further investigation of his sources his most valuable writings are those (wherein at least one part also appears 'borrowed') that define surfaces, bowls, rules and terminologies of his time.*

'Noe High Heeles'!

Severall places for Bowling: First, *Bowling greens* are open wide places made smooth and even, these are generally palled or walled about. Secondly, *Bares* are open wide places on mores or commons. Thirdly, *Bowling-alleys* are close places, set apart and made more for privett persons than publick uses. Fourthly, *Table Bowling*, this is tables of a good length in halls or dineing roomes, on which for exercise and divertisement gentlemen and their associates bowle with little round balls or bullets.

Orders agreed upon by Gentlemen Bowlers: 1. That noe high heeles enter for spoiling the green, they forfeit 6d.; 2. That all gentlemen, and betters that play or come to bett, shall pay no more for their entrance but 6d. apeece; 3. That were the Jack is plaid, the footing to be where it is found dureing the game; 4. That all stamping or smoothing is barred; 5. That none give ground but the players; 6. That no one stand beyond the Jack; 7. That no player or other cross an other mans bowle in the runing; 8. That there be no leading the Jack further than a reasonable throw; 9. That all controversies shall be censured by the gentlemen themselves; 10. That the breach of any of these Orders shal be 6d. to the greenkeeper; 11. That if any gentleman have none with him to take up his bowles, the alleykeeper to find servants, to be rewarded according to his pleasure; 12. That for every lurch, 6d. to be paid by the player or players which lose, to be the Alleykeepers.

Severall sorts of Bowles: Where note in bowling the chusing of the bowles is the greatest cunning, for flat bowles are best for close narrow allyes, round byassed bowles for open grounds of advantage, bowles as round as a ball for green swarths that are plain and levell, Cheescake bowles, which are round and flat like cheeses; Jack Bowles, little bowles cast forth to bowl att, of some termed a block; Studded Bowles, such as are sett full of pewter nayles and are used to run at streight markes; Marvels, or round ivoery balls, used by gentlemen to play on long tables or smooth board romes.

Termes used by Bowlers: Cast out the Jack or block is to throw it out that it may be bowled at; The *Trigg*, or foot the Trigg, is the place or mark on which the players are to set one foot when they deliver their bowles; A *Cast of a bowle* is one throw of a bowle, else a cast is oft taken for the runing of a bowle; *An End*, or got the end, is the wining of one, two or more on that throwing out of the Jack; A *Cast* is one got of the number of the game; A *Game* is at Bowles 5. Very rearly among gamesters doth exceed that number, except agreed upon to make 7 or 9 up.

Up or *Up-cast* is the end of the game, the wining of the betts; a *Rub* is a stop in the bowle's runing; *Narrow* is when a bowle over holds or that runs too much on the bias side; *Too Wide* when the bowle is thrown out to a greater compass than the bias will draw; *Ouerthrown*, or ouer cast, is when the bowle lieth behind the block; *Strike*, or strike him out, is to throw a strong throw to put a bowle out of his place; *Rubber* is two games, either won or lost.

Bowl out the Rubber is to bowl a third game for the betts when the players have gotten one apeece; *Cast*, *Board* and *Game* are three sorts of betts and winings in one game, and in this the betts are never laid but one side is two or the other none if 5 be the game, or at three and none if 7 be the game. In which bett, a cast is the first end won after the bett is layd. *Board* is when the players are at an even number, as 2, 3 or 4 apeece; *Game* is the wining of the game; A *Lurch* is when one party of the players get not one cast in the game; *Back Lurch* is when one side is 4 for none and yet the contrary part wins the game by getting 5 cast together or one after an other; *Bias* is either brass or pewter put into one side of the bowl to make it run more on that side then on the other; *Counter-bias* is to keep the great bias from drawing too much, being smaller bias set on the contrary side.

There is no advising by writting how to bowl; practice must be your best tutor, which must advise you of the riseings, fallings and severall advantanges that are to be had in the game. Onely this have a care, that you be not rookt of your money; and goe not to these places unseasonably; that is when more weighty business requires your being at home or else where.

8

A Struggle Against Death

About five in the evening we went to see a great match at bowling. There was Quality and Rev. Doctors of both professions, Topping Merchants, Broken Bankers, Noted Mercers, Inns of Court Rakes, City Beaus, Strayed Prentices and Dancing Masters in abundance. 'Fly, fly, fly, fly,' said one; 'Rub, rub, rub, rub,' cry'd another; 'Ten Guineas to five I uncover the jack,' says a third. 'D—n these nice fingers of mine,' cry'd my Lord, 'I slipt my bowl and mistook the bias.'

Pamphlet about Bath, 1700

That pamphlet was published two years before Queen Anne came to the throne. Now follow nearly 150 years when the game survived but scarcely grew and eventually almost withered away. The period had its significances: indeed, there is some opinion that today's styles and codes first became identifiable in the second half of the 18th century, and certainly the game had continued to be held more in favour in the North and Scotland, while diminishing in the South. But the conclusion that overall this was a time of vain hope and ultimate crisis is inevitable in a survey of writings contemporary and retrospective.

Throughout the eighteenth century the game retained its hold, and we find towns and villages each with their own green, as a rule attached to an inn. They were generally crown greens; and singles and friendly matches with neighbouring clubs and villages provided keenness, rivalry and topical talk.

Felix Hotchkiss, 1935

We are told the game spread rapidly in the suburbs of the Metropolis in Queen Anne's reign, especially after 1706; but possibly the only circumstances which saved its reputation as a healthy and rational outdoor recreation was the fact that it remained through the eighteenth century one of the fashionable games of the first rank of society. Even in these quarters the game continued to suffer from gambling, but it should be borne in mind that the standard of morality in England, and also in Scotland, was by no means lofty. Our recreations are nowadays much healthier and freer from contaminating agencies than ever they were.

J. M. Pretsell, 1908

A great nuisance in these public greens were the people who betted on the player's skill.

Ashton's *Social Life in the Reign of Queen Anne*

Since my stay at Sir Roger's in the country I daily find more instances of this narrow party-humour. Being upon a bowling green at a neighbouring market-town the other day (for this is the place where the Gentlemen of one side meet once a week), I observed a stranger among them of a better presence and genteeler behaviour than ordinary; but was much surprised that, notwithstanding he was a very fair bettor, no body would take him up. But upon enquiry I found that he was one who had given a disagreeable vote in a former parliament, for which reason there was not a man upon that green who would have so much correspondence with him as to win his money of him.

Joseph Addison (quoted in *The Spectator*), 1711

Stringent legislation occurred in George II's time (in 1728 and 1745) for the more effectual preventing of excessive and deceitful gaming, but neither bowls nor bowling alleys are mentioned, nor were they, as I think, within the purview of the Acts then passed. It is said, however, that after these Acts of George II, alleys were rigorously suppressed, whilst greens began to increase.

E. T. Ayers, 1894

That bowls was still a game of note is instanced by its mentions by the poets. Sir John Vanbrugh (1664–1726), the dramatist and architect, wrote a club song; and the verse-makers went on somehow discover-ing yet more ways to use bowls and bias for metaphors and moralizing.

O thou, of bus'ness and directing soul!
To this our head like byass to the bowl,
Which, as more pond'rous, made its aim more true,
Obliquely waddling to the mark in view.
                    Alexander Pope, *The Dunciad*

It is not every rogue that, like a bowl, can gain his object the better by deviating from the straight line.
                    Horace Smith (novelist and parodist), *c.* 1812

LIFE, like the Game of Bowls, is but an end,
Which to play well this moral verse attend.
Throw not your bowl too rashly from your hand,
First let its course by reason's eye be planned;
Lest it rolls useless o'er the verdant plain,
Like heedless Life – that finishes in vain.
Know well your bias – here the moral school
Scarce needs a comment on the bowling rule;
Play not too wide, with caution eye your cast,
Use not extent of Green, or Life to waste:
Nor yet too straight – in Life observe the same –
The narrow-minded often miss their aim!
Bowling too short, you but obstruct the Green,
Like him who loiters on Life's public scene:
Whoe'er at Bowls – or Business causes strife,
Will rubs on Greens receive; – and eke in Life:
One bowling trick avoid in moral play,
Ah, never – never block your neighbour's way!
These rules observ'd, a Man may play his game
On Bowling Greens – or thro' the World with fame.
                    Anon, early nineteenth century

> Wipe out earth's furrows of the Thine and Mine,
> And leave one green, for men to play at Bowls,
> With winnings for them all.
>
> *Book II*

> Bowling greens
> Of poets are fresher than the world's highways.
>
> *Book III*

> A living Caesar would not dare to play
> At Bowls, with such as my dead father is.
>
> *Book V*
>
> **Elizabeth Barrett Browning**, *Aurora Leigh*, 1857

But the writing was on the wall as well as in the poetry books.

> Driving their ba's frae tee to tee,
> There's no ae gouffer to be seen;
> Nor doucer folk wysing a-jee,
> The byas bowls on Tamson's green.
>
> **Allan Ramsay** (1686–1758), alluding to
> an Edinburgh green rented by a Mr Thomson and his wife

By the middle of the nineteenth century a depression settles over the writings. The picture comes through of a game clung to mainly by the aristocracy and the new, upper-bracket merchant classes: even perhaps in the Northern counties and Scotland, where it continued to be held in higher favour.

It was at one time a fashionable game, and to this day there are well-frequented greens in many principal towns which command the attendance of the most respectable residents, and if the game be now less fashionable than formerly, it still remains extremely respectable.

> **Blaine's** *Encyclopedia of Rural Sports*, 1870

Although it cannot be said that in recent times bowling has been a very common amusement, nevertheless it is a favourite pastime with many persons belonging to the higher classes of society. Greens are to be found in most of the principal towns of Great Britain and are attached to many private residences in various parts of the country. In the city of Glasgow there are (beside public greens) at least six which belong to private clubs. These include about 500 members, many of whom are merchants of the highest status and influence.

A Glasgow club rule-book, c. 1860

By degrees many of the old greens have vanished. Some have been built over to afford greater accommodation to the inns to which they were attached and some have been turned into the more productive kitchen garden; but for one reason or another these greens are not found so often as they used to be, while the introduction of lawn mowers has effectually done away with the industry of lawn mowing by hand, for it was no ordinary wielder of the scythe who was regarded as good enough to mow a first-class green. Fifty or sixty years ago a man who had established a reputation for this kind of work was always in demand, and in many cases he could command his own price ... Today we find comparatively few greens within easy reach of London and we may perhaps regret that the game has to some extent fallen into desuetude.

The Field

Let me not be misunderstood when I describe the two centuries and a half which followed Tudor rule as the dark age of bowls. However, notwithstanding the rational delight the game still continued to afford many worthy folk, there is no doubt that during several generations bowls was boycotted and despised as a people's pastime because of its depressing and degrading environment. Every sport on which the curse of gambling and the blight of excessive drinking have fallen is doomed sooner or later. How long the period of neglect and dishonour might have lasted it would be idle to speculate, since deliverance did ultimately come, though from an unexpected quarter, and bowls at length took its legitimate position among the noblest games of the world.

J. A. Manson, 1912

9

The Great Revival

The Session directed the drum to go through the town, that there be no bickering nor plays on Sundays, either by old or young. Games, golf, alley, bowls, &c., are forbidden on Sunday, as also that no person go to Ruglen to see plays on Sunday.

Annals of the Kirk Session of Glasgow, 24 April 1595

The Pioneer Heroes

To the Scots we owe the salvation of bowls. They stripped it of its undesirable surroundings and made a beautiful game of it: an open-air pastime without violence, second to none in its scientific and strategic possibilities. They gave it laws, demonstrated what constituted a perfect green and fostered the game's most valuable social feature, its democratic spirit. The whole credit for this rescue and revival belongs to Scotland. This was an unexpected quarter whence aid should come, for though bowls, along with its winter analogue, curling, has grown to be the national game of the people there, the pastime was unquestionably of external origin and developed amidst serious difficulties.

In Scotland bowls first took root in Glasgow, probably in the latter half of the sixteenth century; for when the Kirk Session in 1595 forbade Sunday play it is fair to suppose the game had already acquired formidable popularity. Some have claimed Edinburgh or Haddington for its birthplace, but Dr J. G. Wallace-James informs me that the earliest mention he found in Haddington's records is dated 1662, when the frugal grant of £160 was sanctioned for 'the laying out of ane bowling green on the sands'. But Glasgow's right to pride of place is incontestable. In 1695 the Council parted with ground in Candleriggs to Mungo Cochrane solely for the construction of a green. The Willowbank club claims to be the lineal descendant of those who played here from the very first and in that case is much the oldest club in Scotland.

Dr Thomas Somerville, of Jedburgh, asserts that bowls was a

common amusement in his youth (about 1741) but that in his later years many games, though not discontinued, had fallen out of favour; he implies that bowls was among them. That there may have been a period of reaction and temporary decline is probable, for it is significant that, barring a casual metaphor, bowls is not alluded to in any of the poems or songs of Robert Burns, a people's poet if ever there was one. Nor did the game contribute an idiomatic word to the dialect or language. The sudden renaissance of the game in mid-Scotland in the early Victorian period (coincidental with the 1845 repeal of the old bans, including Henry VIII's!), however, proved to be the turning-point in the history of bowls and, as appeared many years afterwards, was of world-wide reach and influence.

The Nestor and Solon of modern bowls is William W. Mitchell (1803–84), who had begun to learn the game at the age of eleven on Tom Bicket's green in Kilmarnock.

J. A. Manson, 1912

Fifty years have come and gone since we played our first bowl on Kilmarnock Green, at that time situated near where the George Inn now stands. It was under the charge of Tom Bicket, himself an excellent bowler, well known as landlord of an inn in Fore Street and proprietor of the theatre. The green was under the patronage of the gentry of Kilmarnock, who have long been favourably known for their love of manly sports and the promotion of social and friendly contests between their workmen and themselves, more particularly on the ice. Curling in winter and bowling in summer have, time out of mind, been their favourite pastimes.

Many an exciting scene have we witnessed on that old green. There, in the summer afternoons and evenings assembled numerous and enthusiastic parties, all busy as bees extracting pleasure from the game. The long and costly war waged by England and her allies to dethrone the usurper Bonaparte, as the first Napoleon was called, had, by the money recklessly squandered on it, feathered the nests of the inhabitants of that day and put them in good humour. Merchants, manufacturers and artisans had all profited by it and, with bankers, bailies and retired gentlemen, flocked with one accord to spend their leisure hours on Bicket's green. A more exhilarating sight than that which it generally presented during the summer season of that prosperous period cannot either be easily imagined or described.

At that time each player played with three bowls, all of which were biased by means of lead, with which the inside centre was loaded. They were numbered, 1, 2, and 3. Number 3 was called their greatest 'borrowing' bowl and described a somewhat large circuit; No. 2, a less one; while No. 1 ran nearly straight or, in the bowling phraseology of that day, 'did not "pay" much'.

Bowl-playing, to use an American phrase, is fast becoming an institution of the country. Thirty years ago it was chiefly practised in rural districts and generally by elderly gentlemen who had acquired an independent fortune and, with leisure at command, delighted in spending the evening of their days at this, the most gentle and pleasant of our outdoor pastimes. But during the last decade, a vast change has taken place and bowl-playing has made prodigious progress: clubs pervade every nook and corner of the land and it is by no means an over-estimate to state that there are upwards of 10,000 true and trusty bowlers within Her Majesty's ancient realm of Scotland who frequently meet in friendly conflict and battle without shedding blood or inflicting pain upon themselves or any other.

The game has obtained so strong a hold on the susceptible affections of the people that ere long it is not unlikely to become more thoroughly national than the very ancient one of curling. And why not? Our winters, from whatever cause, are gradually becoming shorter and less severe, while our summers are becoming warmer and proportionally prolonged. Besides, bowl-playing generally is practised in the evening, when the toils of the day are over and the cares of the counting-house are left behind, whereas curling can only be resorted to by day to the absorption of valuable time. In point of fact, but for volunteering and the fascination connected with the handling of a gun, bowl-playing would become nearly universal; and the West of Scotland may meanwhile be regarded as the headquarters of the game.

In 1848, a general friendly meeting of players was held in the Town Hall of Glasgow, which was attended by upwards of 200 gentlemen principally belonging to the Glasgow clubs but including representatives from Paisley, Greenock and Falkirk. The meeting was presided over by the Hon. Alexander Hastie, MP, President of the Willowbank club. At this meeting it was suggested by one of the speakers that a National Bowling Club should be formed on the same principle as the Royal Caledonian Curling Club. This idea was received with great enthusiasm and the Glasgow clubs appointed delegates to meet and consider it.

In March 1849, a meeting was held accordingly at which the subject was fully discussed and shown to be impracticable: it was therefore abandoned. But as one of its chief advantages – that of providing a uniform code of laws for regulating the game – came within the delegates' province, they resolved to attempt to provide one; and for that purpose named one of their own number from each of the clubs represented to meet as a consulting body and appointed the present writer as general secretary. He, having accepted the office, drew up a complete code of laws, which was ultimately adopted by the whole of the clubs in the West of Scotland; and these ever since have formed the standard laws of the game.

W. W. Mitchell, *Manual of Bowl-playing*, 1864

'He, having accepted the office, drew up a complete code.' . . . in such modest terms Mitchell chronicles the fact that, singlehandedly, he tackled the delicate and complex question of legislation. His success has been mainly posthumous for, though in literary form his laws were susceptible of improvement, they constituted the substance of the code which regulates the rink, pairs and single-handed games on level greens throughout the British Empire.

On the initiative of James Brown of Sanquhar and James Pretsell of Edinburgh a conference was convened in Glasgow in September 1892, and, without flourish of trumpet, created the Scottish Bowling Association, which is to bowls what MCC is to cricket and the Royal and Ancient to golf. One of the earliest tasks of the new body was to promulgate a revised and enlarged version of the statutes on April 24, 1893. It was a manifest advance on Mitchell's pioneer labours, but not beyond improvement.

Mitchell had died in his early eighties in 1884, so his laws remained unaltered during his lifetime. They had always been deemed faulty in expression, were not free from personal opinion, in some points confused the essential and of course could not have provided for difficulties that did not arise until the potentialities of the game were realized. Still, his code offered a sound basis for further enactments and has not been gravely affected by the passing years; and his name, deservedly, is the greatest in the history of bowls.

J. A. Manson, 1912

The bools row – the bools row,
    Your ain as well as mine,
O bonnily the bools row,
    When summer days are fine.

O gin the wins wad stop their blaw,
    O gin the sun wad shine,
O gin the snaw wad melt awa',
    An' summer come again.

For then wad the bools row,
    An' games be lost an' won,
An' clubs contend, an' tournaments
    Be talked of, or begun.

Then let us pray for summer suns,
    To mak' the grass grow green,
That we may ha'e some bonnie runs,
    Wi' fremmit or wi' frien'.

For bonnily the bools row,
    When summer days are fine,
O bonnily the bools row,
    Since ever I ha'e min'.

To guard, or rake, or ride, or draw,
    The back han' or the fore,
Is then essayed, 'mid loud guffaw
    O that thrice happy corps.

But winter comes wi' chillin' breath,
    An' leaves begin to fa',
Which brings to a' a thocht o' death –
    For man is like the snaw.

Ah! some no more the grass will tread,
    Nor ever again will play!
While others lively, look ahead, –
    'Thus runs the world away.'

Yet I ha'e played on Christmas day,
    Before gaun hame to dine,
An' never looked on better play,
    When summer days are fine.

Thus summer's sun, an' winter's win',
    Ha'e been alike to me,
O may they be alike to a',
    Until the day they dee.

W. W. Mitchell, January 1880. (Mitchell had just, at seventy-six,
played four hours at Willowbank, Glasgow)

Mitchell tells us that in the early days of 'touchers' the bowls were not
marked by chalk but in a more primitive method, and it was a proud
man who heard his skip declare, 'That one deserves a spittle.' Thank
God public-health work has spread where it has; but we should all doff
our hats to the memory of a modest man who accomplished more than
most people for the advancement of this game.

George T. Burrows

*The modest Mitchell, amid this great revival on increasingly perfect
greens of sea-washed turf, doffed his Victorian hat to another hero. I
see him now staring out from Charles Lees's classic 1850 golf painting
of 'a grand match at St Andrews': Archibald William Montgomerie,
13th Earl of Eglinton and Winton. In 1860 he would be a factor
behind the first open golf championship at Prestwick; in 1857 he
presented a cup to be played for annually between the combined
bowlers of Glasgow and Ayrshire. The first match, on the greens of
Glasgow, was won by the city team with 1444 shots to 1109.*

The Earl himself, at the head of five rinks from Ayrshire, played on
Willowbank Green, acted as a driver of the middle rink and was
supported by Mr C—, a somewhat demonstrative admirer of his
lordship. In the course of the game, his lordship having played a bowl
as directed by Mr C—, the latter began to flatter it as it coursed up the
green by exclaiming and repeating, with greater and still greater
emphasis, 'I like you, my lord! I like you, my lord!! I like you, my
lord!!!' . . . but suddenly and involuntarily changing the phrase as he
saw the bowl approach and pass without effecting the object intended
into, 'O Lord! you're too strong!' This ejaculation not only moved the
risibility of his lordship but sent a general titter through the players on
the green and even communicated itself to the gay and fashionable
assembly of ladies and gentlemen who crowded its banks.

    That year his lordship said, 'Much as I value the game for the pleasure there is in playing it, I value it still more for the way in which it brings classes of the community together and promotes good fellowship between town and country.' He also declared: 'The encouragement of such games as curling and bowling, especially among the poorer classes of our countrymen, will do more to promote their comfort and welfare and tend to their good conduct than all the beer bills and Sunday-trading bills the legislature has ever passed.'

Although suddenly stricken down in the midst of his benevolent and patriotic career, he lived long enough to witness the beneficial effects of the policy he had so frequently inculcated and so heartily carried into practice. The series of matches he instituted mark a new era in the history of bowl-playing. Since they began the game has steadily taken root amongst us and is yearly throwing out new shoots and branches.

W. W. Mitchell

A blessing rest on Eglinton!
　An' on his princely ha',
An' blessed be the memory
　O' him that's noo awa'.

He greatly loved his fellow-men,
　But saw a gap between,
An' closed it up, an' syne ilk class
　Became ilk other's frien'.

O weel he liked to see a' roun',
　As happy as could be,
An' oft at bowls, or on the ice,
　He bore awa' the gree.

He played the back han' or the fore,
　But aye by boolers' law,
An' gentle folks an' semple folks,
　He brought together a'.

He was indeed a nobleman,
　A prince o' a' his kin',
An' weel he liked a game at bools
　When summer days were fine.

W. W. Mitchell, 1864

Left: The 13th- and 14th-century representations often advanced as evidence of the birthdate of bowls — notably by Joseph Strutt (see page 34)

Below: 'A Lesson in Bowls' by Arthur Hopkins, 1893. At this time Scotland had recently formed its Association but, according to E.T. Ayers and Humphrey Dingley (see page 101), playing in rinks was a comparatively recent introduction in England and the game still showed many differences from that of today

'In the reign of Charles I bowls attained its highest favour, as no royal patron was more enthusiastic.' He even played while a prisoner

Charles I, a captive, playing his favourite game.

Sketch for Picture   Copyright.
Humphrey J. Dingley. 1893.

Two pioneers of the modern revival — W.W. Mitchell, the game's law-maker, and the 13th Earl of Eglinton and Winton, supporter and benefactor

W.W. MITCHELL·

ARCHIBALD WILLIAM

13th Earl of EGLINTON.

The Woolpack Inn, Parramatta, claimed as the birthplace of bowls in New South Wales, which formed a bowling association years before even Scotland did

Dr W.G. Grace (*above*), not only the colossus of cricket, but the driving force behind international bowls

'The Poor Brethren of the Charterhouse: A Game of Bowls in the Garden' by Frank Dadd, RI (from *The Graphic*, 1907). Note that the play is from corner to corner

'Often while playing within this sheltered, old-world spot one may glance up to see, towering above the walls, one of the largest ships in the world.' Southampton Old Green — reputedly the oldest green of all — and the *SS Aquitania* in 1925

D. Irvine Watson (*right*), EBA champion in 1914 — 'never once raised his arm to strike viciously; his delivery was the most studied, most careful and sweetest of all men's'

Jimmy Carruthers (*far right*), first ever EBA singles champion, whose career spanned two world wars

'Women are taking active interest, and although in many places their presence is not too welcome, they will not easily be persuaded to leave the greens.' Early action at Wimbledon

Old Bill Lacy (*left*), 'a legend in the crown-green world . . . was 70 when he began seriously competing in the big tournaments'

Percy Baker (*below*), 'a legendary figure for four decades', with four EBA singles championships — a record until David Bryant came along

Percy Baker, second from left, during a tense moment for Dorset in 1966

Ecstasy! Wiltshire *v.* Leicestershire in the Middleton Cup in 1986

Agony! England *v.* Ireland, 1985

'The ladies gave the impression that nothing short of a cyclone would have curtailed their game.' The EWBA Championships, 1974, echo Julie Welch's viewpoint (see page 241)

Three great forces in modern bowls: television, Tony Allcock and David Bryant

'The Greatest Contest So Far'

Tuesday morning broke bright and beautiful. The 'auld toun' of Kirkcudbright was early astir; streamers fluttered in the July breeze; the artillery boomed a hoarse welcome to the auspicious day; and at 10 o'clock the grand bowling tournament began. Some competitors whose names had not been drawn took horse for Dundrennan Abbey, Anworth or other places of interest in the neighbourhood, while not a few rambled among the beautiful walks of St Mary's Isle and other sweet spots on the estate of the Earl of Selkirk. In the evening the *Countess of Galloway* steamer, decked in gaudy colours, left the quay with a goodly complement of pleasure-seekers. Many a fluttering yard of cambric bade her good speed, and amid gladdening hearty cheers she steamed away for bonny Ellan Vannin [Manx for the Isle of Man].

Wednesday came and the play went on; some of the mighty had fallen, others stepped in and took their places and the day wore joyously away. A match at cricket also came off that day between a picked XI of the county and the first XI of the town, the former proving victorious by four wickets. A goodly number of the fair sex graced the ground with their presence, but the bowling green detracted considerably from the assembly that at any other time might have been expected.

Thursday dawned; again was the contest renewed with increasing ardour. More of the knights had succumbed to the prowess of their adversaries, yet still the Marshal's command, 'Opponents get your bowls', met a ready response. Friday looked forth with grey horizon on greatly diminished ranks, and yet two-fifths were running for the goal. More intense grew the interest, and the 'beauty' turned out in overwhelming force, lining the green with a perfect cordon of crinoline. The *Countess* sailed that evening for Liverpool and we doubt if ever the old boat has seen such a living mass on Scotland's shore since she left the building yard of Tod & McGregor in 1847. But while the splendid brass band of the Kirkcudbright Volunteer Artillery was discoursing sweet music, the heavens gathered black as a pall overhead and down came a deluge of rain in torrents to which a patent Mackintosh even would scarcely have proved impervious. The consequence was a hasty 'skedaddle', with disastrous results to starched muslin and gossamer high-flyers. Thus Friday night closed in amid drenching showers.

But 'after a storm comes a calm'. The sun beamed from an unclouded sky on the last day of the tournament. Once more the signal guns disturbed the morning air and but thirteen were standing to dispute the mastery. The play was splendid and much admired by all onlookers, and among those that fell Anderson of Kirkcudbright, Shanks and Simpson of Kilwinning and Woods of Preston deserve honourable mention. At the time our last parcel left (4 o'clock Saturday) the excitement of the spectators was wrought up to its highest pitch: Creelman had defeated Sheddon by 21 to 12, and Craig and Currie were playing, the former falling shortly after, 19 to 21.

The eighth tie was then commenced: Craig versus Sheddon and Currie versus Creelman. Sheddon fell to Craig 12 to 21, and Currie and Creelman stood alone upon the green. At a quarter to seven the last bowl was thrown. Slowly it pursued its course, anxiously watched by a thousand eager eyes; it stopped, rolled over, and kissed the jack; and amid thundering huzzahs William Currie of Troon was proclaimed the champion of this, the greatest contest in which it has ever been the fortune of a bowler to participate. Currie 21, Creelman 13.

The prizes were distributed by Provost Cavan, who said: 'Ladies and Gentlemen, I think I am but anticipating the unanimous opinion of all who have attended when I venture to characterize the tournament as the most brilliant affair that has ever taken place in the history of bowling. Mr Jenkins, the secretary, gathered together from England, Scotland and Ireland such an army of bowlers as was never before heard of; and not ordinary bowlers either, but all, every one of the 292, picked men, mighty men of valour and renown, and he has given them an opportunity of trying their strength and exhibiting their prowess in the presence of thousands of eager and delighted spectators.' The Provost then handed over the prizes as follows:

	Value
William Currie (Troon), 1st prize, tea service	£50
W. Creelman (Kilmarnock), 2nd prize, a handsome French timepiece	£30
David Craig (Kirkcudbright)	£10
Hugh Sheddon (Largs)	£5
J. P. Tinnion (Troon), special prize	£5

The greatest concourse that had ever gathered on the Kirkcudbright green then dispersed. If one thing gave us more pleasure than another it was to see that gambling was a stranger to the tournament.

Glasgow Morning Journal, 3 August 1864

The tournament at Kirkcudbright which took place in July was the means of drawing bowlers together from all points of the compass and appears to have gone off with considerable éclat. So far so good. Great care, however, will require to be exercised to prevent such miscellaneous gatherings from degenerating and making an opening for the censorious. Lovers of the game, therefore, will see the necessity of guarding these matches from taint of any kind, and, as far as possible, keeping them within their legitimate sphere of an innocent and recreative pastime.

W. W. Mitchell, 1864

The Standard Bias

When the Scottish Bowling Association started, one of its objects was to establish a minimum standard of bias, under which no bowl was to be allowed in any match played under its laws. Almost the first act of the Association was to appoint a committee of three bowlers: D. D. Clark, John Scott and James Brown. I was asked to join them as technical advisor, and the use of the Albany club green was secured and put into as perfect a condition as was possible.

I made an inclined plane, or shute, with a 'sweetly' curved run-off on to the green to prevent jar. I also made a number of bowls, all slightly varying in bias. The three committee-men also brought a number of old bowls, all of which had a good reputation.

We spent about a week on that green, testing and re-testing, until it was finally decided to adopt one of my new bowls as the standard. The bowl is carefully preserved by the SBA secretary and a good many duplicates have been made: for private clubs, practically all of the Colonies and the SBA, who have sent them to their different bowl-making officers to work from – and if these officers have not been able to reproduce the correct bias the fault is certainly not that of the SBA.

Thomas Taylor (quoted in *Lawn Bowling*, USA, 1927)

Meantime, Back in England . . .

The grand north of England contest which has excited so much interest amongst the bowling fraternity of the Border counties began at Brampton on August 4. Seventy-two competitors entered the list, being six representatives from the following clubs: Newcastle-on-Tyne, Hawick, Langholm (old green), Langholm (new green), Penrith,

Cockermouth, Silloth, Wigton, Thornhill, Dumfries, Moffat and Brampton. The prizes were, first, a solid silver cup, value £6.10s.; second, a handsome timepiece; third, a pair of bowls.

Each club divided its players into two rinks of three each; each game in every round consisted of 21 points; the numbers scored by the two rinks from the same club were added together and the club having the largest total score stood. The minimum length was twenty-seven yards; the jack not to be placed within four feet of the edge of the green; each leader to have the power of placing the jack within the prescribed bounds.

The first prize was presented to Hawick and this brought to an end, we think, the only bowling competition or tournament that ever took place in the north of England.

Report, 1864

I have found that south of the Tweed there is no authorized work on bowling and that though the game is extensively played in the north of England there is no written law. Moreover, the custom of one club differs materially from the custom of another in such a way that it has proved impossible to reconcile them and reproduce anything intelligible, so I thought it best to turn to Scotland, the home of the real, bona fide game, and adopt that played there as the best for my readers.

Undoubtedly the cannie Scots are greatly skilled; indeed I remember, during a visit to Glasgow some years since, to have been greatly struck by witnessing a grand match between two clubs, the members of which were reckoned great adepts. It was hardly possible to believe that such power over the bowls could be gained; they seemed to do with them just what they liked. Nor was I the less impressed by the rosy cheeks and fresh, healthy looks of the players.

I should be glad to know that so simple and healthy a pastime were as extensively patronized in England as in Scotland, where it has proved a far more seductive agent to draw working-men from the gin-shop and beer-house than all the preaching and tract-distributing ever yet accomplished. If bowling is to become a popular amusement with the artisan class, those who desire to promote such an end must take care to have the greens established away from the atmosphere of public-houses, which in a short time would make the game only an excuse for drunkenness and dissipation in strong liquors.

Sidney Daryl, *Handbook of Quoits and Bowls*, 1868

England now has a vast number of greens, each with its club attached, and in some districts there are professionals making their living at the game: over 400 players contended in a tournament in Blackpool in 1893 and the electric light was called in requisition.

Scotsmen, who have at least 364 clubs with 30,000 members, also possess fine greens and play with great nicety, but their methods of play vary in many respects from ours, at least in Norfolk and Suffolk to where my play has been confined. To my mind, the dead-level they appear to aim at in laying out their greens tends to sameness (not to say tameness) of play. Inequalities in the surface, if not too great, are distinctly interesting and an improvement, and mostly so when originally unintentional. Moreover, the Scots divide their greens into 'rinks' or sections, about twenty feet wide, one of which is allotted to each set of players, whose play is confined, up and down, on that particular spot.

In the northern counties of England the game is played much in the same way as in Scotland, but the midland and southern English usually play 'all over the shop': the various sets may cross each other in play, and though collisions now and then occur ample compensation is supplied in the perpetual changes of ground necessitating corresponding varieties of play. The expressions of annoyance or glee of the players when an advancing bowl collides with one of another set or the foot of a crossing player can be better imagined than described!

E. T. Ayers, 1894

The greens up to fifty years ago were all 'crown' greens: that is, slightly raised in the centre and falling away in every direction from the crown.

Felix Hotchkiss, 1932

In England (differing from the Scotch game) the jack or kitty is thrown from the last finishing place in any direction. The leader has a jack with the same bias as his bowls, thus enabling him, by observing the course of the jack, to profit by any irregularity of the surface. Rink playing, if played at all, is comparatively a recent introduction. The Scotch game is gradually growing in favour.

In the large wildernesses of stone and lime the city bowling green is an oasis; and to the jaded followers of Mammon the mere suggestion of green grass is a relief, though the turf may have a hard struggle for existence among the smoke and poisonous vapours of a great manufacturing centre. When the game is so keenly enjoyed surrounded by smoke-begrimed walls and towering tenements, how much more are the senses appealed to in the suburbs and country, 'far from the madding crowd'. Sweet Auburn had surely bowls on the village green in mind when –

> All the village train from labour free
> Led up their sports beneath the spreading tree.

There are, unfortunately, narrow-minded souls who think they see all the sins of the decalogue in such innocent pastimes and predict fearful things in the future for such as indulge therein. These are they who with 'fads' seek the regeneration of mankind by their own particular methods and who –

> Compound for sins they are inclined to
> By damning those they have no mind to.

Their lack of commonsense may be likened, as Scott says, to an uninstructed bowler who 'thinks to attain the jack by delivering his bowl straightforward upon it.'

Gambling, which characterised the game in time's past, was simply the outcome of a profligate age. Socially, few games compare with bowls, where liberty, equality and fraternity are component parts. 'Tis true that asperities and ebullitions of temper are not unknown, but exceptions only go to prove the rule: that a very general tolerance of little personal peculiarities exists nowhere in so marked a degree as on the bowling green, yea, not even in a meeting of ordained clergy.

Why do our moral teachers not mingle more in the secular pastimes of the people? In a Clyde watering-place not a hundred miles from the Gantocks there are eight or nine placed clergymen of various alphabetical denominations who are conspicuous by their absence from the sweet recreation, and this is only one instance among many. Perhaps the impression prevails among them that members of bowling clubs have already reached such a state of perfection in morality as not to require any restraining influence.

Humphrey J. Dingley, 1893

10

The Years of Grace

If modern bowls owes its life to Mitchell and other Scots, England, Ireland and Wales largely owe their foundations and examples to Doctor William Gilbert Grace, the colossus of cricket. It was the turn of the century; in 1899 his association with his native Gloucestershire had finished; he now came to London to manage cricket and other sporting activities at the old Crystal Palace...

A Countryman in Town

Grace was over fifty when he returned to London. His eye was still chirpy and shining and, for all his ponderous bulk, he retained unusual energy for outside sports. His inimitable trademark, the Old Testament beard, still hung, flat, shapeless and long, down his barrel of a chest.

The despair of the manufacturers of shaving equipment, Grace never, so it has been said, stropped a razor in his life. In fact, there is some photographic and circumstantial evidence to suggest that for a brief period around 1871 or 1872 Grace did make a few desultory passes at that luxuriant growth. But somehow the beard kept symbolic faith with the Grace story. Wispy and straggly as W.G. ventured, youthfully and hopefully, to establish his claim, it soon dropped from the cliff-edge of his jutting chin like a raven-black cataract as he stormed in triumph through the 1870s. Gradually, as he slowed a little, it mellowed, lightened in colour and was mottled with grey. Finally, in his later years, it hung, fully grey-white, like an outsize in Santa Claus disguises, many inches toward his rather gross waist. Although its pigmentation altered, its characteristic thickness was never enfeebled.

His eagerness for country sports never weakened either, despite the urbanization of cricket and of his own life-style . . . Not that he stuck to hunting, shooting and fishing, or even golfing. Interestingly, he adopted bowls, which had been widely taken up by town-dwellers, for its relatively confined arena was most suitable for the public parks and recreation grounds of urban districts. W.G. probably spotted that bowls was not always the peaceable and relaxing pastime that on the surface it appeared. It is, and can be, played with ferocious intensity, and W.G. entered into the company of bowlers with all the will and exuberance with which he tackled any chosen pursuit.

He was inordinately proud of the smooth beauties of the Crystal Palace green and quickly became an adept, his finely tuned judgement of length giving him a decided advantage. He captained England in the first ever bowls international, against Scotland in 1903, and he was an England bowls player for the following five years as well. Indeed Grace has sometimes been labelled 'the Father of International Bowls'.

Curling was yet another sport he enjoyed, whilst indoors his devotion to whist and long sessions of billiards was unremitting. He was also an occasional, never a persistent, gambler. The major omission to this life-long engagement with sporting diversions was lawn tennis, prominent since 1874 and with the first Wimbledon championship competed for as early as 1877. One might guess that the feminine association with tennis and its then mild air of effeteness would have been off-putting for W.G. He was very much a man's man in his choice of pastimes, and women, it was his implied view, should be relegated to the kitchen and the dance-floor.

Eric Midwinter, *W. G. Grace – His Life and Times*, 1981

Imperial, Imperious England!

Cricket and cricketers were largely responsible for the initiative that promoted not only the growth of bowls in England but overseas tours and international matches; and it was in 1899, Grace's last year of international cricket at the age of fifty-one, that a group of men who loved both games met during the England *v*. Australia Test at The Oval for a discussion that was to have far-reaching effects. The group included John Young, then president of the New South Wales Bowling Association, Charles Wood, president of the Victorian game, another Victorian named Major Wardell well known in cricket and a Mr Yelland from Hove, England. The subject they discussed was an Australian bowling team to tour Britain. At that moment it did not seem practicable but the seed was sown and it fell on fruitful ground. In 1900 a meeting of Australian and New Zealand bowlers was held in

Melbourne and it was agreed to try to raise a team to visit England. There was not much confidence that many names would be forthcoming, but to the surprise of those interested forty men not only promised but actually by arrangement appeared at the Great Central Hotel, London, on May 28, 1901, ready to play.

That Australian enterprise discussed at The Oval in 1899 had revealed an embarrassing shortcoming: we in England did not have a national bowling association to organize the tour. John Young, the Australian, was behind a meeting of clubs here that year and the 'Imperial Bowling Association' was formed. The question of laws under which the matches would be played was the first matter to be considered and it was found that the Scottish laws had been copyrighted and the Scots were reluctant to allow the IBA to use them. The IBA officials were not baulked: they simply made laws of their own, somewhat akin to the Scottish, and went ahead. The tour was a success.

Subsequently an 'English Bowling Association', separate from the Imperial BA, had been formed, with Grace its president, and for a while it seemed the sport might be split. Grace and his colleagues approached the IBA for a conference but were informed that 'in all but name the duties of an English bowling association are already discharged by the Imperial Bowling Association'. It would appear the IBA wanted the EBA to disband and join them. Mr Stonehewer, the EBA secretary, sent Mr Price, his IBA counterpart, on March 7, 1904, a resolution which Grace's EBA committee had passed: 'that this Association cannot entertain the question of dissolution, but if your Association will recommend your clubs to join *this* Association a fair and just representation will be given to them on the Committee.' In Mr Price's opinion this put an end to the negotiations and he resigned.

A few months passed, but it was evident that the two associations must eventually come together. The resolution which caused Price to resign could not remain the stumbling block, and on November 13, 1905, an amalgamation was agreed. The 'C. Wood Australian Challenge Cup' which had been presented by Charles Wood to commemorate that first Australian tour was handed to the new English Bowling Association; the first team to win it were Newcastle West End, the club of the great player James Telford; and today it is still the trophy for fours in the English championships.

E. J. Linney (bowls author), 1932

The Imperial Bowling Association did good work for the game, but did not make a strong appeal to the man on the green. Perhaps this failure was due to the general impression that it was a very exclusive organization in which there was no place for the little men belonging to small clubs. Perhaps the name it bore suggested it was in some way connected with a political party: probably the word 'Imperial' was due to the desire of the founders to create an organization which would become the governing body of the game throughout the British Empire.

Without Dr Grace the English Bowling Association might have died within a few years of its birth. His co-founders were well known in bowls but not in sporting or social life. Grace on the other hand was a national figure, and the success of the EBA in its earlier days was largely because he was behind it. The EBA owes its strength and prosperity to the work done by its founders in the early days of the century, and the greatest of those pioneers was England's greatest and most popular sportsman.

Bowling World, c. 1937

Start of the Internationals

Dr Grace's interest in the game may be taken as beginning with his official connection with the Crystal Palace. In March, 1901, he applied on behalf of its London County club for affiliation with the Scottish Bowling Association, which occupies the same position in the game as MCC does in cricket. Then, after London County were admitted to membership of the SBA, he invited me as secretary of that association to bring a team of two rinks to London and engage a similar number of rinks of his club on the Crystal Palace green. The doctor skipped one of the rinks and played a capital game. So pleased were the Scotsmen with their reception, for they were hospitably entertained by him, that they presented Dr Grace with a pair of silver-mounted bowls.

The following summer, 1902, Dr Grace sent another invitation to me to take a team to London, which I did; and he and his players returned the visit in August of that year. Edinburgh, Glasgow and Ayr were visited, and at each of those places his presence caused great interest, several hundred bowlers and cricketers viewing the games. Dr Grace soon realized the good international contests would do, and during his visit he urged their claims. A ready response was given by the Scottish players, who already possessed a national association comprising between 300 and 400 clubs.

England, Ireland and Wales had not at that time national bodies, but at the request of Grace I approached J. C. Hunter (Belfast) and W. A. Morgan (Cardiff), two well-known bowlers in Ireland and Wales respectively, who agreed with the proposal to establish internationals. Conditions and rules were adjusted and the first matches took place in London (out of respect to Dr Grace) at the Crystal Palace and South London greens in July, 1903. After a most exciting finish England won, and this result gave the game in England a great impetus and Dr Grace great pleasure. The following year the contests were played in Scotland, then in Wales and after that in Ireland; and until 1915, when the contests were abandoned through the war, this routine was followed. In 1906 Grace, through his friend Sir George Riddell, procured from the *News of the World* a magnificent challenge trophy for international competitions, the winning country holding it for a year. This trophy was presented to the International Bowling Board in Ireland that year, England winning it.

During the first two years of the internationals Grace won five of the six games his rink played, the other game being drawn, so during that time he was undefeated. For six years he captained the English team, his last game taking place in Edinburgh in 1908. On that occasion he dined with the members of the Carlton Cricket Club in their pavilion and in his speech advocated international cricket between Scotland, Ireland and Wales.

His connection with the game was most beneficial, especially in England, Ireland and Wales, and it was largely through the internationals that the associations of these countries were formed. His striking personality was a great asset and his keen eye a great help to him in picking up the points of the game. He was a good, enthusiastic opponent, and while his players were sometimes reminded in the doctor's own way that better play was expected of them, he had encouraging remarks for them, too. No man enjoyed a victory better; but in defeat he was a good sportsman, extremely popular at all the internationals in which he took part and as fond of a practical joke or bit of fun as anyone.

Andrew Hamilton, in *The Memorial Biography of Dr W. G. Grace*, 1919

Putting Your Foot in It . . .

Grace frequently took the London County team to various places and always thoroughly enjoyed himself on these excursions. On one occasion his side met the Heathfield club on their excellent rink at Wandsworth Common and the play proved exciting and close. He was skip of his team and loudly urging his colleagues to play to a certain position. After one shot had gone wide the huge doctor, growing highly excited and anxious to win, shouted to one of his men, a Highlander, 'Play to my foot, man, play to my foot and it will get there all right!' Then came the retort from the Scottish international: 'Play to your fut, mon, play to your fut? Why your fut is all over the green!' The joke was greatly appreciated; but Grace remained quiet for several minutes.

E. A. C. Thomson, in *The Memorial Biography of Dr W. G. Grace*

. . . and Your *Back* Into It

J. G. 'Jimmy' Carruthers, who defeated Grace 21–9 on his way to the final of the first EBA singles championship, won half-a-crown from him during the internationals at Cardiff in 1905. Grace wagered that Carruthers, a comparatively small man, could not carry him up three flights of stairs. Carruthers accepted, but Grace made two conditions: first, two strong men would have to follow them up the stairs; second, should Carruthers achieve this physical feat he would spend his winnings in the bar!

George T. Burrows, 1948

Waking up England

When Grace and his men began the English Bowling Association and frankly adopted the Scottish laws, their next problem was to overcome the inertia, engendered by years of *laissez faire*, of the smaller clubs, especially in outlying districts. Many did not take themselves very seriously and some attached almost as much importance to liquid refreshment as to the pastime. In a number of cases the greens were poor: not that they were neglected so far as rolling and cutting went, but they were made of meadow grass, the wear and tear of which were left to Nature's cure, and were often so small that play took place from corner to corner and not up and down.

Moreover, there was variety in the methods of play. Unenlightened London – that is, the clubs other than those which had splendid greens – had one code, East Anglia another, Devon and the South-west a third, and so on. The rink or Scottish game was, in the vast majority of instances, an interloper. What was good enough for their fathers was good enough for them: why should they change?

But surely, if slowly, change began. The English instinct for sport saw there *was* another side to the question, even of playing bowls. Where it was impossible to re-lay a green for want of room or money, committees were induced to spend more care on their greens and to effect repairs with the best turf available. New clubs were formed in ever-increasing numbers – for when bowlers realized the game had become as regularized as golf or cricket, they saw it was no haphazard recreation for a bank holiday or a Saturday afternoon at a suburban tavern but just as worthy as these other sports of being methodically and constantly pursued for its own sake. Then, when a club had built or improved a full-sized green of the best quality members were readily induced to abandon the antiquated methods of playing 2- or 3-men a-side and to take up the rink game.

In England clubs must in the long run be organized county by county, a reform which was systematically started in 1911. The shire is the obvious unit and the clubs within it will constitute a county association. The three estates of the bowling realm will then comprise (a) the club, (b) the group of clubs, or county association, and (c) the EBA, composed of representatives from the county associations. If the EBA possesses the necessary architectonic quality this is the ideal structure it will rear.

J. A. Manson, 1912

When is a Scot not a Scot?

Brilliant play has been exhibited in the International Matches since they began nine years ago, but they lack the hallmark of genuine internationalism. The question of nationality has been unceremoniously shelved, the English, Irish and Welsh teams being largely manned with Scottish bowlers – on the transparent pretext of club membership.

It would have been more profitable for, say, England, to rely on her own unaided efforts, to suffer defeat during a long series of years, to go through the furnace of trial, difficulty and despair and so be drilled and disciplined into the resource, energy and skill that leads to conquest rather than snatch periodical victories with the help of bowlers of other nationalities, whom one were loth to describe as the mercenaries of the game.

Nor is it possible to exonerate the Scot abroad. It is difficult to understand how a Scotsman can think it a privilege or duty to play against his native land and even more difficult to know how he has convinced himself that thereby he is promoting the game in England, Ireland, or Wales. I once heard W. G. Grace advance the plea that it would be a 'national calamity' were Tom Robertson, of the South London BC, to be barred from playing for England, in which country he had learned bowls. That missed the point. Nobody ever dreamed of excluding Mr Robertson from international play: all that was urged was that his proper place was in the Scottish team.

J. A. Manson, 1912

It is to be hoped there will *never* be any qualification introduced in connection with international teams. One can understand it must be hard for some native players to see Scotsmen included in their country's teams, but until the game obtains the same hold in the other countries as it has in Scotland there is little chance of even an English team being without one or two Scots, and men like Robertson, Telford, Muat, Carmichael and others, being members of English clubs, would not be chosen for a Scottish team.

J. M. Pretsell, c. 1912

Today, in 1914, only English-born men play for their own country! This is perhaps the best thing the EBA has done these past few years, and, while England for the moment is paying the price by being defeated each year, the tide must turn when the right men with the correct nerve are picked. They, however, are hard to find, for English-born bowlers are about the most nervous gentlemen I have ever watched playing a game.

London's bowls as a pastime is still in Scottish hands – that is to say the best players are invariably men from beyond the Tweed – but, as Wilkie Bard sings:

Why it should be so
I really don't know!

Scotland has won the lion's share of these international games, and
why the temperament of the men from that nation is more suited to
strenuous and important bowls playing, goodness only knows. I have
spent eight London seasons trying to fathom the reason, but the
enigma is still unsolved.

George T. Burrows, 1914

Big-Match Moments

The first international-match series in 1903 resolved itself into a
struggle between England and Scotland for the championship and
their match had a most exciting finish. Mr Tom Robertson (a Scot but
playing for England!), with his last bowl and the second last of the
game, brought the scores level, a state of affairs which his opponent
failed to alter with the final bowl of the match. Thus ended the first
international in a narrow victory for England, who had the same
number of championship points as Scotland but the better net score
against their three opponents. The game in the south benefited greatly
from this result.

J. M. Pretsell, 1908

Waiving aside the question of nationality and dismissing from notice
the predominance of Scotsmen in all teams, the international matches
of recent years have proved most exciting.

In 1908 at Edinburgh nothing was more admirable than the beautiful precision with which the veteran John Forman (Edinburgh) led or
the graceful accuracy of J. R. Chapman (Sunderland), whose sureness
as second rendered the lead of Robert Fenwick (Newcastle West End)
exceptionally sound since it was impossible that men so absolutely
trustworthy should both fail to do what was needful.

It is in the art of skipping, however, that these internationals afford
the most useful lessons, and at Edinburgh almost every variety of
directing was exemplified. Thomas Muir, of Beith, was steady, safe
and sure, taking no risks and winning all his games. Of a totally
different school was James Telford (Newcastle West End): enthusiastic, and revelling in smashing up his opponents' compactly built
heads. 'Riding' shots are sometimes imperative, but to drive almost as

it were by preference is truculent treatment of the subtler and more delicate science of drawing. Yet it is all in the game, and Telford had the confidence of the *beau sabreur* who, knowing that if he comes to grief failure means ruin, is still prepared to run the hazard. With his white plume shining amidst the ranks of war, Telford always recalled to my mind the lines of James Graham, Marquis of Montrose:

> He either fears his fate too much,
>   Or his deserts are small,
> That dares not put it to the touch
>   To gain or lose it all.

Perhaps the outstanding feature was the excellent form shown by Wales and Ireland. In the struggle between them the score was level with one end to go and the play of the two remaining skips, David Barnett (Belmont, Belfast) and John Pollock (Cardiff), was watched with breathless excitement. Wales were lying shot when the turn of the drivers came. With his second bowl Pollock drew another shot; then Barnett's nerve failed him at the critical moment and the Welsh gained the victory by two shots.

Cardiff and Dinas Powis were selected as the venues of the international encounters in 1909 but the meetings were a Scottish triumph. Save in three games, the Scotsmen overwhelmed their adversaries; their winning every rink game set a formidable record and was a magnificent demonstration of the art of drawing to the jack.

George Snedden's play as a skip was in itself a liberal education in bowls, and against Barnett of Belfast he surpassed himself. Of the 21 ends he won 15, and at the close the score of his rink stood at 25 against Ireland's 6. He played throughout with the utmost deliberation, allowing nothing to put him out. He felt the weight and took the balance of every bowl before playing and did not deliver it until he was satisfied that in both particulars it was adjusted to the task immediately before him. He did not play a single driving shot from first to last. When an Irishman lay on the jack, Snedden removed him with a bowl of sufficient strength, judged to a nicety, to dislodge him and take his place. Once again, Barnett, a first-class skip with plenty of nerve, was outgeneralled.

Snedden's toughest tussle, against an English rink skipped by Tom Robertson, might have been pre-arranged to illustrate my argument on nationality. Robertson's colleagues were James G. Carruthers

(Muswell Hill), one of the few who can lead or skip with equal acceptance, John Fingland (Banbury) and George Muat (South London). Here, surely, the acme of irony was reached when it was seen that Snedden's quartet, all Scots, were engaged in a life-or-death struggle with four other Scotsmen and battling for the honour of England!

Belfast was the scene in 1910 and Scotland won all their matches, carrying off the championship for the fourth year in succession, but Carruthers, again representing England, was one of the delights with his dashing and adroit skipping. At half-time the Scottish rink under John Macmillan (Dumbarton) led by three (10–7), but Carruthers won by eight shots (27–19). Time after time he picked out the Scottish shot by a well-directed drive and taught Macmillan that forcible tactics were not his monopoly.

All the same, as the Scots proverb says, 'a cock's aye crouse on his ain midden', and so, playing at home, both William McLetchie and Barnett had field days against England and Wales. Barnett's play against David Wilkinson was deadly (34–9), and he also even handled Carruthers somewhat heavily (26–13). Sam MacDonald, of Belfast, gave Barnett a perfect lead and every skip knows what that is worth. The Irish meeting was notable for the last appearance for the Emerald Isle of John C. Hunter, who played third to McLetchie and whose game was little short of marvellous in a veteran of more than half a century's practice.

In 1911 the internationals were at South London BC, Wandsworth Common, on a green laid down in 1900 with turf from the Moray Firth, near Forres. England's team had been distinctly strengthened and took the championship, but their triumph was palpably due to the presence of Carruthers and Adam Adamson, both Scotsmen, who skipped with surpassing skill and judgment. Carruthers, indeed, went through the three days' struggle unscathed, being 12 up against Ireland, 7 up against Wales, and 1 up against Scotland.

If all-round merit had been the test, Wales would have borne away the premier honours: her men played with breezy zest and brilliant keenness. As for Scotland, they have never made a poorer show. It had commonly been supposed they could pick a good team almost blindfold, but this belief was pulverized for ever. There was too much new blood in their rinks: of the eighteen men brought south, only five had done duty at Belfast and, though others were not strange to inter-

national responsibility, even the strongest team could not stand so
severe a depletion. It is essential that the sequence of international
experience should not be unduly broken: as a precautionary measure,
therefore, one half of any team should have done duty in the two
preceding matches at least.

Funereal gloom pervaded the Scotsmen's conflict with Wales;
against Ireland they discovered now and again a touch of their
customary skill and dash; but there was a woeful want of staying
power in the fight with England, on the result of which so much
depended. Curiously, however, it was a freshman, W. Blythe, of
Tulliallan, who was *facile princeps*. His combat with Carruthers was
heroically conducted on both sides and he made the shot of the
gathering when, with his last bowl in an end against Ireland, he saved 7
by trailing the jack. But that it should be left to a skip to save 7 –
excepting when the white has been carried, which was not the case – is
inexcusable.

Two abuses at international and other fixtures are ripe for remedy.
One is the wearing of white shoes, which are a perfect nuisance round
the back and constantly catch the bowlers' sight. Another is the habit
certain players affect of addressing jocular remarks and other cheap
chaff to spectators on the banks, ostensibly intended to provoke
laughter but really calculated to put the players on the opposite side off
their game. In cricket, billiards and other pastimes of the highest rank
that sort of thing is regarded as bad form and would not be tolerated: it
is time it were stopped in bowls. One would not suppress every form of
hilarity on the green, but the endless handshakings after every decent
shot, as well as other capers, at last grow tedious and impress the
onlookers as childish rather than funny and spontaneous.

J. A. Manson, 1912

Dashing Welsh, Struggling Irish

Dash and daring are the qualities that most impress one in Welsh play.
Every man is a 'trier' and the performances of the international teams
invariably arouse the spectators' admiration. As in the case of Ireland,
the Welshmen recognize only the Scottish code and through the
excellence of their greens have always appreciated the subtlety and
strategy of the rink game.

In the Principality bowls has owed much to the all-round skill of

John Pollock, who, leaving his native Scotland early in life, settled in Cardiff and found bowls ample consolation for his exile. In the international matches at Edinburgh in 1908 only two skips were up in all their games and Pollock was one of them, his play throughout being a fine exhibition of generalship. Of other Welsh skips mention may be made of David Davies (Cardiff), whose play was sometimes dazzling in its brilliancy; W. A. Cole and F. W. Thomas (both of Mackintosh B. C.) who, while running no foolhardy risks, always meant business; the Rev. T. J. Jones (Penylan) who early in his career proved himself a master tactician; and David Wilkinson (Dinas Powis), an extraordinarily hard worker whose defeat of the renowned Edinburgh skip, George Snedden, at Belfast in 1910 was one of the surprises of the international match.

Through the enthusiasm of such men as Edward Lloyd, Robert Graham, W. A. Morgan, and H. A. Keenor, the organization of bowls speedily reached an exceptionally fit condition in Wales; and the Welsh BA with a view further to stimulate interest extended its patronage to the Welsh Open Championship, an annual fixture, which was first held in 1907. Considering their numbers, Welsh bowlers have achieved wonders and will never eat the leek.

It would seem almost as if bowls were 'forbit by law to grow in Irish ground', since the game has been so slow to strike root in the distressful country. Even in Ulster, largely colonized by Scotsmen, the pastime has had a chequered existence. Still, since the dawn of the twentieth century it has given signs of vitality, not only in the province but in the capital itself.

One club – the Belfast, founded in 1842 – enjoys the rare honour of preserving bowls from extinction in Ireland. Badgered by the builders, it was compelled to lay four separate greens – each, with a pavilion, at a cost of £600 or £700 – before it found a resting-place from which it can never be dislodged near the Royal Botanic Gardens. At one crisis it appeared as if its last hour had struck, but a gallant remnant, setting a 'stout heart to a stey brae', resolved to hold on at all hazards.

Memories as green as the shamrock are still cherished of the exploits of some of the club's old skips like Robert Andrews, John Rose, Joe M'Cready, Andrew Gibson and John C. Hunter. Gibson was a perfect terror and many a Scots team of prowess undoubted sailed back to the Land o' Cakes to tell how 'Dandie' and his men had downed them. But Andrew, like Hunter, was a Scot. Hunter, a native of Kilbarchan, in

Renfrewshire, was a bowler from boyhood, having played first at thirteen. Crossing the water, he joined Belfast, of which he was a member for upwards of thirty-two years until he returned in 1910 to his native place after a service to the game of more than half a century. Hunter was one of the safest bowlers Scotland ever produced and had few equals as a skip. As a man he was geniality itself, a peacemaker, the friend of the friendless and an ornament of that game which appeared to be both meat and drink to him. His retirement might have entailed serious injury to his club had he not remained to see it prosperously settled in a permanent home, where it seeks fresh laurels.

J. A. Manson, 1912

Weakness!

Even with the reforms made, the EBA has years of work before it. Its chief power, in the past, lay in its very weakness! It must still rid itself of its ultra conservatism and must allow within its portals the flood-light of new thought, new conditions and new men with fresh ideas. That, perhaps, is the true secret of its want of real vim and vitality.

The EBA has not moved one firm step towards assuming the national power it should have had vested in its own hands since it took shape in 1902. If it had been ambitious it would have been ere now overlord of *all* the other associations that have sprung into being to govern the crown green game. One would not be surprised if, in the fullness of time, the prevailing North Country associations do not ask the EBA to become affiliated to *them*! They are quite powerful enough to dictate their own terms to the EBA today.

George T. Burrows, 1915

But soon the same writer was to record . . .

The game has long since survived even Acts of Parliament against its vogue and today it is ever increasing in its popularity. It has helped to kill club and even county cricket in many parts of England; and throughout Britain is now well and truly governed by a number of strong and all-powerful associations.

Era of the Amateur

Between the wars was a golden age for the game as a pastime: elegant, social and, even in the parks, somehow private. Professionalism was a dirty word. In reportage, and there was precious little, the prefix 'mister' or initials-only was de rigueur. Bowls was gradually becoming more competitive and more international, but the 'old-man's-game' label was still, with exceptions, fairly applied and the attitude even at top level inclined to be casual. For the second British Empire Games, in London in 1934, Mr E. W. Walker, who happened to be on his way to Britain, was asked to represent Australia in the singles and to ask other Australian bowlers in England to a meeting for the selection of the rest of the team. Two turned up.

Glorious Revival

The months immediately following the cessation of war have produced much towards the advancement of bowls as a national sport. Four to five years of stagnation – for most associations clipped their activities or suspended them entirely – have been followed by a few glorious months of distinct revival, with the promise of this old game taking high rank among the leading sports of the Empire.

New men with fresh ideas have flocked to the game. Comparatively young fellows, straight from the Army, have enrolled as its most enthusiastic adherents, and middle-aged men who stayed at home and perchance grew prematurely old in the strenuous five years of increased labour have likewise joined the ranks – to whom must be added those hale and hearty veterans who, by hook or by crook, got in their games on neglected and deserted greens and kept themselves healthy, both in mind and body, in those years of turmoil through which we all passed.

If proof is needed of the advancement of the game it is to be found in the fact that the Scottish Bowling Association, under whose rules we all play – and that body still remains the Jockey Club, as it were, of our sport – have materially altered many of the long-standing and questionable laws of the game. By changing them in readiness for the new season of 1920 they have shown a desire to meet the wishes of those of us who were always liable to have some little sharp practice put upon us by another who had defined his own rather clever interpretation of such laws and was carrying them out his way, which was not always the legal one. We now start a new season and a new era in the game, with many abuses removed.

It is now made illegal for a marker in a single-handed tournament to display any object in the hand, or otherwise, for the guidance of a player. The law might have gone further and said that markers should keep perfectly still at the head when the contestants are playing: nothing is more disconcerting than a voluble dancing master (oft-times in white shoes!) capering about behind the jack just as one is getting his body down to get a bowl away. A new addition is a clause which provided against a short wood being placed in such a position on the green as to prevent an opponent having a fair opportunity of retrieving a position that may be against him: 'Any bowl which comes to rest within fifteen yards from the front of the mat shall be counted dead.' An excellent change lays down that players not in the act of playing must stand behind the jack or behind the mat, and there are changes in the laws on placing and moving that mat. It is recommended that the mat be not less than 22 by 14 inches, or thereabouts. Had the SBA recommended a certain standard size it would have ensured the observance of the law that at least one foot shall be *entirely* on the mat when the wood leaves the player's hand! Another law has been so altered as to amend an old-time abuse – that of wilfully pitching the jack out of the rink!

'No player shall be allowed to change his bowls in the course of the game.' And law XVIII now states: 'No player shall be allowed to delay the play by leaving the rink unless with the consent of the opponent, and then only for a limited period – not exceeding ten minutes. Contravention of this law will entitle the opposing side to claim the tie.' It is understood this new law refers especially to single-handed play. Of late years the habit of leaving an opponent on the rink and going off either to the bar for a drink or to the pavilion for a short rest and otherwise 'messing your man about' has grown.

The law as to spectators is as important as ever and I for one believe the Scottish Association should have made it stronger. Persons on the banks, it still says, should 'preserve an attitude of strict neutrality'. They do nothing of the sort; and although the garrulous critics who swarm like hornets round some greens cannot be clad by law in gas-masks, something more than a mere wish ought to come from the law-makers as to the prevention of 'barracking', which is practised from the banks of most public-park and not a few public-house greens.

Signs of the progress of the game are further to be observed in the rapid extension of association and league bowls, and here and there we hear of the formation of fresh league tournaments carried out on the principle of the Football League – with, of course, professionalism and the old-time poaching of players discountenanced.

In the south the laying down of private turf (Cumberland and Forres) greens is heard of in all directions. Expert green-layers in the London area severally announce that they are too busy to accept much more work and clubs wishful to lay down their own swards in future will have to call in Scottish experts if the demand on the experienced men in southern England increases. To do the thing properly – with pavilions, water and gas laid on – means an expenditure of £1200 today and a yearly payment of £150 to a greenkeeper of merit.

Reforms which require early and expert handling by the English Bowling Association concern illegal bowls and the range of bias. Also missionary work remains to be done in Norfolk and Suffolk, where, by a little persuasion, the clubs playing under rules modelled on those of the crown-green game might readily be persuaded to adopt the rink style of the national association and join forces with it. There might additionally be established a working agreement with the British Crown Green Association on all matters pertaining to amateurism. Matches might be played with teams of that association in London and Manchester in alternate years.

Illegal woods are being used all over the Kingdom. I have received letters from players in Durham, Kent, Surrey, Devon and Sussex complaining about the dire results of men being allowed to play in first-class competitions with bowls which undoubtedly are straight. In the contests of affiliated clubs hundreds of bowls are used which are illegal by having little or no bias. They are not allowed by the laws, but men still use them.

In county competitions I have watched the antics of woods made in the 'eighties and 'nineties. All bowls made before 1896 should be ordered by the EBA to the refuse heap. The New South Wales BA has a rule that if any bowl be objected to on the ground of illegality of bias and does not bear the stamp of the association, the person or side permitting such bowl to be used shall forfeit one point off their score for each end played and for each bowl played. In London bowl houses and pavilions there are hosts of illegal and ancient pieces of lignum vitae. One man playing with four straight bowls can so smother a jack that the drawing skill of his antagonist fizzles out and he ends up firing and losing his temper.

In Australia each bowler undertakes to return his woods to his association for re-testing in a certain period. I would like to see every bowl more than five years old called in and re-tested, and the EBA (or the Scottish BA perhaps one should say) might make it a condition that all woods be re-tested every five years; and, further, that every bowl should be dated!

Who originated bias? How have its sizes and its latter-day half-sizes developed? What is a Scots maker's three-full is a London man's four. There is no reliable uniformity. In other words, it is perhaps not so much a matter of standard bowls as of standard machinery upon which the woods are turned. The present mode of testing is unsatisfactory, as there is nothing definitely laid down by the predominant association that a three-bias wood, say, shall draw four feet, a four-bias bowl five feet, and so on. The Colonies are perplexed on the point and cannot hope to learn from us what bias is so long as we ourselves have no definite knowledge to go on. What may be a truly reliable three-bias on a Cumberland-turf green drops down, in some cases, to an almost straight wood on a rough grass green. If we could standardize greens as well as bowls, then we should all become Irvine Watson – and then, perchance, the game would immediately lose its interest!

George T. Burrows, 1920

The Team's the Thing

The English championships are played under 'level-green' rules, and there seem several good reasons for this. It is a very different game from the crown-green game – the greens are different, the bowls and jack are different, the rules governing the game are different, and there is no trace of professionalism.

There are two main advantages claimed for the level-green game:

more players can play at one and the same time, and there is a chance for the team spirit to show itself. In crown-green games are generally single-handed – man against man. On flat greens there is quite a different spirit: the player no longer plays for himself alone, but as a part of the rink of four, each playing for the best advantage of the team.

To get as many players on the green as possible is important owing to the expense of a good green. They are generally laid with sea-washed turf from the Solway Firth and a green will cost from £800 to £1000. Neither is the supply of this kind of turf unlimited, though greens of the Cumberland-turf type may soon be produced by seeding at much lower cost than obtains today. A good Cumberland-turf green is a thing of beauty in every way.

Felix Hotchkiss, 1932

Wade's Record

For the first time in history, the EBA singles championship has been won twice by the same man. W. F. Wade, of Leicester, was the English champion in 1928, and in beating H. P. Webber of the Sir Francis Drake club, Plymouth, becomes the 1930 champion.

The final result was 21–10, a most unexpected one as Webber had been playing extraordinarily well until he met Wade. And curiously enough, Wade had not revealed his form until he appeared in the final.

No two men are more unlike. One a fair-headed, straight-backed, athletic-looking youth, cool and collected. The other – well, the old soldier of the game, who follows up his beloved woods with Maud Allan side-steps and other weird limb movements.

The Bowls News, 14 August 1930

Baker's First

The 1932 English championships contest may be regarded as one of the most successful within recent years. The chief factor of all was the ideal weather which graced the week's proceedings; and with the greens the acme of perfection the bowling, generally speaking, was of a high standard.

The Atherley club, Southampton, skipped by Mr James Edney, a bowler of repute both in this country and in the Colonies, was successful in the rink championship; Messrs Arthur and George Bull,

of Wellingborough, following their success in the Bournemouth
tournament the previous week, worthily carried off the pairs honours;
whilst Mr Percy Baker, of Poole Park, Dorset (which club supplied the
pairs champions in 1926–7), won the single-handed contest. Mr E. W.
Fortune was partner in the winning championship pairs last year and
had the distinction of reaching the final stage in the singles this year.

Youth was well represented in the various competitions, one
contestant being only twenty years of age, the singles winner only
thirty-eight, and the pairs champions comparatively young men.

The Bowls News, 18 August 1932

The Difference in Professionals

The winning of the single-handed championship of England puts the
hallmark on a bowler's fame, and since J. G. Carruthers carried off the
honour in the year of its inception, 1905, only one man has won it
twice: W. F. Wade of Hinckley, Leicester, in 1923 and 1930. In the
1936 final, though, were G. D. Goodson, aged thirty, and A. W.
Knowling, Jr, only twenty-four. It seems, therefore, that there is every
chance of Wade's achievement being equalled if not surpassed.

The pairs championship is always keenly contested and no part of
the country has a monopoly, while in the rink event the metropolitan
counties of Middlesex, Kent, Surrey and Essex, strong as they are
numerically, have only won five times since 1905; while Cumberland,
Northumberland and Durham have between them taken the title no
less than nine times, Northumberland themselves securing it on four
occasions. The team spirit seems highly developed in the North.

Valuable trophies held for the year, gold medals and silver cups are
the rewards of winning these competitions – and many watch-chains
carry evidence of success. Should wrist-watches become universally
popular it is an interesting thought how these gold medals will be
brought prominently into notice.

There is a suggestion that 'triples', with two woods each player,
should be one of the features of the national championships, and it
seems almost certain that this game will sooner or later force itself into
acceptance.

There is now no close season. Indoor bowls is fast coming into
prominence, new clubs being formed every winter and enabling

players to participate from January to December. The number of bowlers is also being greatly augmented by women, who are taking up the game and forming clubs and associations.

As the game is spreading over wide areas, imperial and international, its influence grows and will continue to grow, steadily but surely. The Arts of Peace are no less powerful and directive than the Arts of War, and among the former bowls is playing a significant part.

The sport is emphasizing its popularity in a sort of geometrical progression – in town and village, home countries and abroad; whether on the first-class Cumberland-turf greens of the private clubs and municipal parks or on the greens attached to inns. But the game is greater than the man and players must be prepared to sacrifice selfish individual ideas and schemes: the game demands it.

Wherever there is a ball there is movement and life, and the desire to control it is consequent and natural: all ball games are attractive. However, some are spectacular, draw crowds and so give rise to commercial experiment and enterprise – and professionalism. Others, with bowls an illustration, depend on their own values to create and preserve popularity. Trophies and prizes may be won, but there is no 'gate'; and in consequence professionalism finds no opportunities.

In the opinion of many there is a distinct difference between professional and amateur play. In both cases there is the desire to do well – but in the case of the professional he *must* do well or his means of livelihood is jeopardized. There is consequently an inclination to play for one's self, whatever the cost to others, and this in its turn is apt to have an influence on the way the game is played.

The level-green game of bowls is strictly amateur, and the first aim as given by the English Bowling Association in its rules and constitution is: 'To promote, foster and safeguard the amateur level-green game of bowls in every legitimate way.'

Felix Hotchkiss, 1937

Two years later, war again. It delayed the developments envisaged and occasionally feared by the writers of the thirties: younger players, the breaking of Wade's record (by Baker in 1952), triples in the EBA championships (1945) and ultimately, whisper the word, professionalism. Before we turn to those post-war developments and the modern boom, let us cruelly use war as an interval, during which we may catch up on certain aspects already alluded to: the game overseas, crown green and, first, the ladies.

12

'A Graceful Game for Girls'

Mary Queen of Scots was the first lady golfer to be beheaded, Henry Longhurst, writer and commentator, used to say, ominously emphasizing that 'first'! Anne Boleyn was Mary's bowling counterpart; we shall not take the analogy further. It is said she gambled as well as played, and that in May 1532 lost £12.7s.6d. to the Sergeant of the Cellar. Queen Mary also played, or so it is said – the same Mary who forbade the game for fear of conspirators gathering in alleys – and the tragic Princess Elizabeth, delicate and deformed, died at Carisbrook Castle, Isle of Wight, in 1650 from an illness caused by staying out in the rain to watch her father, Charles I, play during his confinement there.

The ladies later virtually disappeared from the bowling scene: to have done otherwise would have been unladylike and unacceptable so despicably had the game been abused by its worst followers. Indisputably the women have become a force in the modern game – which apparently has reminded some men of what Longhurst said. The thought is cruel and unfair!

A Place in the Sun

Some encouragement to our lady players will be afforded by the knowledge that bowls made life sweeter for Eleanor of Provence, wife of Henry III and a sourpuss if ever there was one. She is reported to have played a 'fearful game of bowls' with the unfortunate Rosamund and been put thereby into a better humour.

The King of Hungary, in an old poem entitled 'The Squyre of Low Degree', says to his daughter:

> An hundred Knightes, truly tolde
> Shall play with bowls in alayes colde,
> Your disease to drive awaie . . .

Thus, perhaps, he unwittingly mirrored the first interest of women in bowls – as spectators of their menfolk's games. This first phase was followed in the natural course of events by invitations to the fair sex to try their luck on the greens. Finding it amusing and perhaps no longer mysteriously male, ladies then began to look for a more prominent place in the sun.

Dr John W. Fisher

Bowls is a very nice game for ladies, and nothing can be more picturesque than to see the dear creatures – of course, in the most elegant and bewitching costumes – doing their best to cut Cousin Tom, Dick or Harry out of his advantageously near position to the jack! Such laughing and chaffing, such bright eyes and rosy cheeks, such panting and puffing when their turn is over!

Ah, depend upon it, reader, though Mr Edmund Routledge would try and make you believe *croquet* to be a better game and more suitable for ladies, bowls is equally good for them, and every whit as amusing! Just try and wheedle Papa into appropriating one part of the garden to the establishment of a green. Tell him he will never regret the expense when he sees the healthy tint the game puts into your cheeks, far better than all the rouge or Madame Rachel face-colourings in the world.

Sidney Daryl, 1868

Ladies do *occasionally* join in, though the practice is by no means common, and the wish is perhaps father to the thought that the *custom* of the gentler sex joining their ruder brethren on the green will be revived at no distant date and the charge of selfishness, so often heard, withdrawn from the lords of creation. Hats and umbrellas are quite common as prizes among the men. What sort of commotion would be created if a seal-skin patetot or a duck of a bonnet was offered as a prize for the ladies? There is nothing complicated in the game, and the exertion necessary is not half that of lawn tennis.

Humphrey J. Dingley, 1893

I have always thought it to be regretted that so few ladies play as I am sure they would derive much benefit, the exercise being gentle and enjoyed under the healthiest conditions; and there is no reason why they should not excel. They should use small bowls, and though three ladies could not expect successfully to compete with the same number of gentlemen, considerable energy being employed occasionally by the latter in forcing bowls from the jack, off the green and so on, the sets might easily be formed of an equal number of ladies and gentlemen on either side.

E. T. Ayers, 1894

Bowls – a graceful game for girls.

Girls Realm, headline, 1902

The First Clubs

The first recorded club was Kingston Canbury Ladies, formed in 1910 with about ten members, not one of whom knew the first thing about playing. Nor were they proffered any advice from the men playing on the same green as the latter did not approve of them. However, within a few years other clubs were formed and friendly matches were played on an increasing scale, for since 1906 the London County Council had had a rule that one rink on each park green should be reserved for women if required.

Dr John W. Fisher

To the oldest men's club in the Wimbledon area, Southey, then playing on a green at the Freeman Hotel in the Broadway, belongs the credit of having begun the competitive spirit among English women by holding an annual tournament for the wives of club members. That happened in 1908. Prizes were costly and numerous, for local tradesmen as well as clubmen gave liberally, and 'Ladies' Day' at the Southey green became a red-letter day: an event for rolling out the red carpet, for hoisting gay flags and bunting and for the presence of a chorus of throaty tenors and lusty baritones who sang their bravest to the accompaniment of a little boy pianist.

That boy pianist, son of one of the club's best players, caught the bowling bug in his teens, won the Surrey singles championship as a man in 1932 and, with his father, has since figured regularly in the final stages of many south coast tournaments. At seventy, father is playing as well as ever, while his son has dominated club events at West

Wimbledon for many seasons. Their names? H. J. Cuckney, senior and junior.

Another nerve centre in those early days was the Corporation's grass green in the Dundonald Recreation Ground, at that time perhaps the best sward of its type in Surrey. Here the women composed a club and issued a challenge to the women who were going through the throes of learning on the Kingston Canbury green. This match, played unobtrusively at Kingston some considerable time before the 1914 war, was, so far as my investigations go, the first of its kind to be reported, if it was not actually the first match to be played between two sides chosen among women – who were at that time only beginning to understand the meaning of positional play and the necessity of bowling as a team.

George T. Burrows

'Their Presence Not Too Welcome . . .'

Women are taking active interest, and although in many places their presence is not too welcome, they will not easily be persuaded to leave the greens. Not only in the British Isles but overseas, women bowlers are increasing in numbers and the question of providing greens for their sole use is one for serious consideration in the near future.

Naturally the movement has its opponents, but the main objection is centred on mixed play and perhaps that is merely a bogey. For many years and during 1931, which has seen the formation of the English Women's Bowling Association, I have known the leading women players, but I have yet to learn that they desire to intrude on men's matches. On the contrary, they wish to be left to themselves and to conduct their association affairs, tournaments and championships without interference.

Eastbourne had the first open tournament for women in 1931, this year Hastings had one, and doubtless when the Kingston tournament is revived in 1933 the open pairs, the first event for women held in this country, will again be found in the programme. Some wonderful bowling was seen at Eastbourne. Mrs Tigg (Waddon), who won the single-handed event and, with Mrs Privett, the pairs, is no stranger to competitive play and has little to learn from any male star in the arts and wiles of match-play. She and her partner have been regular prize-winners in the open pairs at Kingston and, wet or fine, their accuracy has been the admiration of every expert onlooker. In the season just over Waddon, through Mrs Tigg plus Mrs Privett and their rink, won the EWBA singles and rink championships.

Wales also has now a women's association, and from the quality of many of the Welsh playing at Eastbourne it should attract a large membership who will follow their menfolk in skill and enthusiasm.

E. J. Linney, 1932

The difficulty, perhaps, is where claims are demanded for the right to play with the men and when the women claim equal ability to succeed. In many walks women are as capable and as useful as men, in some better and *more* capable, but in games it would be a fallacy and a mistake to claim the right to join in and compete equally with men in all cases. Women play cricket, some well; but would the women care to pit themselves against a team with hard hitters, say? Women shine in tennis, but it would be admitted that the best men are somewhat in front of the best women; the same holds good in golf, swimming and other forms of sport. Physical inabilities account for all this – and, with modesty perhaps assisting, they rule the women right out of football of either code. These are the reasons for many of the objections against women playing bowls and particularly against their playing with men.

The question as to whether they should be otherwise occupied, or whether the game is played to the neglect of other duties does not affect the point as to whether the game is desirable and valuable for women to play. It would not be difficult to instance cases where to indulge in the game men have neglected duties which should have been considered obligatory. Many young players in other branches of sport have sacrificed good prospects in business and life through infatuation for games. It should be an axiom that business and responsibility should come first, and this is as applicable to women as to men.

Evidence is overwhelming that men prefer playing among themselves. This is no argument, however, against women playing the game, and, with constitution and organization mutually satisfactory, there seems ample scope for both sexes. New clubs are springing into existence and in other cases become sections of clubs organized originally for men. In these the general rule is to set aside some definite periods, afternoons generally, when the women may claim a rink or rinks as their own. These times are generally arranged so as to interfere with the play of the men as little as possible; but with the growth of women in membership extended facilities may be demanded.

Felix Hotchkiss, 1932

The game for women is still meeting with serious opposition from the men. There are still many men who look on it as an interference, depriving them of the free and unfettered occupation of the green; as an encroachment, for bowls has remained for a long time one of the few games in which women did not take part. Suggested failure of domestic duties, inappropriateness and loss of dignity have all been advanced as arguments against women bowling; but all have failed. The very opposition has been instrumental in strengthening enthusiasm, adding to the numbers of those participating, increasing the fighting spirit of administrators and welding them all together in a stronger and more determined whole . . . it is by no means difficult to visualize matches not only between the Home Countries but also between the constituent parts of the British Empire.

Although mixed play is in vogue it is the exception rather than the rule – and probably this is for the best – and even where it takes place the women do not always receive wholehearted encouragement. The municipal authorities, with their public greens in parks, have been encouraging and helpful: they have placed greens at their disposal on certain days and times and for the present women rely very much on them.

The game is an excellent one for women: whatever virtues it holds out to men it holds out equally to women. They can be just as graceful as – if not more so than – men in pose or stance on the mat and in delivery, and their ideas of general deportment prevent the jumping about and fantastic contortions sometimes seen when men are playing.

Women's hands are smaller than those of men; their woods should therefore be smaller. It will be gathered that, while perhaps economically sound business, it is not always good policy for a woman to use her husband's woods.

Felix Hotchkiss, 1937

Bumps in the Wrong Places

Another physical handicap of the woman is her shape: women have bumps in the wrong places for the ideal delivery. Not for a moment am

I trying to urge the girls to become Amazons, but it would help their game to slice an inch or two off their hips.

A woman's hip usually interferes with the normal backswing, so we must change the mode of delivery. I recommend that ladies crouch more than the menfolk – a lower stance will enable them to have a better backswing, with the minimum of interference from the protruding hip – and that hip makes it essential for a woman to hold her bowl well to the side as she prepares to deliver. Too many are inclined to look over the bowl, which means they hold it in front of the body; then, when they start their backswing, they take the bowl in a sweeping arc around the hip, which generally leads to an unsteady and unreliable downswing.

The general standard is high, particularly when you consider the restrictions placed on most women. They are treated shockingly by most clubs here.

Frank Soars (Australian bowls star and author), 1970

Stormy Start

In October 1931 the English Women's Bowling Association was formed, but the inaugural meeting proved a rather stormy affair. It was first proposed that an association be formed from the three counties of Devon, Essex and Leicestershire. This apparently was shouted down, and a further proposition from Mrs Johns of Sussex that 'an EWBA be formed and officers elected from the women present' was followed by a very heated discussion, as Mrs Greenwood of Leicestershire, who was in the chair, refused to put the proposition to the meeting.

It was then proposed that if the chairman would not take a vote, another chairman be elected and this proposition was duly carried. Ballot papers were then handed round to vote for a president and three names were proposed: Mrs Greenwood, Mrs Johns and Mrs Smith of Surrey. Before the vote was taken Mrs Greenwood resigned and Mrs Johns was elected by 50 votes. Such was the stormy beginning of the EWBA.

Peggy King (county player), 1972

Fired!

Since the formation of the EWBA women's bowls has made phenomenal strides. In 1939 there were 5598 entrants for the national championships. In 1944, 253 clubs had affiliated.

Naturally, the draw is the ladies' strong suit, and I am prepared to wager that, given the right conditions – a neither too-heavy or too-fast green – the star woman can match the average male in this department. Tactics must be conditioned by the feminine physique: hence we find a more delicate type of game, with less emphasis placed on defence in depth. Although the genuine firing shot is beyond the capacity of the average bowler, it is amazing what she can accomplish with a modified version.

My partner and I once struggled through to the semi-final of the mixed pairs at a large tournament, having disposed of several hot partnerships on the way, and there on the green awaiting us was a male lead and a female skip: it was our first experience of this reversal of the order of things and we thought it a piece of cake. The woman skip, who proved a virtuoso of the firm shot, belted us all over the shop.

Dr John W. Fisher, 1948

Clean Daft!

More than 100,000 women are today playing at the flat-green style in all four countries of the British Isles; at the near-flat-green style in East Anglia, Durham, Northumberland and the East Midlands; and at the crown-green style in industrial Lancashire, Yorkshire, Derbyshire and rural Cheshire.

Fortunate indeed are those women who play on the Cumberland-turf greens found in abundance within the flat-green game; little do they know of the pangs of frustration felt by their sisters living in the industrial areas, who make do and mend on rough grass greens upon which their light woods hop and skip as if pursued by some red gremlin and, through the falling 'marks' on these greens, generally finish yards away from the jack. A clothes-prop or a length of fishing tackle has to be requisitioned for 'measuring' purposes!

To watch some women at play on a Yorkshire public green one evening I took my place on a seat and discovered my neighbour was a woman bowler. Resting between her plimsoll-shod feet was a little canvas bag containing two woods. 'A wish 'er'd come. Eh! A do wish 'er'd come,' she chanted repeatedly, and looked with longing eyes towards a row of cottages to her right. At last a prim little woman closed the door of her abode and walked somewhat slowly towards my anxious neighbour on the seat.

'Wherever has tha bin? I've bin waitin' here an hour for thee. A club match is a club match, and tha should have kept tha time w'me,' she shouted at the newcomer.

The latter's reply fairly stirred the electricity in the air:

'That's all very well for a tale. If tha wants to knaw t' truth, my old man walked through t' door just as I was coming out and I had to brew his tea. If tha wants to claim t'match, tha can claim it! Tha's daft about ruddy game, clean daft thou art. Thank God I shall never get that way!'

. . . And with this speech off her chest she returned to the cottage, calling, 'Claim it, I tell thee; tha's clean daft about ruddy bowls!'

And thus no match was played between them, and the woman on the seat received a walkover into the next round.

The others playing appeared to be enjoying their sport over a rough-textured sward which looked as if, in its first existence, it had provided luxuriant feed for fattening bullocks. It had a much accentuated crown, and all the women knew about bowls there was to throw their jack through the crown, to bowl after it as straight as they could with their first wood and then chance their luck, often down a blocked hand, with their second wood.

My mind went back to those fortunate women who play on the first-class greens at Wimbledon Park, at White Rock, Hastings, on the Eastbourne Corporation greens or those delightful swards at Bournemouth and Llandrindod Wells. What a startling comparison! Furthermore, on the flat-turf greens just mentioned there are always two hands open for use by players, and that cannot be said about the straight-edged greens of the industrial areas along which the player must 'trundle' (and 'trundle' is the only word to use) her first wood as straight as a die if she seeks to win.

In short, the woman player of the industrial north knows nothing of the skill of wood placement resulting from the certain use of two open hands and knows still less of that delightful 'feel' emanating from play on a true and reliable turf green upon which 'touch', that gift of silken hands, is closely linked with correct eye measurement and brings accuracy down to mere inches.

George T. Burrows, 1948

Mixed Reception

My husband Frank and I have seen bowls in Australia progress from a sport which rejected women to one which recognizes it will have to accept them. Women, in a suffragette-type struggle sustained for almost forty years, finally have come into their own. There are more than 85,000 registered women bowlers in Australia and thousands more who play but do not belong to clubs. Even some clubs that will not have women members have been compelled to allow a restricted number of mixed days, and indeed the swing to mixed bowls is the most significant recent development in the game.

We remember when Frank could not buy me and my female partner a drink in a clubhouse we had entered to get out of the rain because the staff were not permitted to serve women. We have heard of women playing on greens lent by all-male clubs being refused shelter in men-only clubhouses. For years women have been aware of the hostility. They have acted with restraint, preferring to discount stories of male bitterness, mostly behaving with decorum, always insisting on a strict uniform on the green. Fine bowlers have emerged, from the inimitable 'Sutty' Sutcliffe to Lila Page, who, twenty-five years ago when she was playing against men at Hunter's Hill, Sydney, was the finest woman bowler we have ever seen.

You will still hear males, including many who have become reluctant clubmates of women, challenge the opinion of Mrs U. Wolinski, Australian WBA president from 1929 until 1958, that women are now welcome, or even 'accepted' in more than the literal sense, in the clubs. They claim the 'white leghorns' have intruded, forcing their way into clubs through pressure on their husband-members, forming a disrupting influence and breaking up male friendships that have stood for years. This has not been our experience.

There are great clubs today whose greens are empty because they refuse to allow wives to partner male members in mixed events. Every month we travel hundreds of miles to play with a Leichhardt club, away from where we live in the Sydney suburb of Hurlstone Park. We have tried to get a women's club going at Hurlstone Park but it remains a males-only bowling community. In one Sydney suburb the men's and women's clubs are next door to each other; the men's club will not admit women, but frequently is empty because the members are all at the women's club which permits both sexes.

We have to agree that some clubs have regretted their admission of women: some have even taken steps to rid themselves of them. But Mrs Wolinski, the heart, soul and life-blood of Australian women's bowling for nearly thirty years, takes the wider view. 'The men love mixed bowling,' she says. 'They say they have found mixed days the most pleasant of all. Besides, mixed bowling encourages family unity.' She and her fellow administrators have always stressed that the admission of women has *improved* the spirit in clubs. The ladies are ever active in organizing functions and providing amenities the men would never think of, she says.

Despite incidents such as I have instanced, the general trend is for more men to get together on the greens with women . . . and to find that those women are highly competent players.

Dorothy 'Tup' Honeybone (Australian bowls star), 1963

Matters of Dress

The entire approach to dress is holding back women's bowls in Australia. For the sake of the game, why not modify the clothing to attract more women, particularly younger ones? Why can't divided skirts be permitted? They resemble full skirts and would not have to be worn at such an unbecoming length. There are too many antiquated regulations in women's bowls. One day, I suppose, the players themselves will revolt and make the diehards in the association realize they are dealing with adults, not a herd of St Trinian's schoolgirls.

Frank Soars, 1970

From their first moments of serious play in county and national events, women decided to dress in regulation clothes and in that regard gave a clear lead to their menfolk. Some critics may aver that they have erred in agreeing to play in one set pattern of white dress, but experience has proved that their distinguishing county colours, made very effective in their hatbands, provide quite sufficient variation of colour as well as serving as a means of identification from the bankside during match play. Elegant as were the flowing skirts and floral or feathered hats of the women who started the game in 1908, they were pre-eminently unsuitable for serious bowls, and the regulation costume has everything to recommend it.

George T. Burrows, 1948

13
The Crown Green

To switch from the flat greens of the world and the decorous dresses of ladies to the parishes of northern England and the Midlands, where the greens slope away from the crown, the jack is biased and play goes on all over the green, is to move from privacy to public, from Union to League, from hospitality marquee to pub. The crown-green game in a form may well have preceded the flat-green sport, though a common understanding has been that it followed it. In any case it is a salty, earthy, uninhibited morsel of a sport, with professionals and amateurs both; and all is encapsulated within this conversation-piece reported by George T. Burrows, who played successively on crown and flat and once, as an amateur, challenged 'Owd Toss' – William Taylor, one of the most colourful of the Victorian pros.

'How does tha' play?' asked Toss.
'Same as you,' I replied in my best Cheshire accent.
'Clever, aren't ye? Does tha' tak' coat off?'
'Yes, when I'm keen.'
'Does tha' tak' waistcoat off?'
'Sometimes – if it's hot weather!'
'Does tha' tak' collar off?'
'Very often, if I'm out to win.'
'Oh, tha' tak's collar off, does tha'? Then tha' can only have three start in 21!'

*

At the age of twelve, in the eighties of the last century, I began bowling on the Brook Street green in Chester. It was a spacious crowned green, over which, from corner to corner, a sixty-yard throw could be obtained if one favoured long-length play. The first players of real note I met were the professionals John Peace, Gerard Hart, George Beattie, William Taylor ('Owd Toss'), Dan Greenhalgh, Rothwell, Meadows,

Baston and Richard Hart, who between them, during the decade in which I watched them contesting matches for many thousands of pounds including side-wagers, proved themselves as clean a band of sportsmen as one could wish to meet. Their names are closely linked with match-play during what was the greatest era in professional crown green bowling.

When men began to play for their livelihood I cannot say. They were doing it in the 1860s; in the seventies, when the late Edward Hulton first published the *Sporting Chronicle* (on which later I had nine years' experience), the pastime of bowling got daily recognition in his newspapers; and men who played behind their village inns did so for wagers, then blossomed out into professional players and, quitting their hard work in the pits and the factories, were 'stood' or backed either by one man or a syndicate.

Then it was, in the late seventies, that John Nickson, the proprietor of the Talbot Hotel at Blackpool, hit on the novel idea of a far-reaching Sweepstake, which has by now grown so popular – as carried on by his widow – that it alone has been responsible for extending the Blackpool 'season' quite a month on into the depths of autumn and the frequent heavy rainfalls of October. But weather does not worry the north country bowler overmuch. I have played in a quasi-amateur event at Old Trafford in Christmas week, with a frozen green that rattled louder than do the boards of the Alexandra Palace indoor bowling room, and with a fog obscuring the jack at a twenty-six-yard throw!

Just picture 1000 men ready and willing to back themselves in pounds and shillings; for it is every contestant's aim to secure 'long odds' about himself, hanging on until his fate is sealed. Some of the richer players take their families with them to enjoy the many seaside sensations of Blackpool. The poorer player, however, lives on as cheaply as he can, judiciously betting a half-sovereign here and there and fighting the odds of an unknown opposition right until the end, or until he goes down before the skill of a slightly better man.

It is wonderful what great faith these humble-minded men have in themselves. It is not egotism hard boiled; it is not wilful arrogance; it is just the simple faith of being 'as good as the next man' and strong-minded enough to back one's play against that of any other man put up against one by the luck of the draw. It is all done so decorously and with such good sense. There is no outward show. The gambling is accomplished in the street, in boarding-houses, in tramcars, anywhere a group of men assemble and everywhere a man is frank enough to state his wants in the way of odds. It can be done miles away from the green; indeed, men bet about the sweepstakes everywhere a book-maker can be found willing to lay the odds against an average man, which are certainly nothing less than 500 to 1. Against some, however, the odds are 1000 to 1, simply because they help to beat themselves by their untoward temperaments.

In the early rounds one year I was beaten by a collier who went far into the final stages that autumn. He was still a worker in the pits, and he had been six weeks at Blackpool, failing by a narrow margin at the end. I asked him how he afforded to do it.

'There is no "brass" coming in while I'm here,' he said, 'for unless I go to the pit I have nothing.'

'How are your wife and children going on, then?'

'Oh, they haven't starved. I'd saved up something for them and, you know, well, I've sent them a trifle each day.'

'You backed yourself to win outright, I suppose?'

'Yes, I got £1000 to a pound, and I looked like "copping" it until Thursday.'

What an attractive force the Talbot Tournament is! I saw several finals and can well recall the physical strain it was on a few of the contestants. Yet some of the others engaged may just have been playing for half-a-crown, so utterly occupied they looked with the task that lay before them. They minded not the thousands of eyes watching every throw and the cries shouted across the green at one or other of the players. Some finals have attracted so many spectators that the green has been encroached on and the bowls virtually delivered through lanes of people. Every window and every roof in the neigh-bourhood of the Talbot is crowded with enthusiasts, people stand round the green ten deep and the grandstand would put to shame many a similar erection on a football pitch. Think of that, ye Bowlers of Suburbia, particularly ye who enclose yourselves inside four high walls and no man can gain admittance to your green without having a special key to the gate, or, if he is a stranger, cannot enter without signing a book and swearing an affidavit that he will attempt to spend his own money at the private bar!

One cannot understand the oft-heard outcry against professional bowls. As it is seen in Lancashire, and there understood of the people, there is nothing wrong with the game. Indeed, I would go so far as to say that professional bowls is cleaner than any other phase of the pastime. On the matter of status I am convinced that a professional is the man who has played or is constantly playing for a staked bet. All the rest can go as amateurs. The strict amateur in industrial England is of the middle class – the tradesman, warehouseman, clerk or publican predominating; the professional and semi-professional is the collier, factory-hand and other horny-handed son of toil. Some of the latter, who think for themselves, try to remain loyal to the amateur definition, even against great temptations, but there are countless thousands in Lancashire who belong to neither class.

To Oldham, Blackpool, Wigan, Weaste and other towns I went many afternoons to play in curious semi-professional-amateur tournaments held on hotel greens. The landlords give £2, 30s., or £1 as prize money, perhaps a copper kettle as well, and charge a shilling for admission to the contest and greenage. Now, invariably, a threepenny tally is given to the entrant, and that is the price of a drink which can be bought on the green, or, failing that, it is an unwritten law that the loser of each heat hands over that threepenny tally to the winner.

If I had wanted, I could have bet on the rounds, either on myself or the other fellow! The men I met were colliers and factory-hands, rough-hewn wearers of clogs and caps and scarves – the men who haunt London on football Cup Final day; the 'northern horde', as one penny newspaper once described a Lancashire crowd. They cussed, capered and were rough-spoken, but they played the game and did their best to lower the sails of the booted, linen-shirted, straw-hatted amateur who dared to come and meet them at their own style.

Now these are the men of whom it can be said no association in the world can govern. They have no status they care a hang for; they do sometimes get into amateur affairs but for the most part come and go and skirt on and around the fringe of amateur-professionalism and no one is the worse or the wiser. These are the men you can hardly thoroughly describe as professionals when you think of the out-and-out staked-bet players whose living it is to play bowls.

I do not see any wrong in amateurs being allowed to compete in the Blackpool sweepstakes and still retain their status. As I have said already, it is 500 to 1 against any ordinary amateur ever winning that event. I would lay it willingly against any thousand bowlers of amateur rank. It's a matter of nerves more than skill. Thank goodness I've got over the stage fright of 2000 eyes looking at you, and perhaps 500 voices chipping you or cheering you. The surroundings themselves are quite 250 to 1 against an amateur; the rest of the odds are made up in ability and staying powers. A close game of 21-up will sometimes take an hour and the tension for that hour is remarkable.

The only thing an amateur does in the Blackpool sweepstakes to damage his status is to come in contact with the professional and to 'handle back' his 5s. entry-fee should he be successful in winning his early ties and a few more shillings should he get much 'forrader'. Is there wrong in that? It costs quite £1 a day to live in Blackpool and play bowls – therefore, on the head of expenses alone the amateur who dabbles in professionalism is well out of pocket.

Strange as it may seem, the professionals rather resent the amateur flitting in and out of their events and then going back to be 'whitewashed' as an amateur again. Once, after I had won two heats at Blackpool and the news had gone round that a scribe had stepped into the ring, I found myself the centre of attraction in a crowd watching an amateur event at Old Trafford.

'You still call yourself an amateur?' queried one.

'Why not?' I replied, 'I am not a habitual match-player.'

'You're a nice lot, you amateurs,' he responded. 'I wouldn't be found playing with any one of you!'

'You call this bowling?' he added, heeling round to point to the amateur tournament. 'Would you credit players in open handicaps with such ability? They ought to be chased off the green! Let amateurs remain amateurs. We don't want them coming and going in and out and among us. Bah! No man can pretend to play bowls in a starched collar and shirt and with his coat and hat on!'

My caustic critic was a noted player – a man whose skill has lifted him out of the pits of Lancashire to a position of affluence. I can see him now, fighting a game out, collarless, aye, bootless, coatless and hatless, bowling like a machine, hardly ever speaking except to snap some corrosive comment at a spectator or to accept an offer of a bet from the ringside. As George Borrow loved the pugilists of old, so do I esteem these men who play my pastime for money. I never met a real wrong 'un among them.

George T. Burrows, 1915

Death of a Green

I asked a car-park attendant in Blackpool one dull, dreary autumn evening if he happened to know where the Talbot Hotel and Bowling Green could be found. He looked at me hard for a second. 'Thar's two yards short,' he said, and held his arms wide, in the way bowlers do. 'We'll never hear that cry again. If you could bore through this concrete you'd be on the old green. But there's no green now, only the foundations of a new supermarket and offices. It's a ruddy shame!' The man obviously took it so badly I felt like offering my condolences. As I looked through the hoardings around the site I felt a tugging at the heart-strings. It was like witnessing the destruction of an old and faithful friend.

Later, I met an old bowler having a drink in an hotel close by, and I am positive there were tears in his eyes as he talked of the old days at the Talbot and of the great matches played at this most famous of greens. On the day the demolition began he went along and cut a piece of the turf. Today it is growing in his garden, a reminder of a green that was almost sacred to the men who trod it in their quest to put the premier bowling prize on their sideboards. For every bowler wants to win the Talbot.

Although the old green is no more, the Talbot will go on and is now held at the Raikes Hotel, Blackpool, where it was held for a period during the war years. But when the bulldozers began to rumble and the gangs of men tore into the masonry of the old pub with pneumatic drills, it was the end of an era. The old hallowed grass was mutilated and hacked to pieces by lorry wheels and mechanical shovels. It was the end of a wonderful pub that possessed that magic substance, character; and of a green that had a wonderful feeling about it, too, as if the colour and excitement of past glories had imprinted itself on to the grass.

John D. Vose, 1969

Great Battles

I have seen 4000 present at finals of the Talbot, and perhaps the two most exciting matches were those of 1906, when 'Old Toss' (William Taylor) beat Gerard Hart by inches on the last throw, and 1911, when Fred Threlfall met Tommy Meadows in a final ending in another remarkably near thing.

The final two disputed woods in the Threlfall-Meadows match were so close to the jack that an ordinary measure could not be used. There was a cry for a piece of straw, and the sight of Threlfall on his knees fining down with his knife a frail piece of straw in order to get a true guide as to the winning wood, with the referee, Bill Bottomly, and Meadows watching him and the whole of the crowd waiting in absolute silence was a sight not to be forgotten. Characteristically, Meadows had leaped into the air immediately he saw the woods and his backers had taken this as a sign of victory and cheered. But Threlfall stooped down, put the little wisp of straw between his wood and the jack, and turned to Meadows's wood. It was Threlfall's turn to caper; then another cheer. Threlfall had won.

George T. Burrows

At Preston in 1917 Hopkins beat Yates in a match, 51 up, under remarkable circumstances. Yates was 49 when Hopkins stood at 29. Then Hopkins got the jack and made a run of 21: a lead of one and only one to win. Yates equalized at the next end; then Hopkins got a 'toucher' which Yates failed to beat. At one time the odds were 100 to 1 against Hopkins with no takers. They were against him at the start of the match, but at the last end they were in his favour.

James Hartley, 1922

Old Bill Lacy of Wigan has become a legend in the crown-green world. This man was a dog-trainer and for many years had lived in London working with greyhounds at the race tracks. He took up bowling only when he had retired, 'for summat to do', and he was seventy when he began seriously competing in the big tournaments.

But Bill was a natural bowler, reaching a degree of skill few men attain even after a lifetime on the green. He certainly possessed great spirit and enthusiasm for his new sport as he began his onslaught on the Blackpool 'sweeps', and in 1957 he amazed the Waterloo spectators by winning the famous Handicap. This old man captured the imagination and the hearts of the crowd, and when they realized the wiry wizard was still in the Talbot a thrill of anticipation began to buzz. Could Old Bill do it again . . . the double?

Came the day. The green was packed, the streets were crammed with people striving to get inside, and men were crouched in the most precarious places determined to see the matches. Old Bill came out to play Wally Fish in the quarter-finals, and outside the voices of touts could be heard offering half-crown tickets for a pound apiece. Rarely has a final day had such appeal. Bill's delivery hand was bandaged, which he explained by saying it had been sprained due to all the handshaking over his Waterloo victory.

And what a battle this was! Fish, a real fighter, gave a great show in keeping within striking distance of Lacy. At 18–15 Bill ambled to the side of the green and had a drink of tea from his flask, as unperturbed as if he were playing in a park for a 'tanner', completely ignoring the crowd. Wally took him in the corners and the crowd began to whisper now: could Bill reach? But the green was fast and Lacy answered their suspicions by getting a single: 19–15.

But now came a sudden change-round, for Fish beat the short-mark expert at his own game and on a falling mark took two points: 19–17. Naturally, Fish tried to stretch his man by going for the corners but Bill put paid once and for all to the talk that he was no use on long marks: he scored two and so entered the semi-finals.

He was drawn to play Paul Roocroft, twenty-two, from the Liverpool area. Young Paul bowled extremely well and almost won the day, but Bill, to a great cheer, took the counting point needed for 21 and was in the final.

The old bowler had had a busy day; it was very warm and he'd played long marks, having no easy matches. He was tired, so he had a nap in the interval before the last match. The suspense on the terraces surpassed anything that had gone before. They all wanted the cup to go to the Wigan man – a disconcerting state of affairs for his opponent, Johnny Ball, also of Wigan. Poor Johnny must have felt a sensation akin to guilt as he strove to beat Lacy, but he shut out sentiment and all the distracting influences from his mind.

Again Lacy seemed to have the upper hand and led 16–10. Ball scored five chalks now to creep to 15–16 and was bowling well, but Old Bill went to 17–15, and as he delivered the jack on a favourite falling mark the writing appeared to be on the wall for Johnny Ball. But the unexpected happened, and Ball coupled up to take two on Bill's own 'pantry': 17–17.

Bill had suddenly lost his grip. It was noticeable, and much more so when he struck in an attempt to knock out Ball's two counting woods.

'Evening Bowls' by Peter Unsworth, 1978

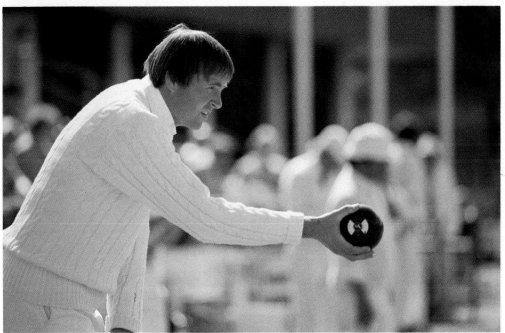

Top: 'Superbowl' pits the top men and women players in opposition.
David Bryant beat Jeanette Conlan in this 1985 match, but
she and other women have added skill as well as variety
to this event

Above: Peter Belliss, who won the world singles title for New Zealand in 1984

Opposite: Noel Burrows: from the crown greens to indoor victory in 'Superbowl'

Tony Allcock, a world champion indoors and outdoors

He missed and wearily trudged up to the mat, trailing now 17–19, a tired, perplexed man. Ball scored a single and clearly had the beating of Lacy; still he gave a chance at the next end when short with his leader . . . but, alas for old Bill, he couldn't reach and was shorter still.

Ball's second wood left him two in and Lacy prepared to bowl what was to be the last wood of the match. It was a fast wood he played . . . but it hit his own short bowl and knocked it past the jack. The lean, weary old man collected his woods and ambled dejectedly off the green; and when he warmly shook Johnny Ball's hand he said: 'Well, at least Wigan's won it – and that's summat!'

Bill Lacy was a great bowler and a wonderful character, but what about Ball? He was lucky to be in the tournament! Earlier in the year he had visited Blackpool with his wife for a few days' holiday but forgot to join the Handicap; it was only on a later visit that he tried to do so but the entry list was full. By a stroke of luck Ball was still on the premises when the secretary had a 'phone call from a Blackpool bowler withdrawing from the tournament. Johnny got the place.

*

'Who is he?' everyone was asking. 'Charlie the Lion-Tamer' was no noted bowler, that was for sure – yet here he was in the final of the 1961 Waterloo Handicap! Charlie Taylor was seventy-one and had spent most of his working life as an assistant in the zoo at the Tower, hence his nickname. It was all rather like Bill Lacy; he had begun to play only when he was in his late fifties. But this was his first really big tournament. Could he win as a local man here in Blackpool? Against John 'The Feather' Featherstone, from Leigh, of all people? Surely not!

The little zoo man came on the green. What a great moment for Charlie as he stood in the centre, the eyes of the crown green world upon him. Featherstone, a publican, winner of big money handicaps and a professional at that, was having his second tilt at the title in two years. There they stood with the referee waiting to start what was to be one of the greatest finals on record: Charlie without his usual black beret but looking quite a studious little man behind his distinguished spectacles; and John, sphynx-like and dour, determined to stop Charlie becoming a legend and, above all, not wanting to go down in the records as runner-up two years in succession.

As Charlie trailed 5–9 it looked as though the Leigh man would have a comfortable ride. Then the local began to settle, his nerves calmed and he was rolling them up much more sweetly: he peeled at 9, then 10, 12 and 13. But Charlie stuck at the unlucky one and John went on to 18. This was it, surely? Age and inexperience of big matches were against the game little 'un.

Not a bit of it! Here he was shaking off the handicaps with a two; then a single to make it 16–18. And now came the extraordinary sight of a seventy-one-year-old setting out to out-throw a man almost twenty years his junior. He knew John didn't favour corner play so he threw out the jack as far as he could, but he slipped up by doing this for both his woods were mediocre and John got in: heartbreaking – and probably the final nail. Charlie must have felt dispirited; the crowd began to leave the green.

But now Charlie's first delivery cannoned off John's wood to put him one in, and he made it two with his second. After playing a short wood at the next end he made up for it with a fine wood to notch a single, and those who had left the green were now trying to get in again. The terraces were roaring on the 'Lion Tamer': 19–20 was the game, and again he turned his eyes to the far corner and proceeded to put down two nice woods. He was in with two . . . but John's last delivery saved one: 20–all!

A hush descended as the game old lad threw out the jack – but he put it in the gutter and had to do it over again, a nerve-racking affair at any time. Even so, he put down a lovely lead wood that came to rest eighteen inches from the block – a grand wood on the long mark. 'Feather' couldn't lick it and Charlie was in. He'd done all he could possibly do that day – it rested now with Featherstone.

He had to play the last wood of the match. And what a beauty he sent up . . . skilfully directed . . . it curled delightfully inside Charlie's bowl and come to rest four inches from the block. A gem to delight the hearts of bowlers but surely it broke the great heart of Charlie Taylor.

*

The 1966 Talbot final was a cliffhanger in the classic tradition. Stan Priestly, a charge-hand joiner in the illuminations department of Blackpool Corporation, played Wally Fish, a tool-fitter at Leyland Motors. Twice Fish led Priestley; three times they were level. At 12–6 it looked as if Fish would win, but Priestley found his best form to go in front 13–12. Fish then took a single to peel at 13. This was the stuff of which great games are made.

Fish got away again and was putting them down so well he led 17–15 and many people were writing off Priestley. But Stan is never beaten and he gritted his teeth to pull back from this tough situation: it would be a hard enough job in any match but a Herculean task in a Talbot final before a capacity crowd of critics and experts. Stan got three chalks to regain the lead at 18–17; then Wally peeled at 18.

Priestley, the Blackpool joiner, was surely home when he came again with two to lead Fish 20–18 . . . but no, Wally Fish ignored the hubbub and coolly scored with both woods! What a match! It was 20–20 and Fish's jack, which made him the favourite. This final end was to provide the biggest shock of all, and one that will be talked about for years.

Wally Fish played a poor lead: short, far too short for a Talbot final. His second wood was no better and lay two yards short along with his first. Priestley was in, and his last wood put the finishing touch to some wonderful bowling. It was dead on target, struck the jack and rolled to finish six inches away. The crowd erupted and genial Stan, the illuminations man, had achieved his life's ambition, with every excuse for getting 'lit up' himself that night! A wonderful final; but Wally Fish had suddenly and dramatically lost his touch at the very moment during his whole career when he needed it most.

John D. Vose

Champion of Champions

There have been many great crown-green bowlers and no definite conclusion can ever be reached as to who is supreme, but Richard G. Meyrick, from Shrewsbury, British crown green individual champion in 1948, 1961, 1962 and 1966, was surely *one* of the greatest. What was it that made him such an extraordinary player? I list some characteristics, not necessarily in order of importance: Great sensitivity of touch or feel, involving bowling to the inch, and fine judgement of distance (target bowls would have revealed his tremendous accuracy) . . . Immense tactical skill, as shown by assessment of opponent, variation of mark, reading of green and conditions . . . Ideal temperament, keen without being ultra-aggressive . . . Ability to deliver from various positions and in different manners which tended to puzzle opponents. Perhaps I can illustrate some of these by referring to specific games where I saw the master in action . . .

Llandudno Oval green, 1951. Wales v. Shropshire: A very difficult green, forty-five yards square, characterized by four shoulders or small humps. Dick was originally in difficulty on a fast-running green against an opponent with much local knowledge. He was down 11–4; then started round-pegging 23–28 yards from hump to hump, eventually winning 21–12. This was my first sight of a bowler bordering on the uncanny as his woods homed their way to the jack.

Dewsbury Rugby, 1957. Yorkshire v. Shropshire, the Crosfield Cup Final: On a treacherous green characterized by strange hollows (now alas no more) he played R. Senior, unbeaten in county matches that season. Dick spent a whole half-hour practising sixty-yard corner marks, then won his match 21–4 on short marks.

Weaverham (Cheshire), 1961. The BCG Final: This green is reputed to have the highest crown in England (nineteen inches) and is a searching test. Dick, in the semi-final, had beaten Bill Dawber (Lancashire), an all-time great, and in the final played Eric Ashton, 1959 champion and another outstanding player. One sensed both were in their prime. Though not the closest, this was perhaps tactically the best final I have seen.

Ashton began with terrific accuracy, led 8–3 and lay two at the next end. Meyrick's problem was immense: he was blocked and could not play a length bowl because of the severity of the slope. For once he studied for some time and decided to play a fast bowl (say eight yards overplayed) off the slope. And he succeeded . . . carried the jack and left himself two. Few in the vast crowd realized the shot was on, but the score had become 5–8 instead of 3–10 and a dramatic change had taken place. He then began a systematic attempt to break up Ashton's length, varying the direction and length of the mark, a very difficult manoeuvre dependent on expert play. His tactic again succeeded and he eventually won 21–16, clinching the game with a superb two to Ashton's jack at the last end.

Rylands, Warrington, 1962. BCG Final: On a foul day, Meyrick had already played five games, winning two 21–20, when he met the Lancastrian Tommy Knott on a green where water was beginning to stand. I felt he would be over-thrown with his rather slight physique, but there was great strength in his wiry frame and he had mastered the technique of wet-weather play.

They came to the last end at 20-across, with Knott leading. On a forty-five-yard mark over the crown, Tommy led brilliantly with a nine-inch wood almost covering the jack: the type of bowl the more you looked at it, the better it appeared! But great champions have a sixth sense or an inner working of the mind telling them what to do. Meyrick reacted instantly, without study, producing a master bowl and playing out Knott's wood like a follow-through shot at snooker. Poor Knott. He had played well and led what appeared to be a match-winner, only to see victory snatched by a great champion who produced a superb shot at the vital time.

Shotton, 1966. BCG Final: Consistent close corner play enabled Meyrick to win comfortably. Corner play was a feature of his game which he developed over the years on changing to heavier bowls. Incidentally, flat-green bowlers might not realize that very large and heavy bowls are a great disadvantage on certain crown-green marks (e.g. fast downhill slopes). I have heard people speak disparagingly of crown green because the woods are smaller, which is rather like saying that a snooker player must use a heavy cue. The truth is that the crown-green player picks the bowl for the job, irrespective of whether it be large or small.

Dick had the correct attitude to the game. Winning was important to him, of course, but he had the knack of putting this in perspective and his matches were always played in a good humoured and chivalrous manner. He was, I feel, the greatest crown-green bowler to the standard jack in living memory, and with present-day opportunities of travel and competition would still have reigned supreme. To win the British championship means winning from a field of about 5000, playing twelve games and more on at least four greens on different days, and this is why it is generally regarded as the supreme test in crown green bowls. To win it once is marvellous: to win it four times borders on the miraculous.

Gwyn Morris (President, British Crown Green BA), 1986

The British Crown Green Association, until the mid-1970s, had 'Amateur' within its title, but now its laws cover most types of events. Years ago, though, the professionals formed the 'Panel', into which only the hard successful core from within their ranks were invited . . .

The Panel Match

I am in the stand at a panel match being played behind a pub in Wigan. I liked the atmosphere as I had half-a-pint in the bar and it is the same in the stand. Good humour is very much in evidence despite the cold wind blowing in from beneath.

'Art gooin' Haydock, Jim?' Check Cap asks his mate, the little tubby man with the Wigan rugby muffler round his size 17 neck.

'Aye,' is the reply; and Check Cap imparts a certain confidential knowledge into his ear, as if he is giving him the plans for a nuclear warhead.

'It'd better bloody win, Albert. Last 'un tha give us had a gammy leg.' Great guffaws greet this remark, even though most of the men around have only heard Jim's reply.

The stand is echoing to the stamping of feet. Breath takes to the air like a great pall of mist and floats off in the rarefied atmosphere towards Wigan pier.

All this is just a fill-in, a prologue of remarks and fun before the real business of the day starts. These men are here for a purpose: they are the betting men of the panel. From all walks of life they come, whenever the chance arises, to write down mysterious data in little notebooks.

The first two men are on the green now and the referee is walking over to the centre. The stamping ceases.

'Gregory's jack,' shouts the ref.

'Gregory wins,' shouts Check Cap.

'I'll tek Gregory,' he chirps as if to confirm to the crowd his faith in the ability of Ingham Gregory to beat Jim Cunliffe.

'Gregory wins for ten.' And as the first end is over, two points to Gregory, they are all at it: 'Eleven to eight I'll lay – I'll lay eleven to eight.' And everyone seems to be laying on Gregory, and looking around me at the chattering, excited men, I cannot help but compare them with the two men on the green responsible for all the yelling, who appear to be bowling with the apparent calm of men playing at who pays for drinks. But it is obvious these men are experts.

'Cunliffe wins. I'll tek ten on t'big 'un.'

Who is this who dares to oppose the shout of the majority? But no one gives him a second look and the 'big 'un' is being hailed as the winner now.

'Cunliffe wins. Guineas I'll lay – I'll lay eleven to ten.' The faces of these men are pictures in shrewdness as they glance, almost slyly at times, at the others around them. It's a battle of wits. Pencilled notes follow winks, nods and strange expressions, and the actual game seems to be of secondary importance even though some wonderful woods are being put down on the slow running green. But really the betting men are watching the game like hawks.

A little fat man smoking a large cigar and answering to the name Gerry says very little, seems removed from the general assembly and continually moves his head, now towards the bowlers, now to the left, now behind to the stand. Suddenly his finger goes up and an answering wave comes from the man in front of me. Magical contact almost – not a word passed and yet both write in little books. Gerry smiles to himself a satisfied smile and slowly moves along the rail – watching, listening and blowing smoke from his rich Havana. An excitable, pleasant round-faced man, answering to the name of Wally, ever on the move, is much in evidence, and every few minutes darts down to the rails for a closer look at the match. He is the very essence of alertness. A big friendly red-faced man answering to the name Seth seems to prefer a wandering role as he walks around searching for takers.

Cunliffe is leading Greg now 16 to 10 and the shouting is hectic. A chap next to me sings his odds: 'Five to four I'll tek; Five to four I'll tek' . . . and I'm sure the tune is 'On Ilkley Moor b'art 'at'. And between his songs he keeps shouting 'All the winners – all the winners,' which I take it is 'panel' idiom not translatable by lay folk.

'Tens I'll take, I'll take tens.'

'Six I'll lay – sixes I'll lay. I'll lay sixes.'

'Tek seven pound to one,' shouts a less ambitious punter from behind, sipping hot tea from a steaming flask. Wally cracks a joke that I can't understand, but it causes a great laugh.

'I'll lay seven halves,' shouts a thin man at the rails to the accompaniment of isolated laughter – but there's little time for laughing a few ends later. For they are peeling at 20 – half way to the 41 up finish.

Both bowlers are really keen now, running after every wood and talking to them. 'Come on, big 'un; thar'l have to do better than that,' Jim Cunliffe shouts to the rolling timber, but he knows it's a short wood. 'Thar's two foot six, Jim,' remarks the referee, who seems a walking tape measure for he can judge distance at a glance. Very often the pro. knows the fate of his wood as soon as it has left his hand.

'How am I?' asks Gregory.

'Thar's in, but a good nine inch narrer,' answers the referee.

But Gregory wants to see for himself and walks all the way over from the corner. The referee, besides being the scorer and in charge of proceedings, acts as impartial adviser to both men and never seems to tire of letting them know how the woods are lying. Greg's second wood is a stormer and he's chasing after it like a sprinter at Powderhall.

'Run away!' It obeys and rolls to nestle against the jack.

A vocal barrage erupts with an almost volcanic quality and I'm certain I'm surrounded, not by men, but by 200 bass baritone rooks.

'Gregory wins,' they chant. 'Five to four I'll lay – I'll lay five to four.'

Men are signalling from across the green now and a tremendous excitement is under way as Gregory scores two more points. A squeaky voice has been piping up all through with ' Greg-ory wins – Greg-ory for six,' hyphenating the bowler's name. But the voice that appeals to me belongs to a dour looking gent in a flat cap. He makes old Satchmo himself sound like a coloratura soprano. 'Tek a pony to four,' he growls monotonously. 'Pony to four Ah'll tek.' He drags out the words as if reluctant to part and the sound is the thickest of gravel.

Some rather rough language comes from the far end of the stand. 'Language up there!' shouts a well-built gent wearing the green blazer of the Association, 'Cut it out, thar not at home thar knows.'

The refreshment room has a great reputation and this is the weather for Lancashire hot-pot with red cabbage. Here men are sitting at tables watching the match through the windows: it's a lot warmer and the hot-pot is superb.

A chap in the hut has just told me that these men are not real bookies in the racecourse sense. They are not allowed to put up stands, for instance. Mostly these men are here just to 'make a quid or two' and for the fun of it. It's in their blood, for they love betting. I feel this is the secret of the whole affair, they really enjoy themselves.

A lot of the punters work on the nightshift and spend the afternoons at the bowls. Most of them aren't out to win big sums. To a retired man a pound made every day in this fashion can be a help. The word 'bookie' is a very loose one in Panel bowling: anyone can do it providing they hold a card which authorises them to take part in 'permitted betting', and the art seems to me to be in taking bets, then laying them off with someone else.

'D'ost want to hear a good story Albert?' It's the chap in the Wigan muffler again. Albert nods. 'This 'ere hippie went t'barbers and asked him for an estimate to cut all his hair off. "It'll cost thi ten bob for that lot," says the barber. Well he gets stuck in and half-way through he asks t'hippie if he went t'Manchester Grammar. "That's reet," says t'hippie, "but how does thy know?" "I've just found thi cap," said t'barber.'

In most sports I find that betting introduces the element of cut-throat commercialism, but not so in this game. There is a great feeling of goodwill here that is never apparent on the racecourse. As I walk down the steps swift glances flash at me. I feel I daren't blink in case they write me down in their little books and I'm almost frightened to blow my nose in case it's taken as a signal that I want to place a bet.

Jim Cunliffe has both his woods round the jack, so 'Greg' decides to strike. It's a good target and his striking wood scatters the jack and woods all over the green. 'Gregory two,' shouts the ref. when the woods have settled. 'He'd have etten his cap if he'd missed with that one,' says a punter. 'Greg doesn't wear a cap,' someone replies. 'Well, he'd have etten his bloody yead then,' comes the rejoinder. 'Greg's bowling very sposmadic,' announces another man very seriously, 'very sposmadic.' 'Pony-to-two,' growls old Satchmo, who gives the impression he wouldn't change his tune if the stand caught fire.

It's hail-storming now. Cunliffe's second wood is skidding along sending up a back-lash of spray as it rolls crash into the jack with a thud. It's something indeed to bowl a length in these conditions. In no time at all the grass has turned from green to white. Their adaptability is wonderful to see as they approach the end of the match.

Cunliffe rallies and it's 40–40. What a din! Hubbub, vocal barrage; the air is full of the shouting of odds, the very essence of concentration written on each face, eyes searching constantly for takers. Still even now they are at it. Even at this stage a man can win or lose.

Greg's wood is a good one – 18 inches, and that's good for corner bowling in a hailstorm. Cunliffe bowls now. He really throws it out and the wood, despite this, seems to make heavy weather in the middle on a bad patch. On it rolls, laboriously and without inspiration, to fall a good yard-and-a-half short. Jim, who only bothered to follow it halfway, shakes his head in disappointment. 'Gregory wins. I'll lay six to four – six to four I'll lay! Greg-ory wins!' The excitement is volcanic.

Greg's second wood is a good one. I like the way it leaves his hand. It has class. 'I like it,' he shouts, striding out behind it, shepherding it over every mushy inch of the way. It beats his first wood and the referee announces 'A foot – 12 inches.' What a task for Cunliffe.

It's all eyes on Jim Cunliffe now. As he bends to his task a hush descends and it's as if all the eyes of the universe are watching the black bowl ploughing its way through the fallen hail. The wood has power. It fairly whirls along.

'It won't be short,' yells Jim. 'Run away,' he shouts, as if to contradict what he's just said. And off he runs, like a charging giant, bending low over the wood, hurling abuse and affection at it in the same breath, stamping behind it, leaving massive black footprints in the white blanket as he gathers impetus. But all is noise now. The wood has found the space between Gregory's woods . . . it's through . . . a foot . . . six inches . . . it's passed the best one and still it rolls . . . what a wood! A toucher – corner to corner on a wet, slushy, treacherous green. 'Weighed in,' announces the ref.

There is an anti-climax now. The first voice I hear belongs to the huge man in the racing tweeds, who looks to me like a racecourse bookie on a day off. 'Well, by the bloody hell – would tha' believe it? Greg's second 'un was a toucher until t'wind give over blowing.' He's obviously lost, but gives a philosophical shrug of the shoulders and peels off a note, and it looks more like a tenner than a quid. 'It was like lightning on Tuesday; today it was like bowling on a ruddy puddin',' announces Ingham Gregory, carrying his woods into the hut.

Now comes the great reckoning, for no money changes hands during the game. Little queues form everywhere and the books are consulted and each transaction is ticked off as it is settled. I hear 'Greenall pays five', and a punter hands over a fiver. There is an implicit trust about it. I like the whole thing – it's different, convivial and, by gum, these pros. can bowl!

John D. Vose, 1969

Flat or Crown?

I left all the happy men of the crown green in 1907, and on joining a London weekly newspaper was asked to write an article comparing the crown green game with the flat-green or rink game which was still in its infancy in the Metropolis. I wrote as I then felt: that I had left behind me a good, open, sporting phase of bowls for one which, if ever I started to play it (and I then had grave doubts that I ever should grow to care for it) was far too confined and restricted, gave little or no exercise and was mere 'finger billiards' compared with the healthy swinging throws one could obtain across some of the big greens of Lancashire and Cheshire.

If the present secretary of the English Bowling Association has all the minute-books he will find pasted down, by Thomas Baines, then honorary secretary, under '1907', a vitriolic article abusing the EBA game and singing the praises of the other. Baines got in touch with me: 'I'm a Lancashire man,' he said, 'and, like you, I'm living and working in London and we both have to do as Londoners do. There is no room for crown green in London and bowlers are compelled to play the rink game. Will you promise me that you will not attack the EBA game again but help it?' I promised I would try.

George T. Burrows, 1915

Not only did Burrows try. He became an EBA councillor and a convert. Sixteen years after penning the above he was to write:

With all its appeal to strength and sheer vitality, the crown green game fails to approach the rink style from the viewpoint of artistry. When a rink on a London suburban green is hot from the day's sun and woods have merely to be dribbled down outstretched fingers, it is then that skilful drawing, delicate placement and end-building made safe from all possible harm are matters that count most. Such are the delights of the rink game, while its companionship is a thing not quite attained at the other style. For pure bowling the northerner's game takes pride of place; for the finer elements of bowl play, calling for generalship and ability to rise to the solving of a hundred difficult problems, the rink game is unsurpassed.

G.T.B., 1931

The utmost that can be urged in favour of crown green is that it yields a sporting though not a scientific game. In a great pastime we have a right to look for qualities somewhat rarer and less fleeting than glorious uncertainty. One might perhaps get a sporting game on a billiard-table with the cloth split right across, but I fancy the champions would soon sigh for a proper one. Presuming that most men play bowls for something more than mere sportiveness, such attributes as judgment, strategy, skill and science are demanded in a far higher degree on a level than on a crown green.

J. A. Manson, 1912

For rink bowling it may be justly claimed that more players can participate on a similar-sized green, and that may be a strong reason for the maintenance of this system of bowling. On the other hand it can scarcely be claimed that rink bowling calls for the exercise of the same skill as cross-green bowling. Rink players are confined to the same piece of land throughout the game, playing incessantly forwards and backwards and so accustoming themselves to the peculiarities of a particular patch or mark. The cross-green style calls for incessant change.

James Hartley, 1922

By understanding both codes, more people may become convinced that there is room for both games. Just as crown-green bowlers should learn that in flat green the positioning of the bowls and the build-up of the head are all-important, so flat-green bowlers should appreciate that in crown the varying lengths, different slopes and variable green, rain and wind conditions can be decisive factors.

Absolutely standard conditions certainly give accuracy, at the expense perhaps of a certain deadening effect. The element of chance adds greatly to the interest in many sports and is certainly present in the bustling, vigorous, thriving crown-green game.

Naturally, there is at the moment great interest in TV indoor flat bowling with its ease and convenience of coverage. This is all to the good, with the important proviso that this should not be at the expense of the outdoor crown, which has perhaps a greater appeal to the young, active and adventurous. Hence, my hope that the stronger worldwide code of flat green can co-operate with and maybe even encourage the thriving but more regional crown green. Variety does give not only spice but also interest, excitement and challenge.

Gwyn Morris, 1986

14

Across the Seas

Whatever their respective origins and merits, crown green today is a parochial game and flat green international. The British took bowls abroad; but as we have seen, in some respects the pupils got their acts together sooner than the masters.

Wherever the Scot wanders he tries his hardest to settle and takes with him – besides his trade and his brains – his Bible, his Bowls and his Burns. When he has found his feet as well as a few brither Scots (not too few, either, be sure of that!) his early concern is to lay a bowling green. And so in quick time the game spreads, and new chums try their 'prentice hand and write to Glasgow, Edinburgh or London for a supply of bowls, the coming of which is awaited with an impatience like that of the panting hart for cooling streams.

J. A. Manson, 1912

Australia – Phenomenal Growth

In Canada we hear of four clubs in Toronto, besides Hamilton, Montreal, London and Quebec, nearly all being combined bowling and curling clubs; Boston, Philadelphia and New York have their clubs in the USA: even far-away Calcutta and Kurachee have their golf and bowling clubs; the Japs have also taken to the game; and every year the export of Glasgow-made bowls is increasing to South Africa. With our Colonial brethren in Australia, the rapid growth in popularity is phenomenal*; and while Scottish bowlers can *now* boast an association, the Australians have had the benefit of such control since 1880, twelve years before Scotland, when the Victorian and New South Wales Bowling Associations were established, comprising many clubs.

The Australian rules are much the same as ours, but some interesting variations may be noted. For instance, rule 6 in Victoria says, 'The jack shall be round and made of wood, not less than 3¼ nor more than 3½

---

* Australia now, in 1987, has about half a million players (men and women) in membership.

inches in diameter, not less than 15 nor more than 17 ounces in weight, and shall be white in colour'; while the NSW association enacts that 'the size of the jack shall not be less than two inches, nor more than two and a half inches in diameter'. In the English game, each single-handed player has a jack made of wood the same bias as his bowls; so that by observing the run of the jack, he is the better enabled to play his bowl. To us rule 20 in New South Wales reads curiously: 'The season shall commence on the first day of October and end on the last day of September.' So the Antipodean bowler goes it all the year round.

Is the day near, when say four crack rinks of bowlers will be sent out to play the best in the colonies? It is certain a deputation of colonial bowlers would be heartily welcomed and hospitably received here. Cricketers made a start in this direction more than eighty years ago; why not bowlers?

Humphrey J. Dingley, 1893

It was in 1845*, at Hobart, Tasmania, that bowls was first played in the Southern Hemisphere, on a green 100 feet long by 36 feet wide behind the inn known as Bowling-green Hotel, where a club was formed. The landlord, Mr W. Turner, issued an announcement in the *Hobart Town Courier* on October 28, 1846, as follows:

BOWLING GREEN

W. Turner begs to announce to his friends and all admirers of that healthful and invigorating old English game of

BOWLS

that the green will be re-opened for play on Monday, the 21st September next (weather permitting), on which occasion a substantial luncheon will be provided for all persons providing him with their company. Gentlemen desirous of becoming annual subscribers to the green may do so on payment of 10s. in advance; and should a sufficient number of subscribers be obtained, they will be at liberty to fix among themselves certain days and hours in each week for bowling, at which time the green will be kept clear for their use.

* Reference books, however, say 1844, credit British bowler Frederick Lipscombe as the pioneer and his 'Beach Tavern' as the Hobart venue. Lipscombe certainly lost a small money match to T. Burgess there on 1 January 1845.

On the mainland of Australia bowls began only slightly later.
Subsequently, on April 11, 1864, John Campbell, a Scot of course,
formed a club at Windsor, Melbourne. He called a meeting, and
although there were not twenty willing to join, he embarked on the
making of the green, incurring liabilities which forced him to mortgage
his property and borrow £30 from friends. The green was opened
October 22, 1864, and in two years he had cleared all his debts.
The club grew: no less than 172 members entered for the first
championship, and thus the seed was sown. Now it is probably the
oldest surviving club.

E. J. Linney, 1932

In 1880 John Young, a wealthy builder and keen bowler, thought it
would be a good idea to arrange an 'inter-colonial' match between
clubs in Sydney and Melbourne: it would give Sydney's comparatively
new players the chance to learn a thing or two from their more
seasoned Melbourne opponents. The tournament was to be on his
private green at Annandale, but the Sydney clubs – especially Parramatta, the oldest and strongest – were irate when they heard what
Young had done. What right had he to arrange such an important
fixture on his own green without consulting them?

John Young was well known for getting things done, often ahead of
time. His father and brothers were builders in Britain. After studying
architecture and surveying, and working as a draughtsman for the
Crystal Palace in London, he settled in Melbourne in 1855 when the
building boom was taking off after the discovery of gold. Big jobs
never daunted him. In Melbourne he built St Patrick's Cathedral and
the interior of the Bourke Street Synagogue. In 1866 he moved to
Sydney and built the GPO, a large part of St Mary's Cathedral, the
Lands Department building and the magnificent Garden Palace (long
since destroyed by fire) to house the Sydney International Exhibition.
He pioneered the use of reinforced concrete in the Lands Department
building and introduced new types of scaffolding, travelling overhead
cranes and arc lights for night shifts to speed work in hand.

When Young built his home at Annandale he surrounded it with
lawns and gardens and laid down a green beside his door. Roads in

Annandale in those days were poor, so the *Fawn*, that 'most pleasurable of steam launches', was chartered from its Captain Byrnes to carry the bowlers to and from the tournament. A German band was hired and a banquet with champagne provided.

The outcry over the venue for the match and confusion over different rules made it imperative that there should be a governing body 'for the general management of the game in the colony', and at a well-attended meeting in Sydney the NSW Bowling Association was formed. After an opening reference to the jealousy that had arisen, it was resolved that the new association would arrange any future inter-colonial matches and prescribe a set of rules for the guidance of clubs. Young, despite the criticism flung at him, was elected president – and held the office for twenty-six years. At the first meeting of the association he donated a challenge cup valued at $50. This was the beginning of today's pennant matches.

Many of the state's leading citizens, including Lord Jersey the Governor, were entertained in the early days at Annandale; and in the 1890s, when Young visited England and he and the president of the Victorian association were instrumental in the Imperial Bowling Association being formed, Lord Jersey became its president.

John Young's influence is still felt. He was a stickler for the tidy appearance of players and their gentlemanly conduct on the green and in the clubhouse. He insisted on a standard of etiquette that has become traditional.

Noel Griffiths, (Australian journalist), 1980

After twenty years of inter-state contests the idea had seized the bowlers of Down Under that the time had come to pit themselves against those of Up Above in Britain, and John Young of Sydney, the grand old man of the Australian game, and Charles Wood, of Melbourne provided the longed-for opportunity. In 1901 the team – twenty-four bowlers from the Commonwealth and eight from New Zealand – bore, each man, his own expenses. An unfortunate misunderstanding led to the secession of the New Zealand contingent ere a bowl had been played, but the rest of the company carried out their campaign without a hitch.

Perhaps the most conspicuous feature of the Australians' play is their predilection for short jacks. Experience has taught them that a minimum jack perplexes their opponents more than a full-length jack does, so they throw one much more frequently than is usual in the United Kingdom. To a long jack, on the other hand, colonial play is distinctly inferior to British, being much too powerful just as to 'baby' jacks the bulk of British play is too feeble. The moral is that play to mixed-length jacks should be more general in both hemispheres.

Fondness for 'riding' bowls – the 'skittles' of irreverent and ignorant bystanders – is a peculiarity of Australian skips. Sometimes this is the only scientific shot possible. Many an English driver – for the Scots skip is seldom loth – is deterred from attempting it through dread of the chaff and ridicule of the banks. The colonial skip, accustomed to big galleries, has plenty of nerve and plays the absolutely correct game at a given juncture. True, he must have an eye like a hawk's. The secret of driving consists in knowing when *not* to do it.

The Australians did well. They played twenty-two matches – ten in England, ten in Scotland and two in Ireland – winning eleven, losing ten and drawing one. Words failed them in praise of the greens in Scotland, but, with several outstanding exceptions, the English greens were condemned as 'unplayable', 'very rough', 'against the bias', 'unreliable', 'not true' and 'tricky'. As to the character of play, the Australians considered that Scottish bowlers exhibited the soundest generalship and possessed the most perfect knowledge of the game, but their methods were irritating. The dilatoriness of the Scots would, they avowed, have tried Job himself beyond endurance, while their habit of capering up the green after their bowl was extremely tiresome. Indeed, in some cases these antics put the colonials off their game. The repeated consultations between the skip and his men, the going up to the head to see how the woods lay before playing and their generally 'dawdling' deportment were features of the Scotsmen's play which the Australians deemed annoying, apart from the wilful waste of time.

Australian greens differ according to the grass. In West Australia and South Australia couch predominates and furnishes a somewhat coarser green. The scarcity of water in certain parts of these States entails heavy expenditure. In the area of the goldfields – as at Kalgoorlie, Coolgardie and Boulder – the supply comes from sources several miles distant. In Victoria and New South Wales there is less couch and, to the eye at any rate, little to choose between the turf of the best greens and that cut from the Solway shores.

Against one serious danger the Colonials must be warned. In many places the game is pursued amidst luxurious surroundings. Besides laying down excellent greens, each costing several hundreds of pounds, some clubs have yielded to the temptation to build commodious and well-appointed clubhouses at an outlay of £2000 or £3000 and upwards. Lavish expenditure upon 'swagger' premises – which, however desirable, are not necessary – involves large entrance fees, annual subscriptions and, commonly, an increase in the cost of management. Every club that approves of a policy which is often both wasteful and demoralizing is unconsciously jeopardizing the most cherished social attributes of bowls. Bowlers will rue the day they sanction extravagant expenditure in connection with the pursuit of their game, for, most assuredly, the next step will open wide the door to class distinction and class sentiment.

J. A. Manson, 1912

The colonials do not strike one as being so keen as the average Scot; at least they enter into it in a much lighter and happy-go-lucky frame of mind than the latter. But then the Scot is well known for his earnestness in all games as compared with his friends from the other parts of the Empire.

Following the 1901 tour, three or four Australians, finding themselves in Britain during the summer of 1907, played one or two games, although in no way officially. Visits to and from Australia mean too much ever to become regularly organized, at least as present conditions exist. They entail too great an expenditure of time and money and few British players could afford the best part of a year and several hundred pounds in order that a team might go out from the Home Countries to Australia. The beauty of the game, and one which is never likely to forsake it, is that it does not lend itself to professionalism. It is impossible; and so long as that is the case organized visits to Australia are equally so.

J. M. Pretsell, 1908

New Zealand – Methodical or Funereal?

The New Zealanders are great sticklers over the observance of the discipline of the green. They believe in the first three players remaining at the end of the rink until it comes to the skips' turn to play, when two processions make their way to each end of the rink. The one consists of the first three players on each side going from the mat to the head, and the other of the two skips going from the head to the mat to play their bowls. This is all very methodical and no doubt good in its way, but it strikes the average Scottish bowler as funereal.

The New Zealand associations have a rule that club colours must be worn in all tournaments and matches. The idea is certainly praiseworthy and might well be followed in the Motherland. Their greens are carefully kept and invariably play keen. With a view to endeavouring to acclimatize the Silloth turf to his native country, Mr W. Wakeman, a member of the team which visited here in 1907, took out a small quantity of the turf and a sample of the seed of the Solway strand.

J. M. Pretsell, 1908

South Africa – Accelerating

The most important milestone laid in the history of South African bowls was the foundation of the Port Elizabeth club in 1882. That began the trundling of woods in South Africa and they have rolled with greater momentum ever since. The progress was slow at first – whether from conditions or the outlook on sport at that period we cannot say. Gradually, however, the qualities of the pastime began to percolate into the minds of men.

The founders, if they were here today, would be dumbfounded at the colossal growth.* The greatest increase in clubs and greens has been in the Transvaal and Natal, so the Pretoria club holds a proud place in the annals of Transvaal sport: not comparable with the mother club of South Africa at Port Elizabeth but great nevertheless.

It has been said that the growth of bowls has outrun its administration. That is a debatable point but plans will have to be made now for future administration because the growth is accelerating. There is hardly a village in the Union of South Africa and Rhodesia that has not a green or is planning to construct one. It is a sign of civilization, the hallmark of a town or village. Where it all will end we cannot prophesy.

South African bowling magazine

---

* South Africa now has more than 800 affiliated clubs, with 1464 greens and more than 38,000 bowlers.

The prevalence of clubs in South Africa is rather what might have been expected considering that the Scot is in truth the only begetter of bowling's geographical distribution, and the pastime is likely to enjoy a long and vigorous career under the auspices of the united British and Dutch peoples.

Probably no bowling community in the world ever went through so unique and anxious an experience as did the Kimberley club, of which Cecil Rhodes was a generous supporter, for their green was exposed to a double danger during the 126-day siege by the Boers. On the one hand it lay within range of the enemy's fire and on the other its existence seemed doomed when the edict went forth enjoining the most rigid economy in the use of water. Yet on the relief of the town by Sir John French on February 16th, 1900, the lawn was found to be in excellent condition, nor had any person suffered injury.

How the turf had been preserved was a mystery, for during the hostilities day after day passed without sign even of 'a little cloud not bigger than a man's hand', and the grass appeared to be denied its natural sustenance. The local theory was presumably right: that some zealous bowler, by an extraordinary lapse of memory, periodically forgot Colonel Kekewich's order and, taking the risk of being bowled over by the Boers, ministered by stealth to the comfort of the turf.

J. A. Manson, 1912

The game is developing steadily in the Zululand, largely due to the fact that most of the sugar mills have put down greens for their employees. The time has arrived when the clubs should form themselves into the Zululand Bowling Association.

The Bowling World, c. 1932

Canada – Awakened

In British North America, bowls first saw the light in Nova Scotia. In 1734 an enclosure was reserved as a green for the officers of the garrison of Annapolis (Port Royal), while the Duke of Kent, grandfather of King Edward VII, had a green laid down in his grounds at Prince's Lodge, Bedford Basin, Halifax, the game then being popular in the provincial capital. These, however, were isolated instances, more than a century lapsing before a concerted effort was made to establish bowls in Canada. The people of Quebec, predominantly of French blood, have never shown any *penchant* for the pastime, though in Montreal and vicinity the rink game is firmly rooted and in Ontario its interests are controlled and safeguarded by the Ontario (1888) and Western Ontario (1896) associations.

Save in three particulars Canadian bowlers accept the Scottish laws. First, instead of a real ditch round the green a space about fifteen inches wide between parallel whitewashed lines is marked off at each extremity of the field of play; secondly, on some greens the rinks are not much more than ten feet wide, a condition tending to overcrowding; and thirdly, when the jack is driven across the side boundary into another rink it is still alive and the end must be completed. As to the first feature, clubs that adopt the Scots statutes should surround their greens with the shallow ditch which, indeed, is almost necessitated by the doctrine of 'touchers'. The second feature is indefensible. In respect of the third, it occasions such constant inconvenience that it is singular the Canadians should ever have substituted it for the Scottish practice, according to which such a jack is dead and the end must be started afresh.

On the whole, the bowlers of Canada are somewhat lacking in the keenness and resource which characterize those of Australia. This is readily explained by the difference of climate, which shortens the season, restricts opportunity for practice and interferes with improvement of the greens. In these respects the Canadians are heavily handicapped. We may develop the argument to its full, logical extent and say that the supremacy of Scottish bowlers lies in the fact that they make their game from youth upwards on greens in the pink of condition.

Canadian greens are never likely to be as good as the best in the United Kingdom. The winter is severe and generally the frost has penetrated to a considerable depth before the ground has been covered with a thick blanket of snow. Then, when springtime comes, the frost does not leave the greens, or even all parts of the same green, equally, so unevenness of surface is inevitable. Intense summer heat follows and bakes the soil, the top becomes pulverized and the roots of the grass have no chance of spreading their fibres on the surface. These two causes are climatic, but the third is artificial and it rests with the bowlers whether it shall be remedied. Night play by electric light, which is installed on many greens, is extensively practised and play goes on long after the turf has been saturated with dews. Consequently, owing to play on the sodden turf, the hard-worked ends completely wear away. On greens exposed to such treatment a truly scientific game is difficult, if not impossible.

In the summer of 1903 the Imperial Bowling Association invited the Ontario association to a series of matches between a representative team from Canada and certain clubs in the Mother Country, and this tour became the feature of the bowling world in 1904. The result of the campaign was disappointing to the Canadians, for they went down on green after green with painful monotony (although their victories were gained over such strong clubs as Bounds Green, Cardiff and Bromley), but it was important to learn, by repeated games, both what a green was like and how it should be made and kept. The trip had been partly of an educational order and had not been taken in vain.

No time was lost in returning a visit. On July 21, 1906, a British team sailed from Liverpool under the captaincy of Samuel Fingland, of Broomhill (Glasgow), with James Telford (West End, Newcastle) and John C. Hunter (Belfast) as lieutenants. It was a team of Trojans and worked with more than Trojan ardour and a great deal more than Trojan success as it swept onwards from victory to victory: twenty-three matches were played and the British won all but two. The gross majority by which the visitors won all their ends was 1,109, which, after deducting the majority of twenty-two by which they were defeated, yielded the extraordinary net majority of 1087 shots.

Though smitten hip and thigh by a team of stalwarts the Canadians were by no means downhearted, and a team of friendly invaders, twenty-eight strong, landed in England on July 3, 1908. They took part in thirty-two matches, of which they won eight. Inexperience of perfect greens repeatedly showed them at fault in timing the pace of the pitch, whilst they constantly overlooked the fact that a full-sized green enabled a much longer jack to be thrown than at home.

Sweet, however, are the uses of adversity, and the stern and strict drill of discipline had been silently at work for the good of the Canadians. In 1910 another team from the Homeland visited Canada and met bowlers whose match-play had vastly improved. Of the twenty-three matches the British won seventeen and lost six. The policy of playing two matches on one day was dubious and against the tourists, for while their opponents were fresh the British team had to do duty twice. However, there could be no doubt that the march of the ever-victorious army of 1906 had had a wonderful stimulus. 'Wake up, Canada!' had been in effect its cry, and her bowlers had responded with an advance that was almost prodigious. Interest had grown keener; individual play had improved; the greens were better. Since most of the bowlers are curlers also, eye and hand are kept in practice all the year round – and such training is bound to tell.

J. A. Manson, 1912

The visit of the British bowlers to Guelph yesterday was one of the most successful sporting and social events the royal city has ever enjoyed. It was a charming afternoon, and the spacious grounds of the club at the Victoria rink were pretty well filled up with the competing rinks and the scores of brightly attired ladies and interested males who watched the play.

It did one good to see the way the visitors bowl – they put their whole hearts into it. Whether a British bowler is standing on one foot with body tense, swaying with the progress of the ball, arms extended intently watching the course of the bowl, or whether he is earnestly following it up and caressing and encouraging its every motion, he is oblivious to all other earthly surroundings. Perhaps they are a shade too keen. They growl over the green if it does not suit them like a bear with a sore toe; they are out for every point in sight; but they play the game.

If a Canadian bowler is four feet off the jack, the skip has generally something encouraging to say; if a Britisher falls down that way his effort is greeted with ominous silence, or he hears about it. They are franker and more truthful than we are, and a player who has much self-respect puts forth his very best efforts.

Guelph Evening Mercury, 16 August 1906

USA – Needs Excitement

Bowling, I read in *Harper's* magazine, is a passion with the Brooklyn people, almost every set or circle including a bowling club:

A page of the *Brooklyn Eagle* is devoted to the bowling matches of seventy clubs, but those are the clubs of skilful, earnest players and do not form a drop in the bucket of the clubs formed by neighbouring coteries all over town.

In an old folio dated 1748 I find in a summary of some of the remarkable enactments of the General Assembly of New England the following penalties mentioned:

> Gaming for money, treble value; use of cards or dice, 5s. Shuffle-board or bowls at a publick-house, £1. 5s.
>
> Quakers: to bring one in is a forfeiture of £100; to conceal one, 40s. an hour; to go to a Quaker's meeting, 10s.; to preach there, 5s.

Poor Quakers! They as well as bowls seem to have been at a discount with the New England Fathers, who doubtless held up both hands in pious horror at the mention of either.

E. T. Ayers, 1894

In the United States bowls has not caught on. This is remarkable enough seeing that Scotland has contributed generously to the population of the Union. The probability is that the game has been deemed lacking in 'purple patches' and altogether too slow for the eager American temperament. Still, though started somewhat tentatively at first, clubs have been founded in several of the states, and the future if not the present will be with the pastime.

J. A. Manson, 1912

In the parks of New York, Boston, Chicago and San Francisco the game is played spasmodically; but when America has developed her municipal parks, the necessary outcome of closer settlement and growing towns and cities, she will tackle the public park's lawn-bowls green subject as she usually does things – right well.

America plays a 'hoodoo' kind of bowls. It is nothing less than skittles as it has been known in Britain for 100 years, but for cheeses the Americans have substituted round bowls. These you trundle down an alley of wood, and if you strike the centre of the alley the bunch of pins are certain to go down. This game has been sent to England and to French and Belgian seaside and health resorts for indoor play. In London it is played underground. I have seen it outdoors all over France and Belgium.

It is only a game for an idle moment or a dull day. There is no skill in it; you just attain the knack of a straight drive and the rest is easy. Yet this hybrid bowls-cum-skittles game is very popular in USA, where it is my experience that no game is loved unless you can hurl all your brute strength into it – just as no story is worth the telling there unless it is particularly long-winded and ultra-marine.

George T. Burrows, 1915

Hong Kong – Wartime Struggle

The firm roots of the game in Hong Kong, which date back to 1897, are admirably exemplified by the experiences of the bowlers in the Stanley Internment Camp during 1942–45. After the capitulation of Hong Kong to the Japanese, many of the luxuriously kept greens were converted into car parks, stables and horse-grazing pastures and the bowls freely distributed to gangs of Chinese juveniles following in the wake of the Japanese. The prisoners, after a month's confinement in bug-ridden, rat-infested Chinese hotels and boarding houses, packed like sardines and inadequately fed on a diet of boiled rice flavoured with chicken's feet or strongly smelling fish, were transferred to the Stanley camp.

Nobody with bowls in their blood could be expected to keep away from the game for long, but the Japanese officers were, to put it mildly, not accommodating. The green adjacent to a prison officers' club showed every sign of neglect. The surface of knee-high rank grass was perforated with numerous small shell-craters, most of the supporting boards had been torn up for firewood and about a quarter of the green had recently been overturned in the shape of a cross as a warning to aircraft. Any bowling equipment was stored inside the prison precincts under the control of the Japanese gendarmerie who clamped down on any release.

Things looked hopeless until two members conveying stores by lorry from Hong Kong to Stanley noticed at the Hong Kong Football Club about eighty bowls strewn around the floor. These were smuggled into the camp under a load of bed-linen; jacks were improvised from old tennis balls filled with plaster of paris and mats from pieces of coconut matting edged with canvas; a plywood door was converted into scoreboards and number discs. On March 12, 1942, with Sir Atholl Macgregor, KC KT in the chair, 104 prospective bowlers held a meeting on the Indian Quarters village green to form a governing body, to be known as Stanley LBA, to serve as substitute for the Hong Kong LBA.

When one half of the green had been rendered playable, it was officially opened on St Patrick's Day with a knock-out competition between England, Scotland, Ireland and Wales, England being victorious. And what a sight it was! The strangest and most assorted garb and headgear were dug out to signalize the occasion: police caps, Wellingtons, multi-coloured military glengaris and the like mingled with the rags and tatters to make the ceremony resemble some grotesque fancy-dress ball. Soon, singles, pairs and rink championships and league competitions were resumed on the pre-war system.

By December 31 the green was in a mutilated condition and had to be closed. It had become a jack-of-all-trades: a popular open-air venue for religious services, health-and-strength meetings, PT classes, and concerts (in particular the performance of sword dances and eightsome reels); it was used as a children's playground, a clothes-drying ground and as a general short cut between the various blocks! Renovation was undertaken voluntarily by half-starved helpers using makeshift tools. The green was ready again for play by April, 1943, in spite of the camp billeting committee, who had commandeered the tiny bowls store in the boiler-room, necessitating storing all the equipment in any nook and cranny, often exposed to the elements.

By 1944 privation had begun to take its toll and several of the regular helpers had to resign. Fourteen of the internees, among whom were bowlers, were killed in a strafing by Allied planes. Crosses were then laid on open spaces, including one on the green. Nonetheless, it was during this year that for the first occasion in Stanley and in the history of Hong Kong bowls a triples championship was organized. The season ended with an open rinks championship played on two narrow rinks squeezed in on either side of the cross.

John W. Fisher, 1956

Europe – 'Bowls of Sorts'

Bowls of sorts has been known in France from the first half of the fifteenth century at any rate if the tradition be well founded which has bestowed upon an area in the north-east of Rouen the name of *Place du Boulingrin*. This appellation has been current, according to the *Daily Telegraph* of January 4, 1906, 'since the soldiers of Henry V and

Bedford played bowls round the walls of the French city in the years just before Joan of Arc was burnt within them (1431)'. One cannot, however, avoid the suspicion that such a recreation was only a casual amusement to pass the time.

The word *boulingrin* is a corruption of 'bowling green' and points to the likelihood of their having borrowed the game from the British. In that case it is probable that the Continental varieties of the pastime are practically survivals of the pristine game. My friend Charles Berjeau reminds me that Vauban and other military engineers employed the term *boulingrin* in fortification for an esplanade under grass and acutely remarks that 'boulevard' is *boule verde*, which translates into 'bowling green'.

Charles Dickens visited Italy in 1845–46 and contributed to the *Daily News* the series of graphic articles afterwards published in book form as *Pictures from Italy*. During his sojourn in Genoa he witnessed many festivals, amongst them that of San Nazaro:

> The men in red caps and with loose coats hanging on their shoulders (they never put them on), were playing bowls and buying sweetmeats immediately outside the church. When half a dozen of them finished a game, they came into the aisle crossed themselves with the holy water, knelt on one knee for an instant and walked off again to play another game at bowls. They are remarkably expert at this diversion, and will play in the stony lanes and streets and on the most uneven and disastrous ground for such a purpose with as much nicety as on a billiard-table.

It is obvious that this pastime, queerly punctuated with sweetmeats and piety, bore not the slightest resemblance to our game on the level green. Yet that it was a variety of the sport adapted to a novel surface and actually known as bowls is tolerably plain from his brief sketch of the scene that greeted him as he left Avignon on a broiling midsummer day:

> The heat being very great, the roads outside the walls were strewn with people fast asleep in every little slip of shade, and with lazy groups, half asleep and half awake, who were waiting until the sun should be low enough to admit of their playing bowls amongst the burnt-up trees and on the dusty road.

In the National Gallery, Edinburgh, may be seen a fine and characteristic example of the seventeenth-century work of David Teniers which shows that three Dutch peasants have bowled while a fourth is in the act of delivering his bowl, an upright peg about four inches high doing duty as the mark instead of a jack – recalling the ancient English version of the game in which a cone was the target.

Bowls is not played seriously to any great extent in the Fatherland. This is to be regretted, for the game is indicated as exceptionally adapted to the temperament and habits of the German artisan and the studious and lettered classes.

J. A. Manson, 1912

For three centuries or more bowls have been played as a pastime in Holland, Belgium, France, Italy and in Spain, where ball games of all kinds have had a particular vogue for long ages. Dutch players of old bowled to a cone with round woods, but today, as also is the status of the Belgian trundler, they bowl with either 'cheeses' or heavy balls of wood at a number of pins. Rather have the people of the Netherlands degenerated from skilful bowl-throwers to pitchers at skittles. I have slung round bowls at pins behind the Rubens Cafe in Bruges for drinks, and one afternoon would have grown quite 'heady' on cheaply earned lager beer so easy was it to skittle all the pins down with a straight right and an eye that plays no tricks.

The French have borne no real love for bowls as we know the game. At Villefranche there is a bowling club which has the base of a disused quarry for its 'green', although the 'course' now is hardened earth trodden down to the consistency of asphalt. Their rules are very similar to the most primitive of British regulations.

The French player at 'expression' could give a lot of weight away to the most enthusiastic Scot or even to the most dervish-like dancer after his woods I ever saw at Blackpool. When about to bowl the Villefranche trundler takes a hop, then a skip, a short zigzag run, next stops dead and the bowl trickles slowly towards the jack. The whole action is a kind of cross between the motions of Tom Burrows, the Nelson hop-skip-and-a-jump expert, and the curious wriggle of Kermode, the Australian who played for Lancashire County Cricket Club.

The Southern Frenchmen plays for *vin ordinaire* (very *ordinaire*, I can assure you), and a good shot means a hurried dive to the nearby jug-and-bottle department and a quick return to the game. I've seen the same thing happen in South London, but the wine is of a different country and is generally mixed with soda.

In Northern France the game is sometimes played on grass, but chiefly on rolled-out hardened sea-sand. The sand 'greens' are about thirty yards long and four yards wide. They are nothing less than specially rolled and prepared plots of sand, protected by rough boards about a foot high, laid lengthways, and by a board three feet high at each end. The bowls, here, are made of lignum vitæ, and while they are not turned on a lathe to get bias, they are plugged with lead, which side of the bowl being played inwards to the green produces the requisite bias. If a drive or skittle shot is necessary the leaded part is turned to face the sky. The jack is a wooden ball about three inches in diameter, and wherever it resteth after it is thrown, to there must the ensuing bowls be played.

George T. Burrows, 1915

Boules, or iron bowls, especially the short game known as *petanque*, can be played in any clothing convenient for the weather, from an overcoat to a bathing dress; any piece of bare ground will serve as terrain; and almost any number can play from two to eight . . . and after that is divisible into matches of lesser numbers. This simple, happy game suddenly exploded into popularity. In less than five years all France was infiltrated – from end to end. In one season Paris was invaded and occupied. On any little piece of waste ground the *boulistes* appeared. The prefect of police, Monsieur Papon, tried to stem the tide but, finding the pressure overwhelming, wisely gave in. *Petanque* crossed the Pyrenees; passed over the Mediterranean; penetrated into Italy, leapt the Alps; crossed the Rhine and the Atlantic; Kennedy challenged Frank Sinatra to a match for the price of a Martini; Canada, California and Australia have outposts already. Now Britain is, I believe, about to succumb to the charms of *boules*. If this does come to pass the benefits will be enormous.

The tremendous impetus imparted to the game by the splendid invention of the steel *boules* (leaping in popularity even far ahead of the cannonball days of Drake) did not reach Britain. We did not know the joy of handling these delightful playthings, but continued conservatively on our way, pursuing silently the old game. But there is some strange magic in the pleasure of merely holding the *boules* and, once sampled, will not be denied. One realizes what a lovely material steel is, surely the most splendid man has created.

Michael Haworth-Booth, 1973

And finally, a brief glimpse into the literature of a sport reputedly illegal in some parts but nonetheless still practised in Ireland: road bowling.

At the butt, the Hammer-man sprang into the air as if he had been shot. All his strength went into the throw. His face convulsed, he gave a gasping grunt, and the bullet left his hand like a rocket. For a hundred yards it drummed at terrific speed along the road. Then it curved towards the footpath. A warning cry rang out, and those on the footpath scattered like blown chaff. The bullet mounted the path and skimmed along like a living thing. Then, without touching the wall, it left the footpath, slicing viciously down the road again. Finally it trickled to a halt and sat dead in the very centre of the road. It was a magnificent shot of over three hundred yards. A soft murmur came from the crowd. To mark the shot another tussock of grass was flung down. In two stages, the bullet was thrown back to the Bridge Wall.

Macklin's arms were astonishingly white, but as he bent down and lifted the bullet, clenching it, the muscles under the skin stood out long and strong. With the sun still shining, another shower swished briefly up the road, but no one paid the slightest attention. All eyes were fixed on Macklin, with a deep hush falling as he walked back for his run. In movement he was sharp and precise, like a soldier on the parade ground. He ran lightly and gracefully to the grass butt, and threw easily, with none of Quinn's exertion.

With a sharp crack the bullet struck the road and sped down the centre, sending up a thin film of spray. It passed through the marker's straddled legs, and dwindled to a faint speck. Gradually it lost its speed, but clung to the dead centre of the road, as though caught in a groove. Finally it rolled wearily into the grassy slough. A moment, and then the shout came up: 'Hind bullet'!

John O'Connor, *Come Day, Go Day*, 1948

15

Peace – and Fiction

It is 1948. The war is over. The lucky ones have returned to their home greens. In this era of relief and ration books Hugh de Selincourt set Gauvinier Takes to Bowls.

Gauvinier's First Woods

Gauvinier felt there was something dashing and peculiar about setting off on his bicycle quite early in the morning to play bowls. He had seldom played any game in the morning, except on Bank Holidays, since playing for the 1st XI at school while the other boys, more than 800 of them, continued their studies in class. And then they rarely started till a quarter to half past eleven. To start off at 10 o'clock on an ordinary Monday much well-formed habit had to be broken down; which increased his uneasiness in inflicting his novicehood upon strange and expert gentlemen.

For that uneasiness he soon found there was no ground. Ten were wanted to make up triples and pairs matches and he was pleased to find he was 2 in the triples: a pleasantly inconspicuous place, he thought, sandwiched between starter and skip. It was all very friendly and nice; indeed almost too friendly, for nobody seemed to mind very much whether an end was lost or whether an end was won. But practice – practice he was seeking and here he was finding it. Practice was the main thing: slowly to build up familiarity with rink and woods and players.

But the too-placid surface was to be rudely ruffled. His No. 1 had sent up two admirable woods which well nigh leaned on either side of the jack. Infected perhaps by this excellence, his own first wood had rolled prettily up to be a pleasant counter, as his skip, voice full of encouragement, informed him. The opponents were yards away, unable to grasp apparently that it was definitely a shortish jack. His opposite number delivered his second wood and groaned in fury, 'Blast it! Too steamy again!'

Gauvinier took the mat in happy confidence. The wood left his hand exactly as he wanted it to leave his hand, the right green obviously, dead on the jack. He stared. Yes, all the way . . . but alas! about half as hard again as it should have been. The sickening thing did not slow nicely down but raced gaily on – crack on the jack, wicked off the leaning wood . . .

'Oh, my dear chap!' came from his No. 1; and the clear voice of his skip answered with no sound of reproach, indeed too punctiliously courteous: 'Just a *little* too strong! They're lying 2 now.'

This shook Gauvinier up badly: all the more so because up to the last half-second of the wood's course he had been fatuously pleased with the shot. A hard, cold light was thrown on his ignorance of the amazing delicacy of poise necessary to register the feel of a right delivery. But he knew enough to know that awareness of a particular ignorance may be the first step towards enlightenment. The hard, cold light shone more fiercely bright upon this ignorance after his third shot, for fear of being too strong caused him to send up a wretched wood yards short of the jack. Yet the oddness and excellence of the game was rubbed in by the fact that they finished two up on that end.

'Not single spies but in battalions', we are told that misfortunes come. For he started off his three in the next end with what would have been in strength and length a beauty, if he had not most unfortunately mistaken the bias: his wood lay, jack-high, on the next green, and there it hideously remained, stupidly, grossly conspicuous.

This was a little more than half-way through the game and what little poise he had till then with tense care attained was scattered. Up till then he had been feeling that he was, slowly perhaps but surely, beginning to make some headway: two out of three shots were not so bad, one or two had been really good. Go quietly on like this, he thought to himself, and you'll be reaching some sort of consistency. Consistency. Consistency – damn it, it shouldn't be too difficult to acquire consistency! It wasn't now so hideously far away – almost within his reach.

Too soon his turn came to take the mat again. 'Just a nice draw, yes, forehand, there's plenty of room. Or backhand if you see it like that. Either way – just a nice draw,' came the clear, encouraging voice of his skip. The see-saw infection of his tone was keyed to smoothe all difficulties that might pop up in his hearer's mind, as a crooner obstacles in some lady's heart. It looked easy – too damned easy.

Gauvinier resented the soothing lilt; loathed crooners anyhow. He made doubly, indeed trebly sure to have the right bias; heroically resolved to do his best, though 'facing fearful odds'. With elaborate care he eyed the jack and stooped to deliver his wood; but he stooped an inch or so too low, his fingers rubbed the turf and the wood managed to crawl a little more than half-way to the jack. The coveted goal of consistency, of which he had caught a clear glimpse, vanished below the horizon.

'Oh, we all strike bad patches,' came a voice, meant to be consoling. But for the rest of that morning all Gauvinier's effort was wholly negative – not to make an ass of himself. Any occasional good one struck him as a mocking fluke. Certainly more in this game than met the casual eye. Certainly, too, he must at the earliest opportunity obtain a set of his own bowls. Yes indeed. His own woods would surely become more amenable than the large heap of impersonals for anybody's handling from which it was the devil's own job to pick and choose a proper lot. To desire them was one thing; to obtain them was quite another, at the end of a long total war.

The gorgeous weather of April, which brought all the flowers in the garden out a good month ahead of their usual time, wavered, faded and then gave up trying even to become a decent summer. Cloud obscured the sun, rain threatened and fulfilled its threats, snow even and hail came and lay for hours preposterously white on the grass and green leaves and flowers. But whenever possible Gauvinier, obedient to the call of practise, practise, practise, bicycled resolutely down to the club. Other stalwarts turned up, too, and, shaking their heads over the inclemency of the weather, rolled up their woods for a couple of hours three times a week in the morning.

On one occasion when the sun deigned to shine there was a newcomer: new, that is to say, to Gauvinier, well known, however, and welcome to members of standing. He was a small man, short and spry, with bushy white hair and bright eyes; an ageless sort of person, to whom Gauvinier took strongly on sight. He was so keen and pleased to be there and delighted with the warmth of the sunshine. Good fortune brought them together in pairs, opponent number-ones, in close company all the morning. He talked happily on without restraint and all that he said was interesting somehow and well-timed; never interfering with Gauvinier's play.

'Just taken up bowls, I hear. You'll find it a lovely game, a lovely game. Been playing for forty years myself. Grrr! You wouldn't think it, would you, after a shot like that, but first roll-up this season and you've always to find your length. Ah, that's more like it! End of last season, a good dry spell: came trickling out of your hand, almost got to hold them back. Today, got to push 'em along. Gor! Too heavy, too heavy!'

Not many ends before he found his length, however, and Gauvinier had the pleasure of watching that consistency in another which he hoped one day not too distant himself to attain. The irrepressible old fellow was not only a delight to be in touch with but was a gift to any learner. How the game went became a matter of quite secondary importance. Who won! Who cared! The score was punctiliously kept and, Gauvinier's skip being very good indeed and his delightful opponent's skip being not so good, it was fairly even pegging. What mattered in the game and what put it in a class by itself was difficult to estimate, there were so many contributory factors, topped no doubt by the old fellow's infectious enthusiasm.

He talked, too, of flowers and his garden and his wishes to try this or that with soil or food for his beds, of new shrubs, of the marvellous variety of heathers, how one thing leads to another in a garden; never-ending fund of interest isn't it, a garden? And always through his talk ran the undercurrent, thrown in casually in a way but as a fact he was not such a fool as to ignore: 'if I live, of course' . . . 'if I'm spared'. And Gauvinier found to his astonishment that these continual references to the inevitable end did not jar in any way but, coloured by a matchless spontaneity, became actually endearing. He had himself lived a good many more years than he would live and he learned even more than how to play bowls from this brave, dear acceptance of age.

But he learned much about the delicate art in the rolling of a good wood, which of course was the main matter in hand, for the old fellow ventured, 'If you will allow me to make a few suggestions . . .

'. . . You've got the makings of a good delivery. Baskerville's been coaching you, you've told me. No, your jack. Let's have a short one, what? (How the old boy managed to keep on the flow of his talk without letting delivery of woods interrupt it, or the delivery of woods be interrupted by his talk, was a mystery Gauvinier could not fathom). 'Fine fellow, very fine fellow, Baskerville. Not everybody's man, perhaps, but luck for the club. Knows the game, see, and keen on the right running of the club. Ah, look at that one. A good little lot that –

make a picture to keep if you could only snap 'em. And as a coach, Baskerville's magnificent. Mag-nifi-cent! But there's this I'd like to tell you – it's fundamental. Your place on the mat you can vary, but your stance and poise and delivery of a wood you must never, *never* vary. The foundation, that, of the delicate edifice of control: the trunk on which to graft the lovely sensitiveness that feels the countless variations of rink and length and can respond in right action. A fascinating process . . . a fascinating process. For the same state of mind that helps you put down a good wood helps you to feel at ease and happy with the fellows you're playing with.'

After the close of the game they stopped on the rink chatting, loth to leave the sunshine; they chatted, too, while changing their shoes in the pavilion. He said: 'There's one thing I don't agree with Baskerville about: but it shows the quality of the man. In a competition he'll let a man beat him just to buck the chap up and make him keener on the game. That I know and . . . well, there it is. He may be right, he may be right, I couldn't say. But there it is . . . I couldn't say. I told him about it. He wouldn't have it. Never do such a thing, of course. But I know it. I know it for a fact. See his old face all twinkling as he solemnly shakes his head and says "Mr Latimer, the truth is I'm not interested, not really, in singles." That fellow cares for the club and the game. But all I really mean is – you do as Baskerville tells you and you'll do.'

They shook hands spontaneously on parting, both expressing a wish to meet again soon. And the old fellow went off, calling cheery farewells, and hurried away anxious not to be late for his dinner.

A member said to Gauvinier: 'Wears well, old Latimer, doesn't he? Eighty-four or eighty-five . . .'

'Never! It's not credible!'

One and another joined in to form a pleasant little chorus of laudation.

'He's challenged the oldest member of the Worthing club to 15 ends.'

'Yes. Some time in July. Home and away, I believe.'

'A few years back he won an open tournament. Torquay I believe.'

'A rare old boy.'

'Good as they're made, Hughie.'

Their general appreciation pleased Gauvinier. He took his painful pedalling home in solemn mood. Whom the Gods love die young. Put the emphasis on die, and what is too often taken as a bitter comment on life acquires another and perhaps a truer meaning. When he was a very little boy it was to an old lady he hurried with any exciting news that had happened. When the spirit conquered . . . And the spirit was? Nothing frail and wispy floating like wisps of mists in the air; no, no, no. Nothing thin and vague – Spirit was the very dogginess of the dog. The more human a man sees himself to be the more divine he may possibly become. The . . .

Oh, damn these aching knees . . . this pedalling business. Twenty years ago he had ridden up this hill with a laugh. Well, now he could not without a good strong wind behind him. He was glad to walk. Queer what an impression one man could make on another! So right that he should think the world of John Baskerville, the old hound. He would, of course. From link to link it circulates . . . Well, anyhow, the hope of meeting Latimer again gave zest to the idea of morning practice; but the sun was coy, cloud reigned in the sky and he saw no more of Latimer for the week or so remaining before he took on Food Office work – the neat writing and courteous handing out of ration cards – which precluded morning practice.

Indeed, he never saw Latimer again. A few days after he had started work (or rather exchanged work for drudgery) he met in the village Sam Bird, who after customary greetings said with a certain odd relish:

'Hear you've lost one of your bowlers.'

'Oh? Who's that?'

'You may not know him – no cricketer, I believe, but a great bowler. A Mr Latimer.'

'Really?'

'Yes. Sudden it was. Found dead, they say, hoeing up weeds in his garden.'

'But when?'

'Yesterday morning. To be buried Friday, I hear.'

'Thanks for telling me. I'd met him.'

Gauvinier walked on, rather dazed, aware of the 'wind of death's imperishable wing', awed at the strange mysteriousness – the end. He would not now take up his challenge of 15 ends with the oldest player in the Worthing club.

Doubtful of the etiquette in such matters, he looked in on John Baskerville to ask if there would be any play on Friday evening . . . out of respect, perhaps? There was no hesitation in John's answer. 'Stop play for him? Not on your life! He'd turn in his grave! He'd like every member to turn up and play as he'd never played before in memory of him.'

'I had the luck to play once with him. I know you're right,' said Gauvinier, and thought that it was the sort of epitaph he would himself like to deserve.

But the good link so abruptly forged, so swiftly snapped, did not fade away there. A little while later John told him the search for woods was over: not to do any more about it on his own, a set was in the offing . . . wouldn't be quite certain for a week or so. Then, after what seemed endless months to Gauvinier's impatience, John called him in to the pavilion to show him two old large cardboard boxes. On greasepaper inside, two in each box, lay black woods, marked L . . . L for Learner, of course!

'As a matter of fact, these belonged to old Latimer,' said John.

'Perfect,' muttered Gauvinier.

Sudden death is apt to lay a man open, may break down defences, as it were, the wind of that wing; it is good when fresh sweet air, like that which fills the lungs when one leans out of a window after a bad night at dawn on a Spring morning, is blown gently and irresistibly through the gap.

'They are worn, of course, but absolutely sound,' John commented.

Gauvinier said, 'Oh, I like them, very much.'

Hugh de Selincourt, *Gauvinier Takes to Bowls*

16

Great Players, Great Matches

As a prelude to considering the causes and effects of the modern boom,
reflect on some of the champions and exciting events the game has
thrown up in the first six decades of this century.

'Most Remarkable Game of All'

The most remarkable flat-green game of all time was played on
Saturday, September 11, 1909, on the Recreation Ground, Chelms-
ford. It was the first final of the Essex double-rink championship
between Valentines Park (Ilford) and Colchester Phoenix.

At the 21st and supposedly final end Valentines Park's No. 1 rink
were 18-all and their No. 2 rink 17-all – a tie, so the game had to go on.
After the 22nd, No. 1 were one up and No. 2 one down – another tie.
At the 23rd end, No. 1 were one up and No. 2 one down – still a tie. At
the 24th No. 1 were one down and No. 2 one up – a tie. Again the rinks
played an extra end, the 25th. Valentines Park No. 1 were one up, but
Phoenix were lying two up on the No. 2 rink. The Park skip, however,
drove the jack out of the rink and made it a dead end, *another* having
to be played. After the 26th end, No. 1 for Valentines Park were one up
and No. 2 one down – a tie once more.

The finish came about in darkness at the 27th head, with the players
striking matches to see how the woods lay. The No. 1 Valentines Park
rink stood three up and their No. 2 rink were two down – yet they won
the championship on the final measure by only a quarter of an inch at
41–40.

Phoenix protested to the new county association. Among their
grounds was an allegation that somebody had moved a wood, or the
jack, after a measure taken had favoured Phoenix; that this alleged
movement was performed by one of the spectators, who in those early
days were allowed to crowd around the head; that it was done under
cover of darkness and hence another measure was demanded and
taken. In spite of these protests the result stood. One player remarked

in later years that the value of a 'toucher' in the ditch was only dimly understood at that time and claimed that at one end Phoenix really had two 'touchers' which ought to have counted but owing to their players' ignorance on this point they lost the benefit of them.

The teams who played were: Rink 1 – *Valentines Park*: J. Stitt, J. Reynolds, D. Smith, G. Burdick. *Phoenix*: C. G. Wilson, W. Glaister, J. B. Hicks, F. Peacock. Rink 2 – *Valentines Park*: T. Brown, W. Bourne, J. Farrow, E. A. Patterson. *Phoenix*: C. H. Humphreys, E. H. Berry, T. Proctor, A. A. Springett.

George T. Burrows, 1915

Snedden's Last Bowl

There was a most dramatic moment in a six-rink match between an Australian team and Edinburgh players before the 1914–18 War. Five of the six rinks had finished; overall the Australians were one shot up, and were lying another on the sixth rink when the great Edinburgh player George Snedden went up to play his last bowl.

He had less than six inches to draw the shot himself. The way to the jack was not clear and it seemed nine chances to one that he would fail. His third player, George Thomson, pleaded with him to strike: for a dubious, a very dubious two. But Snedden, after long consideration and careful study, said, 'No, the strike is too uncertain – I can draw the shot.' Note the confidence of the first-class player. Down came the bowl, crawling slowly along the keen green, past the obstructing woods with not too much to spare, sweeping in on its dying bend and finishing about an inch from the jack. The game, the whole match was saved; the Australians were held to a draw.

W. Stevenson, 1949

Irvine Watson – Virtually Unbeatable

What of the now almost forgotten men who were early champions? One was C. L. Cummings, of Sunderland, who was English singles champion in 1906 and who seventeen years later when he could barely see, for one eye was completely lost to him, played his way through to win the Hastings singles tournament, then followed this up by a similar honour at Bournemouth.

And there was 'Milky' Knights, of Lambeth, who won the EBA

singles in 1908: a giant who joked his way through a game yet could always concentrate sufficiently to outbowl anyone who might be disposed to think he was easy money. When Knights won the Surrey singles in 1921 he mesmerised Arthur F. Warner into submission: slow, elephantine deliberation fairly broke Warner's nerve that evening at Kingston; but Arthur *developed* nerve as he matured and won the EBA singles in 1921.

The real stylist was D. Irvine Watson, who won the Surrey singles in 1913, the English championship in 1914, the London and Southern Counties Gold Badge in 1915 and was virtually unbeatable in the man-to-man game in that period. Yet I have never been able to settle in my own mind whether Watson was a better singles player than he was a skip. He played for England in 1912–19–20–21–22–24–25.

Irvine Watson had perfect balance. His method was that of supreme quietness, making a close study of every end and playing always to have ready certain woods that would prove useful in case the run-through shot came. He admired striking ability in others and built up always with the skittle shot well safeguarded against; but he never fired himself. He could, however, use the 'pound-on' shot with accuracy and never lost, in the ditch or outside the rink, a bowl so played. I bowled with him in several tournaments. He never once raised his arm to strike viciously; his delivery was the most studied, most careful and sweetest of all men I knew.

Watson gave one the view that he crouched as he delivered, but that was not the case. Being a clever billiards player, he used the top of the green for taking his sight before he put away his bowl. He once explained to me that he saw the lay-out of a head better from his crouching position than if he stood up to it. Probably that was why he admired the striking ability of those men who could carve out a wood or a jack from the upright vision and using the Lancashire free-swinging delivery. At short-jack play Watson virtually reproduced the art of billiards on the greensward so delicate was his touch and so accurate were his shots.

What I call the singles Triple Crown of English flat-green bowls – the EBA championship, the Gold Badge and Lord Lonsdale's Gold Trophy – has fallen to only four men: J. G. Carruthers, W. J. Jones, A. E. Godsall and J. McKinlay. With four bowls at singles play or two bowls at the rink game, what better player through the present century, and still in the top class, is there than the Scot Jimmy

Carruthers? Who can forget how he won the *Star* Gold Cup for his Muswell Hill club by having to draw a bowl within one inch of the lip of the ditch – and accomplished that shot without a tremor! His last Lonsdale win in 1936 came thirty-one years after his EBA championship, and he has made nineteen appearances for England since he first played for his adopted country in 1905.

Of Scotsmen whose play has been seen this side of the Border no better single-handed player has appeared than Robert Sprot, of Wishaw, who in the 1934 British Empire Games went unbeaten in all his matches and returned a majority of sixty-two shots in his favour. And of Welshmen who periodically come across *their* Border, what finer exponent of singles play has there been than the late A. J. Stacey, of Llanelly? Stacey once possessed the greatest nerve of any player in the amateur ranks I have known and one has to give him pride of place in being able to bowl more accurately from the mat without going up to look at the situation than any other man in the game – unless the exception be F. G. Curtis, of Southend, who for many seasons amazed everyone by his quick and correct decisions arrived at while on the mat.

Pairs players of undoubted skill included T. C. Hills and G. W. A. Wright, who won two Empire Games titles (1930 and 1934); W. W. Buckell and Robert Slater, four times winners of the Kent championship and twice successful in the English pairs; and the brothers George and Arthur Bull of Wellingborough, whose silent work in action showed complete understanding of purpose. An English rink, Robert Slater, Ernest Gudgeon, Percy Tomlinson and Fred Biggin (skip), proved the finest four the Mother Country ever turned out and their 1934 Empire Games victory was achieved by consistent down-to-the-jack work with never one risk taken.

Other great players of past decades must include William Taylor (Dulwich), H. P. Webber (Torbay), E. C. Redman (Banister Park, Southampton), W. M. Grice (Redhill) and R. Slater and W. Barlow, two Kent men so often single-handed champions of their county. Taylor shared Warner's gift of drawing down to nominated spots in a crowded head; Webber and Redman possessed a delicate sweetness of graceful delivery; while Slater and Barlow could always mix their soft-pedal work with accurate, crashing skittle shots.

George T. Burrows, 1948

My Greatest Shot

A match I recall vividly is one in July, 1939, because during it I played probably the greatest shot of my life. I was representing Oxford City and County in the final of the London and Southern Counties triples at Magdalen Park against Sutton, the Surrey champions. T. Stoker, S. H. Pratt and L. S. Walton were the Sutton men; my colleagues were Dr J. Burrows and J. Holden. After the 13th end we were trailing 14–4; Sutton were playing very well, everything coming off. But after the 14th end the score stood at 14–11.

Burrows and Holden had failed to give me shot, but four of their bowls were lying about eighteen inches behind the jack. Our opponents were lying shot, jack high, fourteen inches to the left of it. I had to decide whether I would force the shot bowl through or try to draw the jack through to my colleagues' bowls.

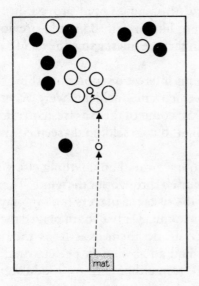

The end Algy Allen
describes. His team's bowls are
white, his opponents' are
black.

Before my last bowl, I had a discussion with my No. 2, Holden, and during it someone among the spectators shouted: 'Go on, Algy, you can do it!' It was the voice of John Paterson, of Surrey, my skip for England . . . I went back to the mat full of confidence. Now I picked up my bowl, delivered it; and, to my colleagues' and my delight, trailed the jack to six of my bowls, making a score of seven. It had the desired effect. Our opponents went to pieces and we went on to win by 25 –18 –seven shots!

Algy Allen (former EBA singles champion, twice fours champion; sixteen times an international)

Greek Meets Greek

When exponents like Percy Baker and Algy Allen, both former champions, meet in the final of the EBA championships one feels entitled to see a fine game, but even the greatest optimist among the faithful few lucky to be present at Paddington could not have anticipated such a classic as the 1952 EBA singles final proved. It was a display that many old-timers who, like myself, had seen previous finals thought excelled all others, in fact the finest game they had ever seen. With this I concur.

No end was without interest or sportsmanship. No shot, however good it appeared, seemed safe. Incidents were occuring in such rapid succession that one lost count of them as fresh ones followed. Shots we so often hope to pull off but so seldom do seemed child's play in these masters' hands.

What stood out to me more than anything else was the confidence each player had in himself throughout the game. There were occasions when it looked as if the risks the players took in playing some of their shots were not worth taking, yet they both played them as though they were certain they could do them exactly as they came off. It just happened that they had an absolutely perfect rink, with both hands playing equally well from either end. And, oddly enough, they both selected the same length jack, just under a three-quarter one – mainly because they knew they could play it better than any other. Throughout the game this length was only varied twice, in each case by about six feet, and at these ends each in turn lost the only fours during the game.

How close was the game can best be judged by saying that Baker scored 12 ends to Allen's 11, and that each player had a four, a three and four twos, the remainder made up by singles. Early on Baker led

4–1 and 5–3; then Allen scored his four to lead 7–5 and carried that lead to 16–10, when Baker scored three, two and four in four ends to lead 19–18. The last four ends finished 19–19, 20–19, 20–20, 21–20.

Who can forget an end with Allen's four woods in a cluster round the jack, none more than three inches away; the shot by Baker, with Allen looking like holding two shots and game, which just promoted his own wood, four inches from the jack, right on to it to make him 20–19; or the near miss of Algy's last wood by a fraction of an inch just to contact Percy's 'sitter', the succeeding of which would have made him game? In this fashion, scoring that one more single than his opponent at the last moment, did Percy Baker of Poole Park (Dorset) create a record by becoming EBA singles champion for the third time – a record I feel might stand for ever!

Jack Jones, 1952

Blind Men with Memories

There is an unfortunate tendency in all walks of life to forget yesterday's heroes when they no longer appear on the stage they illuminated for years. Regrettably, Percy Baker seems to fall into this category.

He became a legendary figure for four decades – the 'thirties, 'forties, 'fifties and 'sixties – capturing the EBA singles title four times, winning a silver medal in the Empire Games singles at Cardiff in 1958 and winning the respect and affection of bowlers everywhere with his inspired bowling, upright bearing and impeccable manners on and off the green. Percy and I have been friends since the early 'fifties.

Now, at eighty-seven, my old friend is blind and was very ill for two months with bronchitis. His wife Elsie died some years ago, but when he remarried he wisely chose Elsie's cousin Winifred, who has devotedly nursed him back to health. I recently drove down to Poole (Dorset) to see him.

Percy is still very upright, the tall, striking figure so many of us remember at the national championships at Paddington and Mortlake and in the international matches for England against Scotland, Ireland and Wales. His memory is keen as he talks about his exploits and bowlers he played with and against. He particularly recalled Fred Biggin (Temple, Surrey and England), who skipped his four in Percy's international debut at Cardiff in 1933. Others were Maurice Ferris (Cornwall), Algy Allen (Oxford), Roy Kivell and Fred Horn (Devon),

G. W. A. Wright (Hants), the brothers Bull, Arthur Knowling and John Scadgell (Sussex).

Edwin Percy Baker was born on 18 July 1895, at Weston-super-Mare, Somerset. Incidentally, David Bryant was born at Clevedon, twelve miles away, in 1932. I had always associated Percy with Dorset, his adopted county, but he is Somerset born and bred. They breed good bowlers there: the good air, perhaps, or the cider apples.

He played for England in the international tournament against Scotland, Ireland and Wales in 1933, '35, '47, '49, '50, '51, '52, '53, '54, '55, '56, '57, '58 and '59. He captained England in 1950 and also that year was in the England team which played Australia in a Test match. He qualified for the national singles by winning the Dorset title for the Poole Park club a dozen times between 1931 and 1968. In 1952 he set a national record by winning the EBA singles for a third time, beating the then equally famous international Algy Allen 21–20 in a gripping, classic battle. Percy received a silver salver from the EBA to mark this occasion. It has pride of place in his sitting-room at home at 3, Park Lake Road, Poole – not far from the delightful greens at Poole Park – surrounded by other mementoes of his career.

He was the obvious choice to represent England in those Empire Games singles in 1958. The gold medal went to Pinkie Danilowitz (South Africa), but Percy took the silver and beat the favourite, Glyn Bosisto (Australia), in the second round. In 1962, partnered by Harry Shave, he won the EBA and British Isles pairs titles; in 1960 Ernie Milnthorpe, Harry Shave and he beat Kelly, Dominey and international Joe Hodgson (Edenside, Cumberland) 13–12 to clinch the national triples. Incidentally, Percy's only son, Cecil, chief inspector of weights and measures in the Isle of Wight, was one of the losing national triples finalists from Ryde in 1967.

When seventeen Percy was apprenticed to a portrait studio in Wellington, Somerset, but in 1914 he enlisted and served in the Royal Field Artillery at the Somme in France and later in Salonika against the Bulgars. 'We chased the Bulgars back,' said Percy, 'and Bulgaria dropped out of the war by Christmas, 1915, the first of Germany's allies to capitulate.'

Demobilized in 1919, he joined a portrait studio in Poole on three months' trial: 'I've been here ever since.' He recalls the advent of the Kodak 'Brownie' camera which proved the undoing of so many portrait studios: the public switched to amateur photography in their thousands and family snapshots largely replaced the more formal portraits. Usually there were three or four portrait studios in the High Street of most towns, but with amateur photography their numbers were drastically reduced. However, Percy's firm remained in business and he continued his work.

He joined Poole Park cricket club in 1920 and after matches would occasionally watch the bowlers on a neighbouring green. Some of these players, with whom Percy played billiards at the local Conservative Club, kept badgering him to transfer to bowls and he finally succumbed to this pressure in 1923. A local tradesman named Wynglade put up a cup that year for a novices competition: Percy's name is recorded as the first winner and the competitive bug had hooked him. He went on to win the club singles championship twenty-two times from 1931 to 1974. At Paddington and Mortlake the spectators *expected* Baker to win and his matches always attracted crowds.

By winning the national singles for a fourth time in 1955, beating J. W. Fletcher (York Co-op) in the final, Percy set a further record, and it stood until 1973 when Bryant set an all-time record of five, capping it by beating Bob Gibbins (Middlesex) in 1975 for his number six. In 1959 Baker himself was a hot favourite to win a fifth national singles, but was narrowly defeated in the semi-final by Yorkshire's Tom Fleming. In 1965 he again came near to winning, losing to Ralph Lewis (Sussex) in the final.

He remembers with pride Dorset's only Middleton Cup win in 1938. In the semi-final against Middlesex, Percy skipped against international Bob Steel, the former Spurs footballer. Another international, Bill Jasper, was no. 3 to Steel and Percy recalls that one of his shots against Steel provoked Jasper to swear about Baker's 'confounded luck.' 'But, of course, I *played* for that result,' Percy told me confidently forty-four years later.

Paddy Orr (*World Bowls* magazine), 1982

'He's Got Me!'

Some terrific shots were played in the last few ends of the 1952 final with Algy Allen, but the 1946 final against Ernie Newton from Berkshire will always remain in my memory. The game was 19–16 in my favour and I lay two shots and game. Ernie had last wood and he took out one of them: 20–16. He favoured a full length and now

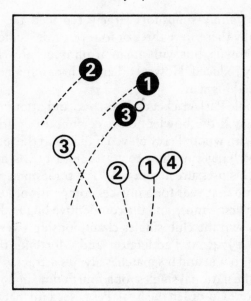

scored two singles: 20–18. On the next end he lay shot and, in trying a
run-through on a short bowl, I pushed him in another: 20-*all*.

   Another full-length jack. Now look at the diagram. Newton played
the forehand arc, N1 and N2 both scoring. My 1 and 2 were played on
the backhand arc in a good position but did not count. Ernie's 3 was
intended to block the backhand draw but ran across, still leaving just
enough room to get through.

   With my third wood I had to make a decision: the backhand draw,
with every chance of being wrecked, or a follow-through on his 1 or 2?
Had it been my last wood I would certainly have gone for the
follow-through, but having already played twice on backhand, my
first wood running only a few inches out of count, there was now an
opening between Ernie's 2 and 3. The invitation to draw between them
was too strong to resist. I played it . . . it was a peach . . . it ran
between the 2 and 3 as intended and pushed the jack some two or three
inches back to bring my 1 in as second wood.

   'He's got me,' I heard Ernie say to his supporters on returning from
inspecting the head, 'He's got me this time.' His only hope left was a
dead draw: there was just about room to get round his 1, but only with
a dead length. He tried . . . and was short. I still had last wood, but
there was no need to use it.

Percy Baker, 1972

Clown and Connoisseur

There is a mixture of the clown, the artist and the actor in Arthur Knowling, of Sussex, whose international career spanned the war years. One cannot say he bowls his woods. Rather he decants them in the manner of a connoisseur lovingly preparing a bottle of vintage port for a golden wedding anniversary.

And having thus decanted his wood, he seems reluctant to let it go. First running, then prancing and finally leaping down the green, he plays a mixture of hide-and-seek and tag with each wood – sometimes staying behind it, at other times overtaking it before letting it squeeze between his hands or feet on the way to its final resting place, which is often separated only by inches from Knowling's nose.

Success elates him. Failure, strangely, leaves him apparently unmoved. There is nothing mean about his enthusiasm. He will unstintingly congratulate both partner and opponents. A connoisseur, Knowling is also an enthusiast.

C. M. Jones

The Forgotten Bowl

One particular Cup match in 1943 is regarded as a classic in South African history. Not only did the match finish on a note of high excitement; it remains unique in that the action of a spectator had a decisive influence on its outcome. The players involved were Tommy Twiss and Hugh Lobban, both nationally famous. In all, five heads were burned during the game while honours were even after the last end, and it was at this stage that the note of drama was introduced.

On the extra end Twiss lay shot, only to lose it to an immaculate draw by Lobban. A tired man, Twiss went to the mat, to explode into excitement as his delivery nudged its way between his opponent's wood and the jack. Nothing short of a miracle wood could now save Lobban . . . and to everybody's astonishment somehow he produced it to edge out Twiss's shot wood. It was an incredible delivery.

Carried away by excitement, the spectators crowded around the head, while a bemused Twiss congratulated his rival on a wonderful last-wood win. Then suddenly a spectator pushed his way through the crowd, and seized Twiss by the arm. 'You've still got one wood left to play!' he pointed out.

The hush that descended on the green can only be described as electric. A slightly dazed Twiss went to the mat, steadied himself . . . and sent down the winning bowl!

Douglas Lampshire, 1961

The Four Musketeers

Those lucky enough to see the closing stages of the 1951 Australian fours championship must have been impressed with the daring, virile methods employed by Glyn Bosisto and his men, who might well be called not Howard Jackett, Bert Rundle, Arthur Davies and Bosisto but Athos, Porthos, Aramis and d'Artagnan. D'Artagnan knew he was good, having round his waist the Australian singles and Victorian pairs and singles championship belts. He looked around for kindred spirits: out of the thousands of bowlers in Victoria he selected Athos plus Porthos from Melbourne and Aramis from as far away as Dandenong to accompany him on his splendid adventure, adopting as their motto 'All for one and one for all'.

To them the Adelaide trip was serious business. As we were mown down and watched others share the same fate, realization was forced on us that we were watching an entirely different approach to the game. 'Draw to the jack, draw as close as possible', was discarded, and 'Take this bowl out', 'Run this through', 'Play up to this bowl and turn it in' were substituted.

When the master plan had been completed by his three companions d'Artagnan came to light and drew the shot. Each man packed a gun in addition to a glittering sword. Occasionally the shot was missed, yet it was here that the 'one-for-all-and-all-for-one' entered the picture. The gallery was spellbound that four men could so completely understand one another and play as one man.

D'Artagnan did not try to pull the whole of the boat himself, but by his own example of pulling an oar he bent the backs of the other three to the oars. I heard d'Artagnan say to Athos (his lead) 'Take that bowl out' -- and the bowl, three inches jack-high, found a resting place in the ditch. The audacious use of the leader as a driving force tears apart the bowling textbooks which stress that the leader's job is to draw to the jack.

Porthos (his second) was asked to place his first bowl a yard behind at five o'clock, but he drew to the jack, a shot that would have delighted most skippers. But not d'Artagnan. He sadly shook his head and said, 'No, no, I want you a yard behind' – and Porthos drew a yard behind.

D'Artagnan would ask Aramis (his third) to roll out his own shot bowl gently and trail the jack a foot for four – and it was done. He would call Aramis up to a clustered head, show him what he wanted and how easy it was to get it. He did not ask him to bowl blindly from 100 feet away and get the shot without any real confidence.

D'Artagnan handled his men as cleverly as he handled his bowls. 'All for one and one for all.' They shared with him the richest fruits which grow at the top of the tree. He was never selfish, appropriating to himself a favourite hand or shot. He was not above freely asking Aramis the shot he would like to play.

'It is easy to unlock the door to victory – providing one has the key.'

W. B. B., quoted in *Bowls* magazine, Victoria, 1951

Tough for Pirrett

The 1954 Vancouver Empire Games singles were played at New Westminster, twenty miles from the Village, and the greens were uneven and tricky. A decision we could never understand was that which resulted in the rinks being put into a hat and drawn by competitors instead of being drawn properly to ensure that a player did not play on the same rink twice.

In the third round I was drawn against the defending champion, 'Ham' Pirrett from New Zealand. He had been narrowly beaten on a particular rink the previous day and now he drew the same rink again – against me. 'Glyn, I'm sorry for you,' he said, 'this rink is full of tricks. I've been trying to play on it for an hour and a half already so I do know *something* about it. The Lord help you when *you* get on it!' What glorious 'psycho' in an Empire Games! There was no doubt, either, that what 'Ham' said was true: he was an hour and a half to the good on a tricky rink.

He took the mat, threw a short head and drew an adjacent bowl on the backhand. With the forehand wide open I played it, and the bowl looked good until it got to the area where it was supposed to run into the jack. Then it just straightened up and failed to respond as it should have. Pirrett scored four in the first hand, three in the second and two in the third. I knew from the moment that bowl straightened in the initial head what I was up against and it did not help when 'Ham', with a smile, said after the first few heads, 'What did I tell you?'

After the champion led 9–0 I struggled along until, down 9–20 (and the match 21-up), I won the mat. I realized he had a ditch-to-ditch phobia because he had played everything short and with reasonable touch, so I immediately threw a ditch-to-ditch length. Neither of us, I might add, knew anything about the ditch-to-ditch geography, but he knew less about it than I did. I gradually overhauled him and at 20–20 got a four on the last head for a 24–20 win!

'Ham' is the outstanding bowler of New Zealand but he could not disclose his true form in Vancouver, nor in Cardiff four years later. I am sure, too, that if he were a top-notch bowler on Canadian greens he would not be the champion he is in New Zealand. The whole touch and delivery on the two surfaces is different. In Canada it is like asking a champion billiards player with delicacy of touch on a fast table to play with the same degree of accuracy on a very slow table – with the cushions out of order.

Glyn Bosisto (four times Australian singles champion)

A Nail-biting, Revealing Battle

The first major championship I reported was the 1954 indoor inter-club Denny Cup final at Paddington. Bournemouth, with the immortal Percy Baker as their inspiration, contested an exciting, nail-biting match with Ascot in front of the 500 or so enthusiasts who crowded into the hall.

It seemed the result was about to be decided by the last bowl of the match, with Baker its deliverer. Dramatically, he did not go to the mat. Instead, he 'killed' that bowl by calling for the umpire and a measure.

With every eye on him, Wally Guiver, who had just retired as EBA secretary, walked calmly and commandingly from his chair to the far corner where the bowls were nestling with the jack. Not wavering an inch or blinking an eye, he walked unhurryingly, got down carefully, measured and re-measured. Probably all that took less than five minutes, but to the watching, breath-holding 500 it seemed an eternity. Then he awarded the shot to Bournemouth and, with it, the Denny Cup. Amidst the pandemonium that followed, only Wally and the always erect Percy remained calm.

Yet the difference in distance of the key bowls was less than half an inch. How, I wondered, could a man's eyes calmly assess that tiny difference with such certainty and assurance?

So almost before my first issue of *British Bowls* (later *World Bowls*) was published, I learned that the seemingly peaceful, relaxed game of bowls contains all the strains, stresses and psychological intangibles inherent in seemingly vastly different games like golf, tennis and motor racing.

C. M. Jones, World Bowls magazine, 1984

The 99 to One Shot

England's 1955 international match against Wales at Cardiff . . . all the rinks apart from mine had finished . . . and the match score stood at 88-all. On our rink we held the lead against the Welsh four skipped by Sammy Day.

On the last end we were lying shot with a wood two inches behind the jack, and, as Sammy had been firing with great success but drawing very inaccurately, I decided the lesser risk was to tempt him to draw. I asked my number three to place his woods behind and to leave the forehand open for the draw. Sammy had not missed with a firing shot all afternoon, so if he fired this time my rink would have the better positions.

Both the number three and I positioned our woods in perfect accordance with the plan . . . but, alas for me, Sammy took the open path and drew a perfect wood that beat our shot wood without touching either it or the jack!

In a crisis, with the opponents holding shot and the tension of the moment, the percentages are strongly in favour of the skip being well up, possibly to move the jack into back woods. Repeat the situation and I would unhesitatingly repeat my tactics, for the chances were 99–1 against Sammy. 'If I'd failed everyone would have praised you for doing the right thing,' he told me, 'but I didn't so you did the *wrong* thing!' Afterwards I was strongly criticized for not blocking the hand. To me that criticism confirmed two things I already knew: one, that only the bowler who has played and thought all the way through a match can thoroughly understand all the possibilities, and secondly, one must accept philosophically when an opponent scores against 99–1 odds.

Norman King (winner of World, Commonwealth and
EBA championships)

Youth *v.* Experience

The brilliant eighteen-year-old Ben Baker back in 1958 struck the EBA championships like a meteor, through both his fine play and the controversy then surrounding the participation of young men in county championships and tournaments. He reached the singles semi-finals against Frank Crockford from the Isle of Wight in a blaze of publicity which added to the psychological advantage his undoubted skill gave him.

But Crockford, a thoughtful bowler, had noticed that Baker's delivery carried a fair degree of skid; and he also calculated that his own experience of tournament play was a good deal more extensive than Baker's, even though the youngster had begun competitions at fourteen. He reasoned that Baker would be able to cope with obvious changes of length but that his delivery and youth might not combat *slight* changes.

Instead of moving the jack and mat in great jumps of six or so yards at a time Crockford contented himself with taking the mat perhaps one yard up the green and delivering a twenty-eight-yard jack one end, then coming back a couple of yards the next time and using a thirty-one-yard jack. In hand again, he possibly moved the mat four yards up green while trying a thirty-yard jack. In a nutshell, he endeavoured to make his changes so small that, even though they demanded a markedly changed touch, they remained scarcely discernible to an inexperienced eye. If they *were* noticed, the underspin Baker was imparting maximized his problems in finding the changes of length.

Consequently, Crockford usually got the advantage first on each end and Baker was unable to achieve enough good saving shots to prevent his opponent winning fairly comfortably. The concentration cost Crockford dear, for he played a tired game in the final later that afternoon and was beaten; but meantime Baker (no relation to Percy, also from Dorset, but a great admirer of him) is still young and good enough to be used as an example of someone out-thought.

C. M. Jones, 1965

I Looked a 'Mug' – but We Won!

Our 1958 Empire Games fours match for England against Rhodesia in Cardiff came fairly late in the series and by that time the wonderful sunshine we had enjoyed had burnt out the grass badly over about six yards from each end of the rink: the green was absolutely bare and it was like trying to bowl on a board. I was leading and using my lignum vitae woods, which are nowhere near as stable on bad surfaces as composition bowls.

However, George Scadgell, our skip, noticed that both the Rhodesian lead and number two were also using big drawing bowls, so, despite the fact that jacks thrown well into the bare, bumpy, burnt parts of the green would ruin my form, Scadgell ordered long jacks every time we won the end. They ruined the accuracy of my two woods; but they had a similar effect on *four* of our opponents' woods. Thus we began each end with virtually two woods' start.

My woods didn't roll along the last part of the green, they bounced – and accuracy on the draw was impossible. Nevertheless, I obeyed the golden rule for bowlers who are out of touch: to get my woods beyond the jack. Scadgell's bowls take less 'land' than mine, so that in end after end his straighter approach was in no way hampered by clusters of woods in front of and surrounding the jack. To any casual observer I must have looked a 'mug', but the *tactics* paid off and we beat the Rhodesians (who won the bronze medals) even though their skip fired well enough to make four 'no ends' during the 21. And we went on to win the gold medal, beating South Africa in a play-off.

Norman King

A Three-minute Measure

When Roger Harris and I reached the EBA championships as a pair in 1959 we travelled up to the Watney's club at Mortlake full of hope, for we were both in good form. Our hopes seemed justified as we made our way through five rounds to the final, where we met Fred Harris and Jim Brayley, from Paddington. Fred has always been a fine lead for he has a smooth style and remarkably calm temperament; he is a double England international, having played in three series of Hilton Cup indoor matches and two outdoor international series. Jim Brayley had at that time just started his way to the top, having begun his Hilton Cup career in the early part of the year. He eventually gained his outdoor England badge in 1962. Brayley belongs very much to the younger school of bowlers and is both imaginative and courageous.

Together Fred and Jim formed a well-balanced pair and were the more dangerous because of their accord over tactics. Roger and I knew we would be involved in a stern contest and this certainly proved the case, the final lasting 4 hours 20 minutes.

We had gone through our share of the 'nears' in the quarter-final when, after 20 ends against Jim Finney and Norman Knight with never more than four shots between us, Norman needed to draw a second shot to tie the score and force an extra end. It was a very long jack and his wood took ages traversing the green to push his shot wood even nearer to the jack. Who held second shot? Roy Richardson, the massive Yorkshireman who was EBA president in 1964, took a full three minutes measuring and re-measuring. Then he rose from his knees and said, in a matter-of-fact tone, 'Clevedon's by an eighth of an inch.'

Our play in the semi-final had been somewhat less consistent, but the positive approach paid off when two firm woods took out opposing woods to net us in the one case a seven, in the other a six, so we beat Loughborough 26–22.

Those two take-outs had turned out well. My efforts in the final were less fortunate. Four times I collected the jack with running woods but only twice did it finish within the strings, though on each occasion we had the best three or four back woods. On another occasion I touched the jack only to run it into five of their woods and put us 9–15 behind. During all this time Fred and Jim were bowling well. *World Bowls* reported the closing stages thus:

> Lion-heartedly, Clevedon fought back to level the score 16–16 after 17 ends. At this stage Brayley switched to short jacks, much in vogue with Clevedon earlier, because of a slowing of the green. During the peak of the day it was running at about sixteen seconds.
>
> The last end proved a worthy climax to a wonderful encounter. With his third wood Bryant glided in for shot amid undisguised elation among the Clevedon supporters. But then, with the shot of the day, Brayley rested his wood delicately on Bryant's, to snatch literally a last-second victory. Said a flushed Brayley, 'I hope I never have to play another shot like that. I prayed all the time the bowl travelled down the green.'

So Roger and I played well and were beaten and I cannot help feeling that fortune was not kind to us. It was virtually our last noteworthy effort as a pair, as Roger later abandoned bowls to return to cricket at a local club.

David Bryant, 1966

Baker Goes Down Firing

Tom Fleming of Middlesbrough, winner of an Empire Games gold medal in 1962 and four times first in Vitalite world drawing-to-the-jack contests, has possibly the strongest claim to the unofficial title of 'world champion of the draw shot' – and he used this shot calmly and with great cunning in the face of repeated shock tactics by Percy Baker in the semi-final of the 1959 EBA singles. Coming from the north, Fleming is accustomed to slow greens – eleven seconds is fast for Yorkshire – but on this fateful Friday at Watney's conditions were the fastest in which Fleming had, until then, ever played. This was the year in which big crowds first began to fill the stands at Mortlake, and as the two men struggled forward in singles and twos the tension became strong. Eventually Baker reached 20–19.

They were playing now to the end at which Fleming had scored best. However he put two touchers right on the jack, only for Baker to fire for and obtain a dead end with his fourth and final wood. Carefully Fleming built up two shots which were almost dead replicas of the previous two. Again Baker fired with his last wood, smashing the jack over the string for dead end the second time. Let Fleming take up the story:

'We played the end a third time, and after Percy's third wood, the fifth of the end, I was prepared to gamble. I was lying shot and a measure for second and every wood up to this end had been played on the backhand, so I played my next right in the draw and just short, forcing Percy to switch to the other hand for his last wood – and he missed. I then drew my last wood on the backhand again . . . it caught my short wood and heeled it over towards the jack, so making the measure unnecessary and completing the most memorable end of my life.'

C. M. Jones

Concentration Lost, Gold Medal Won

Let me clear up a misconception that seems fairly widespread judging from the way people talk and write about my play: that I possess some sort of supernatural power of concentration. How far this is from the truth I discovered anew when contesting probably the most vital singles in all my years as a bowler, against Ian Barron of New Zealand in the thirteenth round of the 1962 Commonwealth Games at Perth.

Victory would ensure me the gold medal irrespective of what might happen on other rinks. Also I had a strong personal incentive to beat Ian and thus win the singles without a defeat. So if ever there was a time for intense concentration, this was it.

But J. Watson Black, the Scottish representative, was chasing me hard, having lost only once – and he was playing on the next rink, against Bradley, the Rhodesian. A win for him and a defeat for me would mean a play-off. My eyes should never have left the rink on which I was playing, but time and again I found myself paying as much attention to Black's progress as to my own and it needed considerable effort to keep sufficient concentration to retain my longish lead.

Fortunately my length and direction were good and I was delivering two, three or even four good woods each end, while Ian was less consistent than usual. Nevertheless he put down one good wood each end, getting either second position or the shot and occasionally running the jack for a couple. My lead was slowly melting away.

Then, on the next rink, Bradley finally got the shot which gave him a 21–17 win over Black and ensured the gold medal for me. I have never enjoyed the game more than in those few minutes between Black's defeat and, with the return of full concentration, the ending of my own match.

David Bryant

17

The Great Explosion

The last few extracts have jumped us into the 1960s – and one can now read them aloud and hear rumblings from within them of the forthcoming explosion in bowls. Percy Baker had long been with us, proving what years ago many had declined to accept: that bowls was a sport of skill rather than luck, that the rub of the green did not always even out to make all players equal and that there were men so consistently sound that they could almost as consistently emerge at the top of the pile. The spectators were beginning to catch on: 'big crowds first began to fill the stands', we are told in that report of the 1962 English singles final. And David Bryant had arrived. (His name will dominate the remainder of this book, because he would come to personify the new image of the young man in the game, earn it publicity, motivate other youngsters to the challenge and set unprecented standards of skill and consistency, nationally and internationally.)

In short, this was a genuine sport and not merely a pastime bordering on sport. One can exaggerate the 'gentle-pastime' attitudes of pre-war: it is clear from writings quoted herein that from early days there were men who, irrespective of age, were ambitious to win, and for things to have been otherwise would have been against human nature. But now, in the 1960s, the pendulum of interest was beginning to swing from the friendly roll-up to the international championship – though not of course to the exclusion of the former. God forbid!

Nevertheless, for those of us alive to the huge potential of bowls these were frustrating times, particularly if one had professional interests. The game needed publicity; it still lacked acceptance as a major force by sports editors and television controllers. Within the game itself those with foresight felt competitive and geographical cramp – and apparently always had *done so . . .*

Then let each true-hearted bowler pray,
That he may live to see the day,
When man the world ower may play,
        At the glorious game o' Bowlin'.
    Edinburgh Bowling Annual, late nineteenth century

It is in the international field that bowls, by comparison with other games, falls short of the status due to a premier sport. Even skittles, with its large American following, not only participates in the Central American Games but has risen to a world championship; curling has its world competition and even once figured in the Olympic Games to enable Britain to win a gold medal; *boule* and *bocce* also have world championships. Bowls has its Empire Games, but these do not cater for non-Empire interests such as the USA, Egypt or Argentina.

The fact that bowls may be considered to be out of place in the Olympics should not exclude consideration of holding some alternative world competition, perhaps on the lines of golf's Canada Cup with two players from each country. Or a start might be made with a world singles championship: with air travel, a competition involving only one representative from each country should not be beyond national resources, and subsequently, pairs, triples and rinks could be added.

We find that although British teams go on tours overseas there is as yet no *British* title for which English, Scottish, Welsh and Irish champions might compete. Could not something be done?

Dr John W. Fisher, 1956

The atmosphere of the English (EBA) championships as held at Paddington is not worthy of the ever-increasing prestige and dignity of our game. The enveloping flats hanging over the greens like some grim spectre – numbers of grey windows unrelieved even by the homely and colourful flower-box or pot – made a depressing background to the great event of the year. Amenities for the players may be satisfactory, but they are not for those who wish to watch – hard iron seats or benches, no cover against sun or rain, no obviously handy place where you could get a snack or drink. No loudspeakers; you couldn't even see the figures chalked on the scoreboard from the other side of the green.

Not even the wonder of Percy Baker could keep my non-bowling friend and myself chained until the end to this unenchanted Cinderella's kitchen when all were craving for a golden slipper, or at least a gilded one; so we left after six ends of the final for the greater comfort and stimulation of Lords, where, on cushions, we watched Lock of Surrey bowl out Middlesex.

Not until the EBA find a better, more appropriate headquarters and green will bowls enter into its rightful kingdom.

'Greensward', (*Express and Echo*, Exeter), 1955

The EBA championships were to leave Paddington for the Watneys green at Mortlake, then move to Worthing (Sussex). That Dr Fisher's dreams and those of others came true, that bowls begat its own British Isles championships, world championships and much, much more within the next few years was due to many factors, but prominent among them, all related, were Age, Ambition, Indoor Bowls, Professionalism, Television and Sponsorship. Let us consider these generic factors and their backgrounds one by one. And let Age take precedence.

Old Man's Game?

That bowls is an 'old man's game' is a recognized fact, for it is the only outdoor game old men can play and there is practically no limit to the age at which a man or woman can play it. Moreover, one can play bowls for a far longer period of one's life than can the devotee of any other outdoor game. A man can take up bowls at a period long after the allotted span.

There are numerous instances of men and women playing in their nineties, and a few proven cases of bowlers playing on their 100th birthday. At eighty Benning Arnold took up bowls in Bournemouth, England, and he played on up to and including his 103rd birthday: he died when 106. A member of the Kettering club in England also continued to play after topping the century by three years. Australia, too, has had its 'Methusalehs'. In the Kyneton club in Victoria is a photograph of John Watson delivering a bowl on his 100th birthday. He was a regular playing member until his ninety-seventh year, when, because of failing eyesight, he retired.

In 1935 Joseph Solomon (Walkerville), at ninety-two, was the oldest bowler in South Australia. He occasionally attended races in the afternoon, played bowls in the evening and topped the day off with a cigar. Until he was ninety, 'Solly' could rest his neck on one chair, his feet on another and invite the heaviest man in the room to sit on him – he stood this test up to 16½ stone. H. C. Colne, until he died at ninety-eight, was the oldest bowler in New Zealand. When aged ninety-three he was captain of a four at Remuera when he pushed the enemy bowl off the jack with his first and trailed the jack for eight with his second.

Bowls Encyclopedia (ed: John P. Munro, Australia), 1951

It is a very quiet game and calculated rather for the steady old gentleman than for his racketty son.

Stonehenge's British Rural Sports, 1861

So many young men are bowlers now that the appellation 'old man's game' does not hold good.

Humphrey J. Dingley, 1893

Nowadays, such is the popularity of the game, such the honours and fame asking to be won, that players are attracted earlier; and no age-limit is to be found in the rules and constitution of any association connected with the game.

Felix Hotchkiss, 1932

Roger Bird, a 6 ft, fifteen-year-old Portsmouth schoolboy, today finds himself a topic for discussion by leading officials of the English Bowling Association. Roger, an all-round sportsman, has just completed his first, full season in the Cosham club and his skill has astonished many older bowlers. He reached the final of the club singles championship; his schoolmaster opponent, however, declined to play him.

Some have now begun to challenge Bird's right to membership of an English club. The EBA rules refer to bowls 'for men'. Is a fifteen-year-old schoolboy a man? The Cosham club, in which there is considerable sympathy for Roger, have applied to the Association for a ruling.

Evening Standard, 1955

The grandads of bowls have taken their stand. Boys under eighteen cannot compete for national championships. This decision, made in the wake of the Roger Bird affair, should be recorded in the minute-book of the English Bowling Association's Council, as follows:

> *Resolved:* That boys under eighteen shall not be allowed to make their grandads look silly by beating them in public. (Laughter).

The laughter is that of the tolerant, warm-hearted British sporting public. Now all we have to do is to reconcile it with the platitudinous patter that is pumped into adolescents: 'Learn to be a good loser.' How can you explain to a schoolboy like Roger Bird that he can't compete for a national championship until he is eighteen because fully-grown men are bad losers?

Jonathan (*News Chronicle*), January 1956

In 1950, ten-year-old Ben Baker, partnered by his father Alan, reached the quarter-finals of an English Bowling Federation tournament in Nottingham. The tournament organizers fixed an age limit of seventeen for competitors in future tournaments. Ben, a frail lad, moved south to Dorset with his family because of his health. The Greenhill (Weymouth) club would not accept members under eighteen, so Ben and his father joined Melcombe Regis. Ben was sixteen when the EBA fixed its championships age limit of eighteen so he could not play in the Dorset championships, one of the qualifying events, until 1958. He practised assiduously at his club in those intervening two years. It was as if he had said, 'OK, I cannot compete in the county championships for two years, but when I am eighteen I shall show you!' In 1958 Ben won the Dorset championship and reached the semi-final of the Nationals.

Paddy Orr, 1959

The Old Order Changeth . . . and Resenteth!

It would be misrepresentation to infer that the increasing participation by young people has not created its problems. In a game as ancient as ours tradition is apt to die hard, and many elderly people resent what they term the 'intrusion' of so many youngsters into their domain.

Through the young players bowls is becoming increasingly competitive, while entry figures for tournaments have risen to record heights. This has brought startling changes in approach. The bowler today knows that average play allied to average health may have been good enough in the old days, but not any more. To win a major tournament now he must be at his peak, physically and mentally; he must be a skilful bowler and in good physical condition. This latter requisite has played an increasingly important role in the deciding of major matches in recent years and most national champions throughout the world are in the prime of life or much younger.

Douglas Lampshire, 1961

The new generation are being attracted more and more to the competitive side of the game. Within limits, competitions are useful, even necessary: they give an added savour to the pastime. But too many condiments are harmful; and there is to be seen in present-day competitions an unhealthy exaggeration of the 'will-to-win' spirit. Too often we see cases of 'win at any cost'. Thus is the sociable character of the game likely to be impaired.

J. L. Stewart (Middlesex bowler)

It is inevitable that with the phenomenal growth of the bowling population the approach to the game should show changes. Greater keenness comes about through greater competition. Competition creates a vicious circle of selfishness: not by the majority but by a few who form a spearhead to contaminate others. That changes in the spirit of bowls have come with the years is a fact that has to be faced. Whether the old carefree attitude which allowed fun to dominate the play and sociability to count more than results was better than the modern competitive one can be purely a matter of opinion. We do know, however, that many an old timer of the green sighs for the 'good old days'.

South African magazine, 1952

Peter Belliss (New Zealand), winner of the 1984 world singles final in Aberdeen after 'the most agonising measure of all time'

Left: Crown-green bowls — 'a matter of nerves . . . the stage-fright of 2000 eyes looking at you and perhaps 500 voices chipping you or cheering you.' Steve Ellis shows his relief at winning the Waterloo Handicap (1984)

Below: David Cutler, youngest winner, at 18, of an EBA title

Above left: John Bell. 'Turned from one of the roughest games, rugby, to one of the gentlest' — and won the EBA singles in 1983

Right: George Souza, Hong Kong's greatest bowler. He won the Kodak Masters at his first attempt — interrupted by a hailstorm

Above: Mavis Steele — 'it doesn't do anyone any harm in sport to have a damn good hiding. It proves you're not as good as you thought you were'

Top: Norma Shaw, who won the singles gold medal for England in the 1981 women's world championships in Canada

Willie Wood (Scotland), former Commonwealth Games singles champion and 1984 world championship silver medallist

The New Aggressive Look

What is happening in bowls can be compared with the revolutionary change that occurred in tennis in the mid-1940s. Before that era tennis was something of a genteel sport, with long rallies featuring fine groundstrokes played from the back of the court. Suddenly the competition hotted up. More young players burst into the sport and began to trounce their opponents with the serve-and-volley game. Certainly the top players still had to have their fine groundstrokes, but more importantly they had to have a more aggressive approach: a killer approach, you may call it.

A similar change is occurring in bowls. A decade or two ago pure draw-shot exponents were dominating the titles; in more recent times most of the major events are being won by the more aggressive players. The reasons for the change are simple: more of the younger generation are taking up the sport; there are larger club memberships and more keen tournaments; more vigorous competition.

Our champions are getting younger. It would not surprise me if in the future Australia's top players were in their late twenties or early thirties. England's Bryant was only thirty-five when he won the world singles title. He is an aggressive player, always looking for extra counters. Even if he is lying a comfortable two shots and has the last bowl to play, he'll be probing for a way to make it four. In Australia the attacking players stand out; and anyone who has seen the powerful New Zealander, Phil Skoglund, will know how *he* achieves results with aggression. By the way, Phil was under thirty when he won the New Zealand championship.

Confidence in attack and unflagging concentration – that is the basis of the modern aggressive approach to bowls.

Frank Soars, 1970

You see, it wasn't the mere fact of youth that was changing the game. Just as it is easy to add later veterans to the list of Mr Munro in his encyclopedia, so it has always been simple to think back to extremely young bowlers: back, indeed, to William Mitchell, the game's lawmaker, who played when eleven. What was different now was the attitude and approach of the new young fellows. They viewed the game as a competitive sport and they wanted to win. But so did other, older bowlers. The diehards worried . . . and looked on the new era as one for the hard men. The tough competitors were there, all right – and not least in Australia, where half a century before they were being accused of lacking the enthusiasm of the Scots but where now bowls was becoming big business, with proud premises, big events and New South Wales clubhouses growing the more commodious the louder the banks of fruit machines rattled and rolled.

Bosisto – Four Times Champion

The feature of Glyn de Villiers Bosisto's game is his over-powering spirit of concentration. Its powers have the effect of eliminating all persons – players and spectators alike – from his thoughts for the sake of the contest at hand. I think that it is in such periods of intense concentration that Glyn has given an impression, by impulsive action and gesture, that has been misunderstood. I have known his preparing to bowl without even being aware that his opponent is standing dead in the line. To know the man is to know that this is the stamp of the champion.

I have sat behind the rink at every one of Glyn's four successive Australian singles victories and feel he is the master of every shot. I saw him defeat some outstanding Australian bowlers for those singles crowns – Charles Boldery of Queensland in Brisbane in 1949; Clem Hooper in Adelaide in 1951 on Clem's own South Park green (a year, incidentally, when Glyn also skippered the winning Australian four); Vic Sharmane on Cottesloe green in Perth in 1952; then that memorable match when onlookers even climbed the surrounding cliffs to see Glyn defeat that great Newcastle bowler Dave Downie at Double Bay, Sydney in 1953. He flattened the field at that carnival and I'm sure I shall never see the like of it again.

I wonder how many bowlers realize Bosisto was so close to making it five-in-a-row? Charles McNeill proved the stopper at Middle Park in Melbourne in 1955 in the quarter-finals. The score seesawed to 19–19, and in the final head Bosisto was lying shot with a bowl in hand and McNeill had his last bowl to play. Charles played a perfect running shot, hitting Glyn's shot bowl and pushing it past the jack to leave him (McNeill) lying two. Glyn played a shot similar to McNeill's with his last bowl, but, as Glyn relates it, with two chances in mind: to find McNeill's shot bowl or to run the jack into the ditch for the match. In the films that were later to be screened over and over again Glyn's bowl was seen to have missed the jack by the thickness of a piece of paper. Charles went on to win the remaining two matches with ease, but the halt to the four-straight singles run – the greatest winning streak in the history of the Australian game – had been fittingly dramatic.

In the process of maintaining this stranglehold on the Australian title Bosisto gave the statisticians some field years. When he won his twelfth club championship at Auburn, Melbourne, in 1951 he had played sixty-eight successive singles matches in championship competition and had not lost a match! These included two Australian singles championships, a Victorian singles, two Victorian Champion-of-Champions-singles, the open singles at the Mildura Carnival and two Auburn club championships. He lost the sixty-ninth match, but by the time he walked on to the Cottesloe green in 1952 to accept the Australian singles trophy for the third time, the record books showed it was his sole loss in eighty-eight matches. He has, in the last eight Australian carnivals, won six events and finished in semi-finals twice and quarter-finals twice.

After some lean years Bosisto seems to be heading for the summit once more. Perhaps I should explain these so-called 'lean years'. In the light of his successes, the story is one of sheer determination in the face of physical disability. His temporary withdrawal from top-line competition was foreshadowed in 1951, the year he won 'everything'. An old back injury, suffered at twelve when he fell from a horse and struck a kerbstone, caught up with him. From 1951 he never ventured out for a game without a tube of balm in his bag. Though he would rub it well in, it invariably meant he would start slowly in a singles match and could count on being five or six down early on. In championship class that is a handicap few bowlers would be prepared to concede.

Things became worse, and midway through 1956 he believed his bowling days were over. He was manager of the important Western branch of the National Bank in the heart of Melbourne's financial quarter. He had to hold on to a table with both hands to get up from a chair. Climbing the stairs from the vault became an endurance test. On the advice of the bank's doctor and three specialists he retired from the bank in the belief that there was no real cure for what they diagnosed as a damaged vertebra.

Bosisto abandoned hopes of playing competitively for the time being and concentrated on treatment. A friend, Claude Hooper, suggested a support belt and Bosisto now wears it constantly. He finds that so long as he doesn't put strain on his back by, say, lifting heavy articles, he can cope. While singles play does not now unduly affect him, the continual standing at the head in a fours match causes considerable discomfort, particularly towards the end of a competition, so Bosisto has developed a method of relief where he transfers his weight from one foot to the other – long enough to get to the point where he can more fully relieve the aches and pains of standing with a brisk stroll back down the rink. None but close personal friends have ever known of the fight he has had to put up.

Sydney G. French, OBE (Past president, Australian Bowls Council), 1963

I read about myself once that 'apart from the brief good shot and the smile of acknowledgment, he wastes no time on pleasantries, nor splits his mind wondering who won the 3.30 . . . to do so may cost him the game.' Quite right. As far as I am concerned, coming second does not count. There is but one opponent when I set out in competitive bowls – myself. It is not the hard shots that can cost a match but the easy ones. You beat yourself if you fail to concentrate on them. I drove off home after playing a round in defence of my Australian singles title in Adelaide in 1951 without so much as noticing my wife, who had arrived during the game and had sat directly behind the centre-line of the rink! I never indulge in banter with spectators.

I can recall numerous examples where matches have hinged on concentration. One was during my first Australian singles championship in Brisbane in 1949. I came up against a player who in the previous round had beaten Gordon Sargeant. After several close heads I led 7–5. We were playing to a medium length. I drew a bowl about two inches jack-high and drew two more eighteen inches in front with barely space for a bowl to go between them. My opponent had two back bowls and with his last he played a fast drive. This was with the purpose of splitting the two front bowls and leaving me with one instead of three. However, his drive was magnificent: it went straight between my two bowls with hardly the space of a piece of paper for clearance and hit the jack dead-centre with such force that when it hit the ditch it bounced over and into the bushes beyond.

I heard him mutter, 'Wouldn't that rip yer! I had two bowls there and should have been three!' But, not content with this outburst, he saw a friend on the bank and walked over to receive his commiseration, too. I could see what was happening, so I moved the mat back and extended the head. I did this on the assumption that his concentration had suffered from his misfortune and that he would fail to cope with the change of length. I was fortunate in drawing a close one with my first. His first was five feet short, the next four to five feet behind. I then blocked his forehand to lie three shots. He changed to the backhand and finished wide and with his last he drove and missed and I picked up a four. Next head I scored three, and from 7–5 I was 14–5. He scored only another two for 21–7 down.

Glyn Bosisto, 1963

If age and attitudes contributed hugely to the modern boom in Britain, so did the indoor game. This also grew; and grew ambitious, independent even. Effectively, it created a new game and developed or claimed its own personalities and champions.

Brimble – the Looker-ahead

One's immediate impression on seeing Peter Brimble in action concerns his complete absorption with the task in hand. His manner is earnest without any suggestion of grimness. His stance on the mat is erect; his delivery clean, smooth and easy. He has no time for thoughtless, inconsequential play. All he does is with a purpose and a mind to what has to follow.

Brimble is one of our young bowlers. He was playing in his early teens: not in competitive bowls because of age restrictions, but nevertheless playing, getting the feel of the game. He was a good all-round sportsman, interested in football, cricket, table tennis and tennis. Natural ball players find bowls a rewarding game: their sense of position, power, direction and judgment of length become valuable assets. Brimble applied them all, plus his remarkable gift of concentration, to indoor and outdoor bowls and has gained unusual success.

He played in the lead position for many years and reaped the reward of becoming expert at singles play. He is a master of skipping: it is the basis of his play although he has every shot in his treasury.

Much of Brimble's indoor experience has been on the rather short and difficult green at Bristol and as a consequence he has become adept at the short-jack game. Short-jack play on fast indoor greens requires superb control and a fine sense of judgment. It is his mastery in this direction that has brought Brimble his many victories.

He gained the English indoor singles championship at Croydon in 1963 when he was thirty-one. Brimble had disposed of a number of strong opponents to find himself matched against George Scadgell in his semi-final. I may have a bias about this match when I claim it to be one of the finest singles games ever seen because I had the honour to be marker, but others have expressed identical views.

Brimble drew to inches; Scadgell with similar accuracy, plus an occasional heavier wood to disturb Brimble's close play. Possession of the shot changed hands many times during each end and end after end. Neither player was safe from the skill of the other, and Brimble came through as winner and finalist only after much distinguished bowling from both. It was a close thing for Brimble and a near miss for Scadgell; the result was in doubt for the two and a half hours.

Brimble went on that day to win the championship. He has a big place for indoor bowling in his range of interests. He likes the absence of those interfering elements which disturb the outdoor player. He is dedicated, a student of the game and its many sides. In his early thirties he has not only gained that singles honour but has represented England as an indoor international every year since 1960.

Possibly his ability to look ahead, to look around and to direct his play toward definite ends and possibilities form the most prominent feature of his game. We are given to understand that the great snooker player, Joe Davis, and other distinguished players of that game look far beyond the particular shot they are playing to envisage a whole series of shots and positions which should emerge if they play successfully. Peter Brimble is the Joe Davis of indoor bowls.

Arthur Sweeney, *Indoor Bowls,* 1966

Professionalism! The word began to appear in Britain and abroad: a subject for conjecture and deep concern (as indeed sham-amateurism would be, also). That concern was deep-rooted ...

Professionalism? No!

If *money* prizes continue to be the rule at public tournaments love for the game may develop into a sordid hunting after 'filthy lucre', and 'pot-hunters' inaugurate the subordination of sport for gain. Good old George Herbert says —

> Play not for gain, but sport. Who playes for more
> Than he can lose with pleasure, stakes his heart.

— and it would be a good thing if all clubs would make a rule that prizes should in *all* cases take the trophy form, say, from the modest 2s. 6d. pipe or vesta-box to the lordly vase of high artistic excellence.

Humphrey J. Dingley, 1893

Complaints are at the present time made of the 'betting nuisance' at the great matches in Lancashire and the northern parts of England where heavy stakes are played for and professionals employed. I hope this nuisance will not be introduced elsewhere. Certainly it would lead to unseemly wrangling and drive from the greens the quieter sort of company, so depriving them of their favourite and healthful exercise and the opportunities it affords for kindly social intercourse. Prize playing may be carried too far, interrupting the play of those who do not care to compete and inevitably causing heated disputes.

E. T. Ayers, 1894

Bowls is one of the few games in which there is no place for the professional. How long this pure, unadulterated, double-distilled amateurism will last it is impossible to say, but as the years roll on it is quite possible that professionalism in some shape or form will get a footing and the game may have its Henry Cottons and Fred Perrys. At the moment, however, professionalism is merely one of the things that may come; one of the things we must keep off as long as we possibly can.

British bowls magazine, c. 1937

A game, to be an all-round, *good* game, should have at least three main qualities. It should provide healthy recreation; should reward skill sufficiently to encourage serious effort; and have enough luck in it to give even the poorest competitor some sort of a chance. Bowls more nearly approaches this ideal than any other outdoor game. Other games may present, especially for beginners and average performers, all these desirable features, but gradually, in the hands of experts, they get so obliterated or distorted that in the end it becomes difficult to recognize such games as games at all and they come to look more like professions.

Technique in bowls is too elusive, too subtle, too heavily offset by other factors, too uncertain therefore in its results, for it ever to enjoy the distinction that it acquires in other games or have any commercial value. Thus, there are no spectators worth speaking of; there is no money in the game, and therefore no fund out of which to pay for the services of a super-bowler. And anyway, factors tending not to nullify skill but to counteract or substantially reduce its advantage have meant that no super-bowler has ever arisen, nor apparently ever can arise, to dazzle us with his brilliancy and disturb our serenity as to the quality of our play.

The game has its own special qualities, though they do not lie in the direction of high technique. Let us appreciate these and be thankful for them, for they are the very fountain of its beneficence. And it is these, therefore, or, rather, these especially, that we should cherish and cultivate if we want to get from the game all the good it can be made to give.

Now, should we be doing this by paying the expenses of visiting bowlers for important matches, as has been suggested? If not, then where's the gain? This proposal is made ostensibly and, I believe, honestly for the purpose of providing more skilful displays. Well, how much greater would the skill be? To what extent would it be appreciable? Would it be worth paying for? And who would be expected to pay? These are all difficult questions to answer. On the other hand there might easily arise an ugly brood of petty discontents, on the sordid nature of which there is no need to enlarge.

John May, *Our Game*, Australia, 1947

Professionalism, in fact, was held off in Britain for another thirty-odd years. And then . . .

Professionalism? It's Here!

Owing to the national preoccupation at the time with such diverse matters as babies and riots at Neasden, the news will have escaped rather a lot of people's attention during March that one of amateurism's last bastions had been divebombed and the sport of bowls went pro. To all those who think of bowls as a tediously stuffy form of exercise for the stiff in joints as well as upper lip, the idea of this pastime taking on the mantle of golf, tennis and cricket will come as something akin to Open Tiddlywinks and the Croquet World Series.

There will be others who, while respectfully aware of the game's exacting demands on skill and concentration, will be convinced that allowing players to earn a living from the game is only a step away from such professional degeneracy as the Love Doubles tennis tournaments and champions advertising lawn fertilizers on the backs of their linen blazers. They can be reassured. As the Kodak Masters tournament continues at such notorious landmarks of hard-bitten professionalism as the Croydon Bowling Club and Beach House Park, Worthing, David Bryant, bowling's first pro, sported no Adidas flashes on his specs and pipe, and the evidence is that if anything has changed at all it is only that more and more spectators are getting hooked on it and more and more players have yet to hurdle their thirtieth birthday. This year's national under-25 singles attracted 600 entries. They used to get 115 and think it was crowded.

You do not have to hunt very far for the reasons why the English Bowling Association has achieved the successful transition to open status. Some of the men who run bowls may look like the sort of old sporting codgers who think the name Kerry Packer is synonymous with moral dermatitis, but their genial determination to preserve the game's friendliness and sportsmanship is matched by a tough-nutted business sense. Bowling is well and tightly organized, but it is also expensive to run. The EBA's members pay an annual sub of 20p, which would just about get you a glass of Coke and some crisps at the pub and, even multiplied by 110,000, the number of registered bowlers, is not an awful lot of money.

'Now we've gone open,' says Hylton Armstrong, the England team manager, 'we'll be controlling the game. Sponsorship money is available and it won't be going to bowling circuses like it has been in South Africa. We are going to organize the sponsors and the tournaments so that the game gets the profit. It will help pay for our coaching scheme for a start.'

It may disappoint prospective professionals to learn that a bowler has little immediate chance of becoming a sporting millionaire. Only David Bryant can so far reasonably expect a lucrative income as a bowls consultant. 'We really just don't know how much the top ones will make,' says Armstrong, 'but there are quite a few of them all with a chance of winning, so even with £4000 first prizes the money is going to be spread around. A pro is still going to have to do another job for his living for the time being.'

The best news, though, for the sport is that at the age of forty-eight, Bryant, that incredible West Country ex-schoolteacher, is still bowling as well as ever and, what's more, intends to do so for at least another ten years. I hope so. However gratifying the sight of all those under-25s streaming to the greens, it is one of bowling's bigger plusses that a twenty-eight-inch waist and a post-1950 birth certificate is no prerequisite of success.

Julie Welch, 1980

Ferment off the Green

The decision of the English to embrace open bowls has placed the game in temporary ferment off the green, although nothing much seems to change on it. England may have been world bowls champions in Australia earlier this year but the Scots can still claim to be masters of the fours game, as yet another win in the international series indicates. But England lead where others follow in an administrative sense, and it is worth reminding bowlers everywhere that their decision to 'go open' has been taken as a means of getting rid of hypocrisy in the game over the question of payments to players and this is being accepted by straight-thinking people everywhere.

That having been said, let us now consider more recent developments. The most significant was the decision of the Scottish, Welsh and Irish outdoor associations to 'go open'. They visualize a licensing system and provisions for players who embrace professionalism on lines similar to those laid down in England, with players permitted to play in national and international competition. This means inevitably that the International Bowling Board will almost certainly be changing its constitution, for it is inconceivable that the 1984 world championships in Aberdeen will take place without the leading players of the four home countries.

Let us now look at another interesting development. During the internationals in Nottingham, Tony Allcock, the twenty-four-year-old triples gold medallist with David Bryant at the recent world championships, signed a contract with Harvey and Harvey, a shoe firm in Leicester, to publicize their products. Tony, now headmaster of a school for mentally handicapped at Tewkesbury, is one of fifty-five English bowlers who have signed professional forms with 'EBA Publications Ltd', although he will continue with his vocation – but the fifty-five face one difficulty. Their contracts cover all their bowling activities, but the English Indoor Bowling Association (and, by its recent decisions, the British Isles Indoor Bowling Association) do not recognize the International Bowling Board and have their own laws of the game. This places the contracted players in an invidious position if they wish to participate in indoor events.

Aware of this and of the need for a common policy in the game, EBA Publications recently offered the English Indoor Bowling Association two seats on their board and an opportunity to acquire an interest in the company. The EIBA considered this offer but announced through their secretary, Bernard Telfer, that they could not take advantage of it: 'The EIBA recognizes the need to respond to recent developments by achieving closer co-operation and liaison between the national organizations. It does not, however, recognize at this stage that the offer from EBA Publications Ltd of EIBA representation on their board represents the most effective vehicle for achieving such close co-operation and liaison.'

It would seem that at the moment there is no way yet out of the maze of open bowls. EBA Publications clearly recognizes that an indoor game exists and needs liaison with the indoor game to find outlets for its contracted indoor players. The EIBA feels that it is a 'big boy' now. Conscious that its influence is growing as more indoor centres are opened, it probably considers that this is no time to play second fiddle to the EBA. Under its constitution and its own laws it could easily decide to go its own way.

Teething troubles were inevitable when the game went open and it will take some time before all the problems are resolved. There are many determined men in the game, but for all their skill and apparent foresight there are times when they are clearly wearing blinkers.

Perhaps the EBA should stop having a 'superiority complex' and stop playing things too close to the chest. It needs publicity. The EIBA should not be misled into thinking that the outdoor game is dying: it is very much alive, especially internationally. The English Bowling Federation, with no international influence but a patron who has linked up with David Bryant in a company to promote him, should remember that one swallow does not make a summer.

The need for unity in English bowls is apparent. But it is doubtful if there is anyone available with the mental sweep, the rational judgment, the freedom from prejudice, the time to spare and the inclination to spare that time to bring it about: if there is let him remember all these qualities are needed. Meanwhile the game will go on showing its pettiness, absorbing its players, spreading its fellowship, making mistakes and giving a lot of pleasure, particularly at club level, as it has done for a very long while.

Donald Newby, 1980

Julie Welch's report of David Bryant's intention to bowl as well as ever for at least another ten years was written in 1980, so he has already kept his promise for seven of those years. He has been fascinating writers for three decades . . .

Bryant – Uncanny Mastery

David Bryant has to be seen to be believed. His play is a revelation of what can be accomplished by youthful keenness, an eminently practical approach and an uncanny mastery of all the constituent parts and performances which go to make the complete player. Bryant has now won the Commonwealth, British Isles, English outdoor and indoor singles championships. And this before he is thirty-three!

It would hardly be fair to describe Bryant as a bowling machine. All he does bears an aesthetic quality which prevents that, but there is a certain consistency, a peculiar purposefulness of action and execution in his play that introduces a machine-like character to his bowling. Even so, Bryant is no automaton, no robot. He is very human, lovably so.

It was my luck to mark the English indoor semi-final in 1964 between Bryant and H. W. (Bert) Smith. Bryant came to this contest with limited experience on large indoor greens but loaded with outdoor distinctions. Smith, a double international and a master of the singles game, arrived at the match in his finest form, having in earlier rounds overwhelmed all opposition. He began against Bryant in the same convincing style, found a hand he liked, a length of extreme accuracy, and soon left Bryant behind. It seemed as though he had the game well in hand.

But Bryant was waiting: serious but not apparently concerned. Being so near both contestants it was possible to study their methods and to some extent share their shots with them. It was clear that Smith was determined to press on and make hay while the sun shone. As an old hand at singles he knew that almost certainly a point would come when the trend of the game would alter. Bryant, too, was waiting and working for that moment of change.

And it came. Without hurry or any trace of anxiety Bryant quietly built up an accuracy of shot and mastery of length and green that soon brought him on level terms and then on and away to a final victory. Smith did not perceptibly weaken or lose that good length of bowl, but he appeared less effective than formerly when measured against the deadly power of Bryant's bowling.

One can learn much from close attention to a master in action. On this occasion Bryant displayed not only superb skill and mastery of shot, he showed that he was master of himself. And it is here that great players of any sport find the secret of success. First master oneself and the mastery of play and opponent follows.

There is no magic wand Bryant uses to influence his games. Every event is a challenge bringing its own problems and requiring special attention. His only magic is his remarkable ability to interpret quickly the requirements and peculiar needs of each match and to apply his exceptional powers to play accordingly. Bryant, whenever and wherever he steps on to the green, demonstrates the value of a lively, studious approach and the vital importance of steady, enterprising, well-controlled play.

Arthur Sweeney, 1966

After watching one of the most brilliant displays seen in Australia, in the 1980 world championships, we spoke with Russell Evans of Wales, who had just been defeated by David Bryant, winner of gold medals in the singles and triples. The almost ruthless way in which

Bryant played from the outset, with complete confidence in his own ability to attack or recover, had to be seen to be believed.

The player from Wales, we are sure, would have beaten almost any other bowler and we mentioned this fact in our conversation. His reply was short and to the point: 'Bryant is not normal.'

A. T. Nicol, *Bowls*, Victoria, 1980

Without embarrassment, the compere introduced David Bryant as the 'undisputed champion, the supreme maestro, the king.' Last time out he had been the 'best bowler in the world, anywhere, at any time.'

Any hint of hyperbole is banished as soon as Bryant gets on with the job. Sucking his empty pipe throughout the final of the John Player Classic at Darlington, he destroyed his Hartlepool opponent, Mal Hughes, in forty-five minutes after only eight ends, beating him 15-2 for the second time in the week. It was rather disappointing for the crowd in the Morrison Centre, but short of making the man play with his hands in his pockets, that is the way it is always likely to be. So the world indoor and outdoor champion marches on, and at forty-nine he may march on a long while yet.

Nothing changes; and yet it did. Bowls will never be the same again after this week. Two women saw to that, beating several of the finest male players in the country in this, the richest and most extraordinary tournament the sport has known.

Ten champions were invited to the four-day contest. Six came from the traditional form of the game, one each from crown green bowls and the Federation game, and two were women. Each woman beat two of the men. Lorraine Hawes finished in seventh place and Norma Shaw, whom many think the best woman player in the world, ended as a semi-finalist.

She faced Bryant yesterday morning and their first end said it all. Mrs Shaw bowled the first wood, a soup plate short of the jack. Her second touched and finished only a saucer *beyond* the jack. It was a near perfect jack sandwich and that, in the first end, was too much for Bryant. He stood upright, sighted the target in that firing position that thrills spectators across the world and delivered an impeccable wood at a speed that would have taken your foot clean off your ankle. The head exploded and they started again. Bryant won 15-8.

Nevertheless, Mrs Shaw and Mrs Hawes did something for bowls –

and for women – that I hope will never be forgotten. Fairly and squarely, they showed they could beat some of the best of men. The next hurdle is an even bigger one: to be able to do so without the men feeling ashamed.

There are other problems, of course. Bryant won £3000, but women may not yet accept money. Mrs Shaw took a voucher for £700 and Mrs Hawes (who is only twenty-seven) took one for £400. And she had a bonus: eight dozen cans of beer. That's something else that may have to change.

David Hunn, *The Observer*, 15 February 1981

I have a theory about David Bryant. It has little to do with his skill, which is considerable, but concerns his concentration. This man can immerse himelf so deeply in what he is doing and what he has to do, and he has a capacity to pour his whole self into a game which really matters to such an extent that his opponents break against his will to win.

Bryant, although the world champion, came to the 1982 Kodak Masters at Worthing with his reputation as Britain's top player tarnished: he had not won the English singles title for seven years and for the past two had had to give precedence in the 'Masters' to Bill Moseley (South Africa) and David McGill (Scotland). Months earlier I had written: 'To remain top of the heap he needs to win the Masters – and he may well do so, for he is at his best when on the ropes.'

But here at Worthing he did not really deserve to be playing for the money at all. Representing England South against The Masters earlier in the week, he lost to Moseley, McGill and Australia's John Snell. If you are to win back a title you have not held for two years you do not expect to be beaten a day or two before by all your main opponents.

Nor can you go on to lose the first two matches out of three in your section. This is what happened to Bryant. He went down in his first game to Peter Belliss, the tall, graceful New Zealander, a massive driver, by 21–16. Then Cecil Bransky, from Israel, who played for many years in South Africa, got the better of him 21–20 and Bryant seemed down and out.

Bryant could not have qualified for the semi-finals without some help from his opponents. McGill, who had won his first game, went down to Belliss, who completed a hat-trick of victories to head the section. Bryant, winner of the first two Kodak Masters, then decimated McGill 21–10, and despite two defeats was through to the semi-final.

In this he had to meet Moseley, winner for the last two years, who had proceeded regally to chalk up three wins to head his section. Moseley's match with Snell, which he won 21–19, suggested that if Bryant was not around a repeat would make a worthy final. Bryant and Moseley met on rink 6 and we thought a close game was in prospect. Moseley is a great bowler despite his awkward, almost complete fixed stance. Just before the point of delivery his left foot, already on the grass, shuffles forward, almost imperceptibly. But Moseley had 'peaked' the previous day: he had difficulty in finding his length, and Bryant, growing in confidence, won fairly comfortably.

And so we came to the final: Bryant against Snell (who had always had the edge over Belliss in the other semi-final) the gold- and silver-medallists from the last world championships. It was played in warm June sun in front of a crowd packed in stands or lounging in deck chairs away on the palm-fringed adjoining green. Both players served notice on the first end what sort of match this was to be . . .

With the first wood, the sun-bronzed Snell, right foot on the left of the mat, left foot standing parallel to it on the grass, bowls a toucher . . . with his second Snell touches his toucher to hold two shots. This won't do for Bryant. He fires and takes one out. Before the end is out, Bryant has the jack into the ditch but Snell holds shot and goes one up.

Bryant is twice short on the next end but takes shot, and on the next Snell goes out into the country on his forehand and falls abysmally short. Bryant, puffing smoke from his inevitable pipe, is not yet in the groove. Of the first seven bowls delivered, four are short. But Bryant squeezes in with his last to go 2–1.

With his first wood on the next end Bryant bowls a toucher and later is holding two. Snell's superlative drive then takes them both out, leaving the jack undisturbed; so Bryant bowls another toucher. Snell promptly drives that off and, after Bryant is short, draws another to go 3–2 ahead. On the next end the Australian draws two to the jack and now it is David's turn to switch to the power game. He fires and misses, and Snell collects three to go 6–2.

Bryant bowls a toucher again on the sixth, laying the foundation for a three, then takes up the mat for the seventh short end. Snell likes it and is soon holding two. Bryant doesn't like that and kills the end. In the replayed end, Bryant draws to the jack beautifully to hold two. But does Snell shatter the head this time? He does not; but persists in drawing on the backhand, dislodging Bryant's shots to take shot and a great ovation. And so it goes on . . . a duel between two true masters. It's 7–7, then Snell goes ahead.

At the end of the tenth, with Snell at 9–7, umpire Gerald Scott has a brief word with the Australian. It transpires that he has pointed out to him that in walking and running up to the head and then stopping he was not observing the rules governing possession of the rink and that it could be disturbing his opponent. Snell, who is not allowed to follow up his bowl in his own country but who has welcomed the opportunity to do so in England, accepts the instruction with good grace; Bryant said afterwards that Snell had not disturbed him.

But the fact remains that Bryant scored a four on the next end and after that never looked back. On the twelfth, Snell took his own shot out to go five behind and on the next he lost another despite trailing the jack. At that time I felt the championship was back with Bryant, and so it proved. Truly in command he moved smoothly to the title and £5000, the largest cash prize since the game went open, leaving Snell to collect £2500.

Afterwards I asked the Australian if he intended to take the money or remain an amateur. He has not been selected for Australia in the Commonwealth Games, so he said he had decided to keep the money and become a professional. Moseley, who has no such problem because South Africans are banned from the Games, won, and will keep, his third prize of £1000.

But David Bryant's capacity to soldier on when all appears lost is enormous. His ability to concentrate in adversity, to hang in, to conceal his feelings when all is not well is even more impressive than his superb skill.

Donald Newby, *World Bowls* magazine, 1982

The Modern W. G.

I have seen David Bryant referred to as 'the Bradman of bowls'. I would rather in a way call him its W. G. Grace. Grace was the first cricketer to become a household name. Bryant is the first bowler to be admitted to that exclusive club – and so far the only one.

It is twenty-five years since Bryant, who was then a schoolmaster, first played for England. He now has more caps than anybody else. But the nature of the game is such that the widest renown is not achieved by playing year in, year out for your country. It is achieved by winning singles competitions, and in that Bryant is unique.

Outdoors he has won the world championship twice, the British Isles championship four times, the Commonwealth Games gold medal four times, the English national championship six times, and the Kodak Masters three times. Indoors, he has won the world championship three times, the British Isles championship four times, and the English national championship eight times. Then there are all the club and county competitions he has won, the miscellaneous events at home and abroad, and the pairs, triples and fours championships at every level.

Now and again you see this or that young player described by some unthinking enthusiast as 'an up-and-coming Bryant' or 'Bryant's natural successor'. Technically they may be comparable. But is it conceivable, this side of fantasy, that they will equal, let alone surpass, what he has done?

In 1960, when he was twenty-nine, he won his first English outdoor singles championship, beating Tom Fleming in the final at Mortlake. A year later he won the British Isles singles at Eastbourne, and the year after that the Commonwealth Games singles at Perth, Western Australia. In 1966 at Sydney he became the first world champion. And at that point we can put a full stop to the statistics. They tell us much, but not, perhaps, the essentials. Bryant has been winning nationally and internationally for a quarter of a century. How does he do it?

He comes as near as is humanly possible to being the complete player. He has all the shots, a technique developed and perfected by endless thought and application, a liking for experiment, an equable temperament, imagination, concentration (to which his ever-present pipe is an aid), the will to win, and a readiness, no matter what the state of the match, to acknowledge good shots by his opponent.

There are other factors, no doubt, but there is one that nobody knows. In cricket it separated Bradman and Sobers from the rest, Pele had it in football, Borg had it in tennis, Muhammad Ali had it in boxing, Barry John had it in rugby. Those who try to pin down everything in life like so many butterflies to a board would call it genius. I prefer it nameless.

It is not fanciful to place Bryant in the same company. His is not a hectic sport, always in the public glare, in which, nowadays, a player can be dubbed 'great' on the strength of a few performances. Bryant has proved his greatness in the only way it can be proved, by beating the best for a long time. Barring the unforeseen, there is no reason why he should not go on beating them for some years yet, with his defence of the world outdoor championship at Aberdeen next year the highest peak in his view.

He is fifty-one and fit, apart from recurrent back trouble for which he took up yoga. As far as such things can be judged, his will to win is as strong as ever. Some critics allege he is not the player he was and wonder if the ramifications of his involvement in the game as a professional and a business man are impairing his skill. But no sooner do they air their doubts than he tends to win again, just as, in singles play, he is at his most dangerous when he is losing.

He is a friendly, communicative and unassuming man to whom everything about the game is of interest, from turf to tape-measures. He plays table tennis and snooker well, goes fishing when he can and wears his fame gracefully. Wherever he appears the spectators crowd round the green, and he will talk to them and sign their autograph books with ease and patience. No sport has a more diligent student of its subtleties, a greater exponent of its skills, or a better ambassador.

Gordon Allan, *The Times*, 1983

David Bryant's victory in the 1984 Gateway Masters tournament was a salutary lesson for followers of the game who had already begun choosing candidates to wrest the crown from his brow before he had finished with it. His performance at Worthing, and the manner in which he tamed the tricky conditions, underlined the fact that when he sniffs victory in the wind any opponent is going to need to play out of his skin on *every* end to beat him.

The most precious lesson that a budding bowler can learn from the game's number one has little to do with style. Bryant's is, in any case, a very personal one and a decent coach can teach a pupil the nuts and bolts of the game in a relatively short space of time. For anyone with championship ambitions it is simply not enough to master the mechanics of bowls; other factors, principally fitness, concentration and temperament are vital qualities, and these have been faithful allies to Bryant throughout his career.

Certainly Bryant is not invincible: he can lose matches he should
have won, although that view is perhaps to disregard the efforts of his
opponents. But, as the tempo of bowls hots up, with increased
sponsorship leading to more and more tournaments and bigger prize
money attracting more contestants, the competition will inevitably
become fiercer and even Bryant is only human.

What appears to make the man just that important bit different
from almost any other bowler is his attitude to the game. I cannot
honestly recall seeing him *look* like a defeated man. I have never seen
him in a dejected or despairing mood on the green. Even after his world
indoor championship defeat by Nigel Smith, which must have hurt, he
was relaxed and full of praise for the young man's brilliant exhibition.
But David Bryant simply never hangs his head. When the bugs briefly
find their way into his game, whatever tensions or furies arise within
him are kept private, and he is the first to applaud an opponent's
killing shot as well as being often the first to recognize it for what it is –
but don't expect him to roll over and die. A fleeting shadow of
self-annoyance is about the extent of Bryant's acknowledgement that
he is perhaps not playing as well as he should be in a match, but that
briefest of looks is rare enough to be an endangered species. The man is
a complete professional, one who seems to regard each loss merely as a
preparation for his next game.

His win at Beach House Park, from a strong field, earned him a
record £5500, but also reminded us that it is unwise to harbour
thoughts that his hunger for success is on the wane. Bryant
still obviously wants to win, *needs* to win and prepares mind and
body to that end. He has, using a diet of his own concoction,
trimmed off surplus weight with Aberdeen in his sights and will
be aiming there to add a third world singles gold medal to the two
already on his sideboard . . . and, really, who can say he won't do
just that.

Patrick Sullivan, *World Bowls* magazine, 1984

Youth Strikes Again

Youth served notice on older generations at the English indoor
national championships that they can no longer be patronized and that
a big change is taking place in the game. See what happened in the
singles. The singles winner was a boy of seventeen, only a few months

out of school, and the average age of the four semi-finalists was twenty-seven.

In addition to the new champion, John Dunn of Tunbridge Wells, two other young bowlers reached the last eight: Keith Benwick, aged twenty, of Spennymoor, and Gerry Smyth, a nineteen-year-old student and a semi-finalist last year. Nor were these the only young players to distinguish themselves. In events other than the singles young skips were baling out their older colleagues and impressing both experienced players and onlookers with their skills. There is, indeed, a revolution in the game.

Two years ago Charlie Burch won the British Isles outdoor singles championship at fifty-nine. Now young Dunn, a trainee accountant who plays bowls at the same tempo as 'Hurricane' Higgins plays snooker when given the chance, has illustrated that clear eyesight, near-perfect co-ordination of mind and body and supreme self-confidence can sometimes combat the rule of experience.

Brash and sure of himself young Dunn certainly is. After he reached the semi-final he was asked by Mike Ramsbottom, the *Daily Mirror* writer, if he was surprised he had gone so far. 'No,' said John. And that was that.

In the final, against Brian Howes, thirty-nine, of Norfolk and Norwich, Dunn, who had been chided the day before for the way he ran up the green to arrive at the head before the bowl, curbed some of his natural exuberance. But the fluency remained, and as end succeeded end it was evident that a photo-finish was likely to develop.

After holding shot Howes moved up the mat time and time again. For much of this match I sat with two of the regional coaches, Joe Burrows and Fred Summers, who were not slow to praise the control of Howes in delivering the jack so accurately.

Yet, paradoxically, in the closing stages, his failure to reach the required length twice cost him the game. On both occasions Dunn, who once asked for a measure from mat to jack, moved back the mat to his own advantage. On the final end Dunn bowled jack high each side of the jack and three times Howes just went through. Howes' last delivery, a fast running shot, removed two bowls – but two remained; and a seventeen-year-old was champion of England.

World Bowls magazine, 1981

Champion at Twenty-five

Watched by television cameras and a record 3000 crowd Andy Thomson, the Kent champion, beat Alan Windsor, the Surrey champion, in the greatest singles final seen since the English championships moved to Worthing in 1973. The packed Beach House Park crowd gave a standing ovation to the players as the twenty-five-year-old indoor international triumphed 21–20.

Against the experienced thirty-six-year-old Windsor, a Woking school caretaker, an England international since 1973 and indoor singles champion in 1976, Thomson led 17–9 and it looked all over; but Windsor, with an eye on the Commonwealth Games shortlist, hit back to score one, three, one, one, two to level. Thomson then drew shot to lead 18–17; next it was 18–18.

Thomson went 19–18, but after three short woods at the next end was in trouble . . . Windsor scored one, but missed a chance of taking out the shot bowl for game. On the following end Windsor held two for game when Thomson got in with his last bowl for second and 20–19. Then Thomson levelled for 20–20.

On the final end Windsor put a good first bowl just short of the jack, while Thomson was narrow. Windsor then delivered two bad bowls, one short and tight, the other wide and just short. Thomson failed to make an impression with his next two, but with his fourth took out Windsor's scoring bowl. Windsor had two alternatives: go for a difficult draw on a full-length jack or go for the shot wood. He opted for the latter but missed it by less than an inch. Thomson was champion!

Ray Potten, *Bowls International*, 1981

Talk of a successor to David Bryant as Britain's outstanding bowler could be heard around Worthing following Andy Thomson's triumph over Windsor.

Windsor, a former British Isles and England indoor champion, was the first to praise Thomson after declaring that, given the same situation, he would still fire with his last bowl ('If I had tried to draw and fallen short I would never have forgiven myself'). 'Calmness is Thomson's greatest factor,' he said. 'It doesn't matter what the situation is, he doesn't show any emotion, he just goes on bowling in the same old way.'

Windsor's assessment was amplified by the National Director of Coaching, Jimmy Davidson: 'He is completely "Scotlandised". He treats each end as a separate match and concentrates fully on every bowl, putting out of his mind anything that happened on the previous end.' Accepting this assessment, Thomson dismissed the idea that he is unemotional.

Certainly Thomson has great skills, plus a splendid ability to produce a great shot when all seems lost: witness one magnificent draw shot that killed Windsor's match-winning brace of bowls, followed by another which cut Windsor's potential 3 into a single.

However, the British disease in sport is fear of winning, and while this can scarcely be attributed to Thomson, there were a few warning cones around for those who research in this field to arrive at slightly worrying conclusions. When discussing the pressure he felt when Windsor had those two match-winning heads, Thomson revealed that the pressure was not as great as when he played his semi-finals: 'Once I was in the final I had got where I wanted.' Those were virtually the same words spoken by Hana Mandlikova after losing to Chris Evert Lloyd in the Wimbledon tennis final; she was content to be a finalist this year, winning could wait.

This degree of satisfaction is never apparent in Bryant in bowls or Borg, McEnroe or Chris Lloyd in tennis. Mrs Lloyd confesses that after defeat in an important final she is moody for three or four weeks. She is the fairest and most sporting competitor one can meet, but put her in a winning position and she clamps right down on her opponent.

Contrast this with Thomson when leading 17–9. He lost five ends in succession and consequently delivered the last bowl four ends running. Facing defeat he twice pulled magical shots out of the air – the old self-preservation syndrome. If he had been hungrier, basically, for victory, would he not have produced just one shot of similar effectiveness? The answer has to be 'yes'.

Thomson learned his bowls from his father some ten years ago. He loves the game and abandoned golf for it because he believed it offered better chances of high-level success. He has developed the talent and a fine ability to survive. The time has now come for him to hunger – severely – for winning.

C. M. Jones (*World Bowls* magazine), 1981

Looking Back at Summer

Before we are all lost indoors, let us glance back at the summer. It was a lovely blue and gold one, not quite so fine, the weather men say, as 1976, but still worth using in the future as a point of reference and comparison whenever – and that probably includes next year – the cool days outnumber the warm and greenkeeper Jock Munro has frequent recourse to the squeegee at Beach House Park.

England won the international series for the first time since 1964. Hurrah, say I, a Scot; we do not mind someone else winning it every twenty years or so. John Bell won the national singles. Hurrah again, say I, a rugby reporter under my other hat; a pleasure it is to see someone turn with such success, as Bell has done, from one of the roughest games to one of the gentlest. Contrast, much more than variety, is the spice of life.

George Souza from Hong Kong won the Kodak Masters at his first attempt, breaking the monopoly of David Bryant and Bill Moseley. Hurrah. Monopolies are bad. The newspapers (those sensible few that pay any attention to bowls) loved Souza for his name, a gift to sub-editors, who could write headlines about his march towards the title and not blush at the cliché. But would Souza have won if that amazing hailstorm had not interrupted his final against Bryant?

I remember Souza's victory, but I remember the storm more vividly, for it seemed against the natural order. If you could have taken a photograph of the whitened green and shown it later to somebody who knew nothing of the circumstances, they would have said, 'What on earth were you doing at Beach House Park in winter?'

Surrey won the Middleton Cup, but, meaning no disrespect to the county where I live, I think first of an intruding squirrel. It hopped on to the green near the end of the final against Somerset and held up play for about ten minutes, just as a dog has been known to hold up a Test match against Australia at Headingley. The players and the crowd laughed their heads off; I felt sorry for the squirrel, frightened as it must have been by the noise and unable to find a way home.

It sent my mind back to the British Isles women's championships at Sophia Gardens, Cardiff, last year, when there was a circus on the other side of the hedge. Granted, no elephants or lions wandered on to the green, but they trumpeted and growled a counterpoint to the click of wood on wood and the cries of 'Well bowled' and 'That's the shot.'

A carnival of the animals, I called it, for three dogs did in fact dash through the gate and on to the green one day.

This year I visited for the first time the English Women's Championships at Leamington Spa. I enjoyed the domestic charm of the occasion, but the almost military rules regarding dress, as set out peremptorily in the programme, made me quake – and I have been in the Army. 'Regulation dress and shoes must be strictly adhered to', 'Officers inspect uniforms before going to play,' and so forth. Not a button escaped.

Most of all to the point about this summer, as far as I am concerned, is the fact that my wife took up bowls. On Sunday mornings she would go to our club for lessons. The coach used beer mats to indicate the shoulder of the green, and once, when another learner, trying to be helpful, stood on one of these spots, she called out to her husband, who was bowling from the other end, 'Just pretend I'm a beer mat.'

Gordon Allan, *The Times,* 1983

Gordon Allan's recollections capture some of the delights of days in the sun. However, the summer game was by now being out-thought and out-paced commercially. Television covered the Thomson-Windsor final – and was lucky in getting for its money reputable weather and a superb match. But only rarely have the cameras attended these finals. The presentation of our traditional events still lacks the 'big-occasion' look and they are also a rain risk. The alternative, for TV, and thereby sponsors, has been obvious.

Great Stadiums . . . Giant Green Carpets

Whether romantics like it or not, the gentle click of lignum vitae on the village green is being replaced by the competitive, curving cut-and-thrust of plastic woods on carpets of man-made fibre. In place of the finely manicured lawns, the game is played in great stadiums, on carpets conservatively green, forty yards square, like giant snooker tables.

Even in the early days fanatics sought ways of playing their favourite game twelve months of the year. W. G. Grace was influential in providing indoor facilities at Crystal Palace as early as 1906, but Scotland can claim earlier pioneers. There was an indoor club in Edinburgh in 1905, romantically bowling by gaslight in the cellars of the Synod Hall! And that was seven years after William Macrae had demonstrated that indoor play was possible, covering a floor with sawdust and girding his bowls with rubber bands.

For half a century indoor bowls remained a poor substitute for the outdoor game, with makeshift, often miniature greens in church halls, schoolrooms and working-men's clubs. Things changed. Indoor bowls became modern and progressive in the sixties and seventies.

Most televised bowls is now played indoors. Sponsors like the guarantee that the show will go on whatever the weather. No longer is indoor bowls the poor relation. Millions watch it, absorbed by the skill, concentration and sportsmanship of the top players. Gentle games like snooker, bowls and croquet have hidden qualities. Seemingly sedate, even somnolent, a match can suddenly ignite. Aggressive tactics can destroy a carefully built-up advantage and initiative can pendulum at a stroke.

There are now well over 200 indoor clubs in England, thirty-two in Scotland and ten in Wales, all busily occupied morning, afternoon and evening with local leagues, friendlies and national competitions. Bowls offers a social and community therapy in times of political stress and depression; a physical and mental therapy for the overworked and the unemployed.

Often indoor clubs are found in out-of-the-way locations. Local people are often unaware of the frenzied activity going on behind the town hall or in the middle of the trading estate. Such modest anonymity certainly applies to the Coatbridge club where the world championships are held: this must be the unlikeliest venue for *any* world championship. It was in 1979 that this unprepossessing yet enterprising outskirt of Glasgow hosted the first Embassy world indoor championship. England's David Bryant won that one . . . and the next two! Since then, two Scotsmen, an Irishman and a Welshman have found Coatbridge a sympathetically atmospheric venue in which to win the top honour in the indoor game. The rink is claustrophobic, surrounded by a thousand or more knowledgeable, vociferous and partisan spectators. It is a unique arena.

David Rhys Jones, *Radio Times*, 1986

The last roller-ball firing shot from the veteran, David Bryant, came scorching down the artificial green at the Guild Hall, Preston, missed the cluster of woods around the jack and blustered noisily but harmlessly into the ditch. John Rednall, Bryant's twenty-one-year-old opponent, who had seen it coming, already had his hands gleefully in the air, making up for an evening of painful self-control. Like a promising pupil expecting praise for an outstanding exam mark, he jogged up the rink to meet the master, and Bryant good-naturedly bestowed it.

After nearly three hours of nagging accuracy from the fresh-faced Rednall, which he had countered with varying tactics and fitful brilliance, Bryant was eliminated in the second round of the UK indoor singles championship. Like several others during the week, Bryant had become the ungrudging victim of his own dictum: 'Bowls is a young man's game which old men can play.'

Not that Bryant, at fifty-four, is an old man, but he wishes he were twenty-five years younger. 'I keep myself pretty fit, but mechanically I can't be as good as I was then. The main need is for suppleness. I think in some ways you have to be fitter for bowls than for golf. It's all the controlled bending. And the faster the green, the slower and more controlled the bending has to be.' It was Bryant who in his time did more than anyone to make the young swallow their jibe about 'old men's marbles', just as it was Bryant, with his involvement in coaching, mail order, promotion, the management of players and the building of indoor greens, who went on to become, as the Americans would say, the 'role model' for professional bowlers.

Even so, it wasn't just for the wily skill of his play or for his eminence in the game that Bryant would be missed from the rest of the championship. It was because he is such a character. Bryant is a cartoonist's dream, a compendium of distinctive mannerisms: the praying-mantis crouch before delivery, with elbows on knees and the ball held at arm's length towards the jack; the long backward walk from the head as the exact deployment of the woods is printed on his mind; the glinting concentration behind the metal-framed glasses; the empty pipe clamped between the teeth (an indoor green is one carpet that ash isn't good for).

With men about like the extrovert one-time Cumbrian full-back, John Bell, and the athletic Tony Allcock with his wrist-flicking delivery, you could hardly say that bowls lacks characters. But mainly they are characters within their own circle. There is something in the elaborate etiquette of bowls, the snatches of conversation between

opponents, the applauding of each other's good woods, which inhibits
public displays of temperament. It may be a professional, or, to be
more precise, an open game but it still has the social graces of the club
green. It is the *niceness* of the players which is one of the game's main
assets, just as it used to be snooker's. The question is whether their
restraint will survive increasing exposure on television and progressively larger tournament prizes. In the case of several snooker players it
didn't.

David Harrison, the championship director, is involved as a pro-
moter in both sports and it is he who negotiates all the TV and
sponsorship contracts on behalf of the governing bodies of indoor
bowls. 'We are,' he says, 'where snooker was six or seven years ago.'
Last year's equivalent of today's singles final attracted a TV audience
of 7.8 million. And although Harrison says he is anxious 'not to screw
the sponsors', preferring them to get to like the game, each of the home
countries has already received £10,000 to subsidize its international
tournaments, and he hopes to more than double that – to the benefit of
stadia and coaching schemes – by the end of the season.

By snooker standards the rewards for the players are still fairly
modest (£6000 to today's Preston winner). But like the isolation of the
rink compared with the chummy, busy surroundings of the club green,
even three-figured prizes demand some adjustment by the players.
After winning his second-round game John Bell said, 'It was only at the
end that it occurred to me that £500 was hanging on the last wood.'

The same immaculate green carpet, mounted on ninety wooden
pallets levelled by laser beams, is now used in all the major tournaments. And this is what allows the players to achieve their uncanny
accuracy. No moisture, no worm casts, just a little speeding up of the
green as the hall gets hotter. Given these ideal conditions, the simplicity of the rules, the matching up of the red or yellow discs on the
bowls with the colour of the players' shirts, indoor bowls provided
some of the most gently absorbing hours on television last week.

Bryant is sure that it will eventually overtake snooker (which as a
young man he used to play with daily devotion). 'The one thing it has is
it's not repetitive. Although I can watch safety play for hours, the
potting can become boring. With bowls the jack is moved and you've
got a totally different situation.' All the game needs now, perhaps, is a
little less composure and a little more devil.

Geoffrey Nicholson, *The Observer*, 1985

The Art of TV

In your ears comes the constant jabber of jargon as the disembodied voice of the producer pans camera three, zooms in camera one and generally organizes his video hardware. The action is at the far end of the green and your monitor isn't much help to your head-reading as the picture is extremely foreshortened. Your headphones are slipping, splinters from the rough wooden bench are making their presence felt and the commentary box twenty feet airborne is swaying in the breeze.

'What do you think he's going to do with this?' asks David Vine, expecting an intelligent answer. There are perhaps four million people out there waiting for you to speak. Three million, nine hundred and fifty thousand of them know nothing about bowls and are demanding an incisive, helpful and knowledgeable explanation; 50,000 bowlers are ready to jump on you if you make a mistake. What are you going to say?

In fact you haven't been concentrating, you don't know who lies shot and you're not even sure whose turn it is to bowl. An expert summary is called for, though. You respond to the challenge. 'Well, he's got to be thinking he's got to do something with this!' you say knowledgeably and decisively. And later you score a notable triumph in the school where you teach when the sixth form are mightily impressed that *Private Eye* has printed your inane comment in the infamous 'Colemanballs' column.

That was me, in 1979, during my first Kodak Masters. I think I have learned since then, but I am still aware that the business of talking for television is much more complicated than I first supposed.

Editing, for example, imposes a string of conditions. In the Kodak, we talk for about eighteen hours over three days, but only about three hours will survive the editing and reach transmission in September. I think with regret of all those gems – the bits of personal history, tactical explanations and general propaganda for bowls – that I was so proud of at the time but which never reached the screen. Conversely, there are the embarrassing mistakes, awkward silences and wrong predictions remaining for public examination.

Then there is the *timing* of what you say from the *technical* point of view. It is tempting to go on talking at the completion of an end, because that is when the more interesting aspects of tactics can be seen clearly in retrospect. However, you must make it possible for the editor to cut conveniently, so talking through from one end to the next is not allowed. One of us (normally in the Masters this is David Vine, for he is the professional) must say something succinct and final as soon as the end is over, leave a gap of a few seconds and pick up the next end as if a completely fresh start were being made.

Again, how much should you say? There is an increasing belief that commentators say too much. There is nothing worse than a commentator on television who tells you what you can already see. Indeed, there are times when most of us have wished that the incessant chatter of the commentator would cease and we could be allowed to watch the action in peace. Johnnie Watherston, producer of 'Jack High', believes that silence is golden and I agree with him. However, this introduces another consideration: to speak or not to speak, that is the question.

The 1981 Masters will be the fourth the BBC have turned into a 'Jack High' series: Johnnie Watherston will have produced all four. Bill Malcolm has produced all the Embassy Indoor programmes from Coatbridge; Keith Phillips produced February's 'Grandstand' coverage of the John Player Classic at Darlington (and has considerable previous experience of crown green's 'Top Crown'). These three producers are gradually accumulating a body of expertise in the covering of flat-green bowls. No longer do we see isolated woods rolling down the green unrelated to mat, jack or head. The producers have caught on to the fascination of watching the wood approaching the head: it looks a good one . . . I think he's got it . . . he's on target . . . yes, well bowled!

Producers have been covering tennis, cricket, soccer and rugby for so long they have it down to a fine art. There is an optimum moment in tennis for cutting from camera one (a close-up on the serving player) to camera two (behind the player receiving the serve). The exact moment for change of camera is the instant *before* racket hits ball. This split-second timing is taken for granted now, but originally it was learned by trial, error and experience.

Camera-work for bowls is coming through the pioneer stage. One thing learned is that in bowls, as in tennis, there is an optimum moment for cutting. As it takes longer for a bowl to traverse a green than for a tennis ball propelled by, say, Tanner, Borg or McEnroe, the timing clearly is different. If the green is running at, say, thirteen seconds, the first four or five seconds are not particularly instructive in terms of the path of the wood towards the head. During this time it pays camera one to linger on the man on the mat. His concentration and commitment are likely to be photogenic and as the wood approaches the shoulder of its curved path, his body language should be indicating the success or failure of his efforts.

This is the moment to cut to camera two, which is either above and behind the head so that we can see the head itself with the wood approaching it or at the mat end with a zoom following the wood into the head – the bowler's-eye view. In either case, the camera should be placed as high as possible to minimise the effect of the inevitable foreshortening. Of course, interesting shots may be interposed to provide variety – crowd shots; the player's opponent, unable to watch; the player dancing down the green – but that is the basic formula.

David Rhys Jones, *Bowls International,* 1981

In these torrid times, what of the ladies? Hilly Janes's reference to their game later in these pages is disconcerting. Nonetheless, the women, too, have produced their champions of skill and consistency.

Nerves of Steele

The dress regulations in the programme for the English women's national championships at Royal Leamington Spa set the tone for the event: 'Skirts must be below the knee, and below the crease at the back, and two inverted pleats front and back. Sleeveless and transparent blouses must not be worn.' 'This makes for bending tidily, even if you're a bit plump,' explained the EWBA's honourable secretary, Mrs Nancie Colling, as 192 hatted females, many of them of mature years and ample bosom, bowled in the fours section.

The atmosphere was earnest but highly competitive; there were 41,000 original entries for the 700 places available in the championships finals and even the doyenne of the game, Miss Mavis Steele, who has represented Britain in international competitions for twenty-seven consecutive years, only qualified for one event, the fours. For a solid three hours the ladies bowled with a dignified, knees-bent swing, then adopted the familiar hands-on-hips stance to follow the wood's progress in an arc down the green towards the jack. 'There's nothing you can do once the wood has left your hand except hope for the best,' the president, Mrs Elsie Walters, said. 'There's a lot of skill attached to bowling and it's very ladylike, but that doesn't mean people don't swear under their breath,' she explained; but she made it clear that John-McEnroe-type tactics would not be tolerated. 'If he turned up, we'd throw him out. We like polite people in bowls.'

If the players' decorum was faultless, the weather was anything but obliging – grey and blustery with squally showers – but even this did not deter the stalwart bowlers. They stretched shower-cap-shaped covers over the brims of their regulation hats, fitted white wrap-around plastic skirts over their pleated uniform ones and played on. 'The only time we stop is when the greens are under water,' said Miss Steele, who has been playing for forty years.

Miss Steele, who has a cabinet full of trophies in her Middlesex home, has been national singles champion three times and runner-up twice. 'My parents were bowlers, so ever since I was a child I've been near a green. My father taught me but my mother encouraged me. I suppose I was something of a natural but you don't get anywhere without hard work.' She trains daily, often in the local park, to 'keep my arm in trim', and still expounds the competitive philosophy which has kept her at the top for nearly thirty years: 'I thoroughly enjoy competitive bowls; I don't like going down to the green for a roll-up.' She admitted it can, deceptively, be a demanding pastime. 'When you've had a real hard game you can come off the green physically and mentally tired, it's the concentration . . . you're always learning. The beauty of it is that you can go out and play a cracking game and an hour later do exactly the opposite. It doesn't do anyone any harm in sport to have a damn' good hiding. It proves you're not as good as you thought you were.'

Bowls is making strenuous efforts to attract younger women, but they face a battle for the greens from their male counterparts. 'There are half-a-million bowlers in the country, one third of them women, but it's the men who control the clubs,' explained Donald Newby, consultant and journalist. 'They demand the greens in the evening, so women can only play in the afternoons' – which seems likely to perpetuate the image of the game as a retirement sport.

Carol Thatcher, *Daily Telegraph*, 1985

Women's bowls has, to a degree, moved with the times, though not sufficiently to attract Press and TV like the men's game. The sport has

*its world championships and it does have incentives to the young:
national under-25 championships, for instance. The game, perhaps
correctly, worships its tradition – though perhaps not its reputation –
more than it wants its fame. Certainly days like those described in the
Sunday Express magazine have no ending . . .*

Storrington Ladies were playing at home to Petworth on a muggy
summer afternoon. Chestnut trees drooped lethargically over the high
road where a steamroller exhaled damp clouds of breath like an
exhausted athlete. A thunderstorm hung in the air, but the ladies gave
the impression that nothing short of a cyclone would have curtailed
their game.

The fixture against Petworth was a favourite one for the small
Sussex club. Of course they liked to win, but basically they went out to
enjoy themselves. It wasn't like when they played against the huge
clubs from nearby Worthing, some of whom boasted eighty members
and really brought out their competitive instincts. 'We feel, gosh, we'd
like to beat *them*. That's human nature!' Home or away, the mainstay
of any match against Petworth was the tea interval, for both Storrington and Petworth had *rather* a reputation for their cooking.

They told me Storrington was a private club, whose thirty-five lady
members subscribed £17.50 a year to enjoy one or two matches a
week, daily casual games ('if the men are here we join up, just like
that') and the Friday spoon drive, a mixed game for which the prize
was a teaspoon silver-plated in Sheffield. Miss Botting, the match hon.
secretary, said the green was looked after by the club's own men,
unlike those in Worthing which were maintained by the council. '*Their*
greens are miraculous . . .' but three or four clubs had to share them
and consequently they did not have Storrington's sense of identity.

That afternoon, the ladies were playing triples. Normally it would
have been fours – '*the* game,' said Miss Botting – but owing to holidays
and club touring commitments Storrington had a womanpower crisis.
Miss Botting soon hoped I would call her Jill: Mrs Bramham, the
chairman, became Kay and all the other ladies shed the formality of
their surnames to be Amy or Meta or Jean or Peggy or Sheila.

Tea was to take place approaching four o'clock and was spread out
on tables in the clubhouse. Plates overflowed with dainty scones like
pound coins, cup cakes, two kinds of chocolate cake. Before every

match, once the team was selected, a list went up on the noticeboard with four headings: Jam, Milk, Cakes, Flowers. Underneath each was room for three signatures. 'We have a little laugh sometimes,' said Miss Botting, 'because some people will always sign for jam and milk if we're not careful.'

Brightly chattering, the ladies descended upon the clubhouse. 'In here, girls.' 'This way, Ruby, Beryl.' 'It isn't heavy going at all.' 'Black or white tea?' 'At least you've got three woods.' They were all smartly dressed in ivory skirts and blouses and good sensible shoes: and some wore cream trilbies, though these only became compulsory dress at the semi-final stages of county tournaments.

Mrs Amy Capewell, the captain, made the speech of welcome and on behalf of Storrington looked forward to the return match in Petworth next month. Replying for Petworth, Mrs Jean Hurst congratulated Storrington on how well their green was playing, 'considering the pasting it had all winter'. Miss Botting whispered that Mrs Hurst was a marvellous bowler: 'She taught me all I know.'

In fact, Petworth was looked upon as the backbone of Sussex bowls. They had only twenty lady members, but many of those were quite outstanding. There was Mrs Hurst and Mrs Vera Cocksedge who had competed at the Nationals and were entitled to wear the Sussex county badge, six larklets on a blue background, on their blazers. But Storrington had their stars, too. Mrs Meta Joyce was a county player and Miss Dorothy McEvoy, who had been in international cricket, played in the Johns Cup, a nationwide county knockout competition: 'Mac,' said Miss Botting, 'she's my buddy.'

Mrs Bramham, who had been in the village almost all her life and whose late father had played here, and who lived with her artist husband in the wide-windowed studio on the road into Storrington, recounted the history of the club. 'Colonel Ravenscroft lived at what is now the convent and was the village fairy godfather. His daughter married a baronet who was killed in the war. He presented the land, and his gardener structured the bowling green – very well considering he wasn't a bowling-green expert. The men's club has been going sixty-four years, and originally the players were all British Legion, but as the years went by the Legion got smaller and the British Legion club became the Storrington.'

The ladies' section was started twelve years ago. Miss Botting (she had been a schools PE inspector) thought most of those playing that afternoon were retired, though immediately there were dissenting voices: 'Hazel's in one of the shops here'; 'Dorothy's a driving instructor'. The club was one of many in Storrington that included the WI, church organizations, tennis, golf, several bridge clubs of course, but 'it plays its little part'. Storrington inhabitants had been on the elderly side, but now a new estate meant younger members. 'Thank goodness, they can take over when the time comes.'

The main room of the clubhouse looked out on to the green and the men had panelled it in wood. Once it had been barred to the ladies, who were confined to their own sitting-room-cum-kitchen built on the side ('We had to have our tea in there and ooze out of the door'), but later a third room was added and the men could retreat into that. The room for the ladies had chintz cushions over the lockers and pennants round the walls. There was one from the Airport Bowls club, Luton. A plaque from Neath was waiting to go up.

There were no embargoes on when the ladies could play. 'Not written, anyway,' said Mrs Bramham. Miss Botting said, 'Things . . . creep in.' For instance, in the mornings the men seemed to get the green to themselves. 'Well,' said Miss Botting briskly, '*we* have our chores to do then!'

They made good friends through the club, and it was nice for widows ('It *is* a game for older people, isn't it?') to get companionship. Mostly, everyone got on awfully well together. 'You know, within a community you get odd bods but we've got such a lot of nice people here. Anyone who comes in to be awkward, they get their edges ironed out straightaway!'

A recent innovation at the club was a new sprinkling system, on which they had spent £3,000. They showed me the programme for the Gala Day on 10 August, by dint of which the club was paying for it. There would be an 'Inauguration of Automatic Watering System' and a 'Men's Invitation Triples Tournament' with prize money and an exhibition match with the great David Bryant partici-pating and TV coverage (to be confirmed). A sponsor had been arranged, though in certain quarters feelings were a little mixed about that.

As far as that day's match was concerned it was not the best of performances for Storrington. 'We're being beaten on every rink,' admitted Mrs Joyce. 'We only had ten names up and had to choose nine, and one girl hasn't played this season,' said Miss Botting. 'I'm not making excuses, Petworth have some very strong players, but we're being walloped.'

When the game ended, the ladies of both sides sat down together on the chintz cushions, chattering as they changed out of their brogues. The flower vases from the tea tables were rinsed out and left neatly on the draining board. Miss Botting checked with Mrs Capewell about availability for a coming fixture. Mrs Bramham made sure those who were on the list to clean out the clubhouse had fulfilled their obligations: '*All* have to help. Not left to the willing few.' Later, sitting at the spotless Formica-topped table, still wearing her cream hand-knitted bowling jersey, she furnished her own story: 'I took up bowls in self-defence because my husband was always off painting. And Daddy had his membership of the club and was president and I've followed in his footsteps.' She said it was a very enjoyable game. 'Fresh air and no hassle.'

Then they began to discuss the afternoon's match. 'Their Number One was fantastic,' said Mrs Bramham. 'So was their skip,' said Mrs Russell. 'Had these enormous woods.' 'Like bombs,' marvelled Miss Botting.

Leaving Storrington, the impression of their liveliness and friendship lingered over several days. Miss Botting had given me one of the teaspoons silver-plated in Sheffield, and I shall treasure it.

Julie Welch, *Sunday Express* magazine, 1985

Bowls, at this point in its development, happily maintains its extremes. At one end the congeniality of the club – for men as well as for women. At the other, the biting tension of the major championship . . .

The Best Ever

In competitive sport, even at world championship level, a high percentage of matches are lost by one player rather than won by the other. Nevertheless, in epics, there are more examples of the victor telling himself, 'I really *won* that match.' That relates to the Willie Wood *v.* David Bryant match in the 1984 world championships, right down to the last delivery: it robbed Bryant of a place in the final; scored a single and that was it.

It was, in my view, the greatest singles match ever played, certainly in the British Isles. Westburn Park, Aberdeen, hummed with the excitement of it after 27 pulsating ends. At no stage did either man look in fear of defeat or show negative, fear-to-win signs. So what specific factors were at work for each man? Self-confidence led the field: the self-confidence which grows from having 'been there' a multitude of times and knowing how to escape from the crisis. That, consequently, derives from sound technique. In turn, sound technique is the child of self-disciplined and intelligent practice. Nothing is more valuable in a crisis than the knowledge that one can succeed with the necessary shot.

Among factors of the mental-toughness family, technical proficiency and relaxation rank highly. So, too, does realism and a mature philosophy which realizes defeat in bowls is an occupational hazard. Not in the slightest degree does that mean any reduction of will to win: the reverse, in fact. But in daring to win you must 'pay the fees'. In this case, it is realizing you have no guarantee that such a shot may come off . . . but also knowing that it has been practised assiduously, with successful results in the past.

When all these requirements have been met, one is in ideal-performance state when stepping on the mat. Fragmentation of time should automatically eliminate all thoughts of past and future. Backed by sub-conscious know-how of what is needed, one can concentrate completely on the present; on the bowl and the green. Before delivering, one should visualize a vivid picture of the shot one is going to play. That visual should be backed by strong, positive exuberance in the chest and brain and total relaxation of muscles and body. Having 'seen' this perfect shot winning the end and, when applicable, the match, the champion delivers with firm determination – and a repetition of the mental rehearsal which has just succeeded.

Wood was Commonwealth champion; Bryant, the master bowler and holder of the world singles title. They began at a splendid level, scarcely dropped during the middle section, then rose to a peak for the last five ends. One, the 27th, was killed and replayed.

Subjectively, Wood thought his bowls (Drake's Pride 5 1/16", 3 lb 6 oz) straighter running than Bryant's (Henselite 5 1/16", 3 lb 6 oz). He also thought his switch to 'mat-up-short-jack' tactics were the key factor in his win. Bryant agreed.

There were seven such ends, five set up by Wood, two by Bryant. A study of Bryant's 27 deliveries on those ends (he didn't dare use his fourth on the 28th end) shows that 12 of them drew into the 'dustbin lid', an imaginary circle of 15 inches radius with the target, normally the jack, at the centre. Another four were correct in length but not in land, leaving 11 that went adrift. On the first six of those ends Wood scored seven shots and lost only one. Bryant, on the edge of defeat, delivered three outstanding shots in succession to score three.

The other awesome feature of the match was Wood's gossamer touch with gentle take-outs, promotions and positional wicks. He used one or the other on ten different ends, cutting out 16 potential scorers for Bryant, so clearing the way for 10 shots for himself. That performance praises Bryant, also, for how well must one play to suffer conversions of 26 shots and still only lose 21–18 by a breathtaking last bowl?

The match was a classic of concentration and mental toughness. Remember, Bryant did not lose, Wood dared to win – and did so with one of the best shots of his lifetime. Such talents are acquired skills within the capabilities of many more bowlers than might be imagined. The key is intense, unwavering self-discipline.

C. M. Jones, *Bowls International*, 1984

Agonizing

With slightly trembling hands and a dry throat, umpire Jim Muir from the Sighthill club of Edinburgh had to make what must have been the most agonizing measure of all time on the last end of the 1984 world singles championship at Aberdeen. A quarter-of-an-inch (or now that flat-green bowls has gone metric, 0.55 cm) separated the two bowls of Scotland's Willie Wood and Peter Belliss of New Zealand.

Played in glorious sunshine, with just a hint of a cross-wind and in front of a 3500 capacity crowd, this was a match of three distinct phases. For the first five ends it was cut and thrust, with Wood, 5–1 down, getting a double with a good drive on the fifth end. It was then the turn of Belliss to display his skills: bowling with the mat well up he scored two, three, one to lead 11–3.

At this point the Beatle-mopped Scot suddenly began to find both his line and length as the sun dried off any remaining moisture on the green and light increase in speed and wider draw resulted. With a run of 11 shots in the next seven ends Wood advanced to a 14–11 lead and on the 19th end got a single to lead 18–13. It seemed that the news of Scotland's crushing 30–15 win over Hong Kong in the fours that gave them the bronze medal was an additional spur for Wood in his chase for one of gold.

The 20th end proved crucial. Wood, holding three for the match with a superb trail, had to watch agonizingly as Belliss drew a superb winner with a backhand draw. Then, with Willie again in a match-winning position, Belliss killed the next end and scored a three on the replay to narrow the gap still further.

Again on the 23rd end it could have been settled. By then it was 19-across and Wood was holding two shots, but Belliss 'killed' the end with a slightly misdirected drive that wicked off a side bowl and took the jack off the rink. On the next end it was Belliss's turn to agonize. He held the shots he needed, and after a long pause to assess the situation Wood calmly played a forehand shot with weight which turned his own bowl lying third into the shot.

In the grand shoot-out at 20-all both men put their first two bowls into nervous no-man's land. Willie then drew jack-high shot; Belliss one just behind. It all seemed settled when Wood drew a forehand shot with his last bowl just in front of the jack. Belliss then took a calculated risk to play the shot out with a drive, which succeeded brilliantly.

And then it was up to the umpire. Having abandoned the electronic measure, he used a tape . . . and Belliss's gamble had paid off: 21–20!

Said Belliss: 'I shook Willie's hand straightaway because after all one of us had won, although at that time I hadn't looked at the bowls in the head. I was glad the measure wasn't settled by the electronic measure, although when I saw the umpire's hands trembling I wasn't sure which was the best method.'

It was New Zealand's first singles gold medal and only the second gold they had won since the world championships began in 1966.

Bowls International, 1984

Bowls today, judged by television and newspaper coverage, is bigger than ever it was. Some feel it should be even bigger; occasional writings indicate that a few suspect the game has already gone far enough in compromise over scoring, attire, prize-money and other factors to woo TV *and sponsors. Meantime, the trend toward youthful*

champions and challengers continues – and the indoor 'Superbowl',
begun by Granada Television in the north of England, has helped give
the game new dimensions in terms of atmosphere, entertainment,
excitement and the combining of flat-greeners, crown-greeners, men
and women. The victory of Noel Burrows, known for crown green,
over Bryant in 1985 was a break-through in more ways than one.

Jack-the-Lads' Revolution

With his fresh-faced good looks and trendy earring nestling in a
stylishly cut mop of blond curls, Russell Morgan looks more like a
football star than an expert at flat-green bowls. But at twenty-one he is
already an England international. Last month Russell took on David
Williams, a twenty-two-year-old gasman from Brighton, for a place in
the final of the Kodak Under-25s National Singles Championship. It
was a close game in which, perhaps, sleep – or lack of it – was the
deciding factor. David, who is likely to be found sporting his suntan
and streaked locks around the Brighton discos of a Saturday night, got
to bed at two that morning: Russell turned in at four. David was the
winner.

What is it that attracts these jack-the-lads to revolutionize a game
that was associated more with over-60s than under-25s? David has no
doubt: 'I like winning. When I get to the stage where I am no good any
more, I shall give up.' Retirement at thirty, perhaps? Nearly 1000
players entered the Kodak championship this year and most would say
they are just as competitive.

The placid face of bowls is also being changed by sponsorship and
television coverage. Cash prizes have enhanced the thrill of winning.
That, too, is helping to attract younger players. Russell Morgan, who
works in his father's antique shop, would love to make his living from
the game, joining the small band classed as professionals such as
Bryant and Allcock.

A further attraction is that with so many indoor greens you can now
play all the year round instead of being limited to the official outdoor
season which starts in May and ends in September. Because of the
increase in facilities, membership of indoor clubs rose from 21,000 in
1971 to more than 53,000 ten years later and is still rising. Bowls is
even starting to become popular in schools. Derek Bell, national coach
for the northern region, enthusing on the spread of the game among

comprehensive school pupils in Hartlepool and Darlington, says: 'Children who don't like contact sports find themselves more at home in the quieter, concentrated atmosphere of a bowling green.' In Hartlepool's case, though, there is an ulterior motive: the town holds the national club cup for indoor bowls – equivalent to the FA Cup in football – and is anxious to keep up a steady supply of young players.

Almost half the pupils who have taken part in schools bowls in the north-east are girls. Most of them, according to Mal Hughes, the England team manager, have shown considerable promise. Yet it is unlikely that they will become the female versions of Russell Morgan and David Williams, for ladies' bowls has not progressed very far beyond portly posteriors and pork-pie hats. Men and women still have separate clubs and a separate governing body and girls are put off the game by the old-fashioned regulations on dress. Working women find they are excluded from matches because most ladies' clubs play in the afternoons.

Meanwhile it is a veteran who underlines one of the least expected aspects of bowls: its knife-edge suspense. 'It takes fifteen or sixteen seconds for the wood to end on the jack and there are not many sports where you have to wait so long to see the result,' says Charles Wigg, the eighty-four-year-old president of the Worthing Pavilion club. Judging by the way players run after their woods, flapping their arms like a farmer's wife chasing a wayward chicken, the tension is never far from the surface. It even gets to the young stars. To reach the final, David Williams played three matches, each lasting two to three hours, in one day and finished up almost exhausted.

One of the most pleasant aspects of bowls is its egalitarianism. As Dale Wilson, one of the Under-25 contestants, says, 'You can find yourself playing – or having a drink – with anybody, from company directors down.' The EBA has a commitment to democracy reflected in its annual competitions. Anyone can enter; there is no seeding. You play your way through club and county until you get knocked out. 'It doesn't matter who you are or what you are,' says Jimmy Elms, the EBA secretary, 'you are recognized for how you play.' He is one of only two paid staff who run an organization that has more than 2660 clubs. These, in turn, run like clockwork, mainly thanks to retired members who are keen to put something back into the game. For many, indeed, it is a lifeline. With time on their hands after giving up work or losing a spouse, bowls is a way of keeping fit and maintaining social contact. 'I dread to think what would have happened to some people if they had not taken up the game,' adds Jimmy Elms.

With the influx of the young stars bitterness has sometimes erupted like a molehill on the smiling surface of the game. Some older players have had their weatherbeaten noses put out of joint when players young enough to be their grandchildren started walking off with all the prizes. The hostility is breaking down, though, probably because the old timers realize how much the youngsters have done for the sport's image.

Young and old now play side by side. Russell Morgan, for example, is a member of the reigning British fours team and the ages of the other three range from teens to sixties. A rush of success over the last two years may make Russell feel that 'it has happened so quickly and everyone is out to get me'; but if he manages a few early nights he could still be at the top when he is eighty.

Hilly Janes, *The Times,* 1985

Crowning Glory

Noel Burrows, a forty-one-year-old Manchester publican, displays a rather thoughtful innocence when he's playing. He has a placid temperament. It belies his professional approach and an obsessive desire to win every game he plays. He is a marvellous corrector of the next bowl. If one of his shots is two feet short of its target, he will make sure the next one is a lot nearer. Known primarily as a crown green player, he created a major upset in the Granada TV Superbowl competition, where the racy, rumbustious nature of the spectators, linked with the unification of flat-green, crown-green, men and women competitors makes it top televised entertainment.

In the final with David Bryant Burrows demonstrated how much he had learned over the past couple of years about the flat-green game. It was his ability to play the 'yard-on' shot that won him the match, as he used it so effectively in times of trouble.

The first set, which lasted nearly an hour, was crucial to both players. Burrows, having led 3–1 after four ends, was 6–3 down after seven. On the next end Bryant tried weighted shots for the first time and failed to disturb a two-shot advantage to his opponent. The Clevedon man was again two shots down the next end but this time fired effectively to kill the end.

The Manchester man then played Bryant at his own game. Bryant had been very successful during the week on short jacks, but Burrows set up a 'shortie' and despite a close, dramatic firing shot by Bryant survived to get the two shots he needed for the set.

Play in the second set was of the highest quality, but it was becoming evident that Burrows was beginning to outplay and out-think Bryant. On the sixth end he demonstrated his skills with a backhand trail that gave him two shots from a two-down situation and put him 6–4 ahead. Three down on the next end after Bryant had successfully fired, Burrows cut it down to one, and got a single on the next to win the set 7–5.

Following two sets that had lasted ten minutes short of two hours, the third set was like a Whitehall farce: just three ends and over in eleven minutes. The best that can be said in Burrows' favour was that he had three consecutive bad ends to lose the set 7–0 but was able to get it out of his system in time to produce his best bowls in what was to prove the final set.

There was some magnificent interchange of shots, delicate draws, good trails and some great 'take-outs.' In the last few ends Bryant set the crowd buzzing with some thunderbolt firing shots and brought the scores level at six-across, having previously killed the end with a fantastic firing shot which removed Burrows' shot bowl cleanly without disturbing anything else. On the next end Burrows was a little overweight with a jack-trailing shot; but he held on to the one shot he needed to win the set 7–6 and the match by three sets to one. Superbowl had given the crown-green code and the unification of bowls the biggest boost it has ever received.

Chris Mills, *Bowls International,* 1985

More Than Life and Death

Tommy Johnstone swigged a glass of the sponsor's brew and wiped the remains from his mouth with a flourish of the sleeve of his faded scarlet jersey. Still unable to catch his breath after a comprehensive defeat in the Waterloo of the favourite, Allan Thompson from York-shire, the wide-eyed, twenty-five-year-old plumber from Withington, Manchester, could not fully comprehend his achievement: 'I'm still shaking . . . the Waterloo is the one every crown bowler dreams of winning . . . I suppose I could retire now!'

The cheers of his loyal supporters would not be stifled amid the fiercely partisan 4000 crowd. It had been great stuff to watch and experience for one more used to the mild ripple of applause for a resting toucher in the Gateway Masters or a muffled gasp for an expertly played drive during the English ladies' championships at Leamington. This had not been a matter of life and death, it was more important than that – a Yorkshire *v.* Lancashire Waterloo Handicap final.

Bob Warters, *Bowls International,* 1986

Super Superbowl

Superbowl has such a macho, gladiatorial ring to it that it came as a relief this week to see an Irish umpire, Stanley McIlroy, caught with his tape measure in the sort of tangle that would drive the average DIY enthusiast and his wife up the wall. The fact that Stanley got himself into such a fine mess in front of a national television audience at a crucial stage of a match in the Liverpool Victoria Insurance indoor bowls championship was embarrassing for him but fun for everybody else. And it makes a pleasant change to find some fun in sport.

This Superbowl could not be further removed from the armour-plated football extravaganza of the same name played in the United States in January. What we have here is the world's most sophisticated and lucrative indoor bowls tournament played on the rink of the Rovers Return, Coronation Street – although the location's official title is Stage One of the Granada Television Centre in Manchester.

The game itself, delightfully skilful, deceptively simple and usually sedate, is cocooned by technology, a genuine studio sport: lights, camera, action and an audience of 1000. A few months ago, Stage One was the scene of Najib Daho's forlorn attempt on the world super-featherweight boxing title. The arena was then swiftly transformed for a more vicious fight as the Westminster Debating Chamber in Jeffrey Archer's *First Among Equals.*

With a total of £34,000 to be won, and a first prize of £12,000, the Superbowl has a keen competitive edge, the more so because it draws together the finest flat and crown green players, women prominent among them. This year the crown green players have prepared well for the tournament at the many indoor centres in the north of England. These bowlers are accustomed to an altogether livelier code of head-to-head confrontation, an intense gambling game as opposed to a trundle in the park.

Tony Allcock, the world indoor champion, a personable fellow of thirty-one whose blond locks give him a striking resemblance to Barry Foster's Van der Valk, welcomes the introduction of the crown green players, but points up the void in etiquette: 'It's rather like a street-fighter conforming to the Marquis of Queensberry rules.'

The exemplary David Bryant, who seems to have been the dominant figure in bowls ever since the invention of pipes with curved stems, has experience of this difference in attitudes. Last year, a crown-greener, Norman Fletcher, played his normal game against Bryant but, to the flat green bowler, appeared to be roughing up the great man. This week Bryant was ruffled by the aggressive style of a 66-1 outsider, Robert Crawshaw.

Crawshaw, aged twenty-seven, a former schoolboy basketball champion from Wilmslow, bounded down the rink as if still wearing vest, shorts and sneakers. He beat Bryant 7-6, 7-6 in the first round and apologized yesterday for his behaviour after progressing to the quarter-finals with a 7-6, 6-7, 7-1 win over Jim Muir, Scotland's British Isles indoor champion. 'When playing David Bryant I got over-ambitious chasing my bowls and forgot the etiquette of the flat green game,' admitted Crawshaw. 'I was just over-excited. Today I made a special effort. I refrained from running, and everybody said how well I observed the flat green rules.'

Bryant compares the manners of bowls with the ethics of golf. We spoke about this during a world championship, and he said: 'In golf, anybody who shows his emotions gives an incentive to the other bloke to lift his game. You get the same in bowls, although you face a totally different type of pressure than in other sports.

'In golf, if you can play a good shot the other chap has to match it: he can't do anything about your ball. In darts, if a chap makes a good score then the other fellow again has to match it. He can't do anything about what you've thrown, can't alter it. And in snooker you can only do something when you get to the table.

'Now in bowls, you can bowl three good ones and the fellow who hasn't can all of a sudden wipe out all the good you've done with one bowl and score several shots.'

At which point, etiquette demands that you smile and congratulate him, the way Muir smiled and congratulated the excitable Crawshaw. 'I found the boy to be a very good sport today,' Muir said.

There was a smile, too, from Willie Wood, who shed a stone and a quarter in training for a campaign that has taken him to a meeting with Crawshaw in the last eight, and another from Jack Hodson, a fifty-seven-year-old retired Blackpool postman who had never won as much as his £500 from the first round until yesterday, when he guaranteed himself a further £1000 by reaching the quarters.

Jim Baker, another quarter-finalist, spoke of how success rubbed off on the folks back in Northern Ireland. 'Mine is a small country,' he said. 'When I won the world indoor bowls title in 1984, people started to play bowls. When Dennis Taylor won the world snooker title, people started playing snooker. And when Barry McGuigan . . .'

'Aye,' interjected Gordon Dunwoodie, a Scottish journalist, 'everybody started fighting each other!'

                    John Roberts, *The Independent*, 17 October 1986

Sudden Fame

Stephen Rees went to a Welsh Cup soccer match between Swansea and Newport last night to be introduced to the crowd. A few days ago few people had heard of him. Then he ambled into people's homes via the television screen.

On Sunday, Stephen, aged twenty-six, beat David Bryant to win the CIS Insurance United Kingdom Championship after a seven-hour marathon. It won him a cheque for £7000. Now he is back in a Swansea warehouse, where he works in the despatch department of a plastics firm.

Bowlers excelling in television programmes explode into the public eye, because bowls is not exactly noted for frenetic enthusiasm, for making the turnstiles click or for producing fodder for banquets. Sportsmanship is paramount. Partisanship from the bank is frowned on. A criticism of one's opponent is just not done, and the tempo of the game is slow.

All this suits young men like Stephen Rees, a shy bachelor who lives at home with his mother and father Bryn, a British Rail driver. Despite his modest bearing Rees has a considerable record. At the moment he is the British junior outdoor singles champion, a title he won at Paisley in July. In company with John Price, another brilliant singles bowler from Swansea, who is about the same age, he has won the Welsh pairs title twice. They offer an unusual sight on the green, the willowy Price contrasting with the bulky Rees.

Last weekend Rees crushed three of the world's leading players. The first was world champion Tony Allcock; the second, Ireland's David Corkill, winner three weeks ago of bowling's biggest cash prize of £12,000 in the Superbowl, and, finally, the great Bryant, who had started as a strong favourite.

Rees's victory over Bryant was brilliant. His accurate drawing to the jack end after end enabled him to build a four-set lead, which, translated into shots, represented a 28-8 advantage – almost unheard of against a man of Bryant's calibre. When play started again in the evening, Bryant, whose refusal to be beaten when the odds are stacked against him is well known, ground away for more than three hours, determined to win the remaining five sets.

'I wasn't worried when David reduced my lead to 4-2,' Rees mused yesterday. 'When he got to 4-3 a doubt or two crept in. But when it was 4-4 I relaxed. I didn't have to worry any more if he was going to catch me up, and I knew the cycle might change – it often does in bowls. I scored a two, then a one in that final set, and I felt then that nothing was going to stop me winning, not even Bryant.'

Donald Newby, Daily Telegraph, 12 November 1986

Heed the Warnings!

Today's affluence has created new standards of discipline and morality. Victorian standards (those maintaining when modern bowls began), which were considered harsh and unreasonable, have given way to a freedom of thought and expression evidently leading to nowhere but open rebellion to all forms of authority, whether right or wrong. Hooliganism, vandalism, violence and aggression are common occurences; the firearm and bomb the common medium of protest and enforcement of will. Comfortable prisons have a waiting list, like reserving a seat at the Savoy Grill, and if the television programme is not favourable they are quickly reduced to a burnt-out rubble.

The greed, aggression, indiscipline and materialism of our economic and social lives has now infiltrated into our sports and leisure to such a degree that winning, and the success associated, has become the predominant feature. In many sports money purchases the time for practice and the equipment for success. In others, the dedication of the skilled is stimulated by the end product, fame and fortune.

The media still exploit the simple and physical sports (which naturally became popular in Victorian times as a psychological outlet from dismal lives), stimulating glamour, gods and partisanship for those simpletons who worship these shrines to a point of fanaticism bordering on maniacal hysteria. Sponsors eager to sell their wares and image provide the main stimuli.

Whatever way we may try to organize bowls to attract money and the media, sports like this which hide their true qualities in the quiet serenity of the environment and placid behaviour of the participants will remain unacceptable to the public as a whole, irrespective of what the 'professionals' might think, until such time as there is a complete social change of society's thoughts and attitudes. The main dangers to bowls as we know it will arrive if some radical changes are made to its characteristics for the benefit of the media and sponsors, and book-makers line the outside of our greens.

Rowland Tait, *World Bowls* magazine, 1981

18
Miscellany

There are writings to which no historical label can be attached. Here are some . . .

Woods

At Penshurst in Kent, home of the Sidney family since the fifteenth century and within a mile or so of Lord de l'Isle's famous 'Place', there is a secret chamber guarded with all the care of the Kremlin itself. Why? Because it is the room in which they give the bias to bowls, and none but the trusty workmen who operate the process is allowed in lest the precious secret be made public – or given away to competitors. All bowls have a bias, but not all bowls have the same bias. The importance of the secret machine at Penshurst is that it will give you bowls of the exact bias you want and guarantee them accurate, not by trial and error, after shaving here and trimming there, but automatically.

First catch your hare, said Mrs Beeton, or so it is commonly reported. First get your bat, said the great John Wisden. First get your lignum vitae, say the makers of bowls, for bowls must be made of a wood that is really hard, and lignum vitae, the hardest wood known to the bowls-maker, costs money. Lignum vitae will turn the finest blade, and if when it is cut it is not immediately varnished the wood will dry and crack. So bowls-making is not a job which anyone can light-heartedly undertake and the number of people who do it is very limited.

Assume the arrival of a hundred logs of lignum vitae: they weigh a lot, so a hundred logs would be a reasonable cargo. The ends of the logs when they arrive are varnished. That was done before shipment to prevent cracking on their journey from the West Indies. That's where the wood comes from. The first operation is to saw off a dozen blocks with a power-driven circular saw. The turning of bowls is done on a machine which, for all that it is nearly sixty years old, is still on the secret list.

The big name in the making of bowls is Taylor, of Scotland, who, in the early nineties, designed a revolutionary bowl-turning machine which gives 'micro-accuracy' of bias. This very quickly superseded the then existing rule-of-thumb methods. But Edinburgh of the Victorian age did not offer the scope for which Mr Taylor was looking, and he brought his invention to London. There he fell in with Mr Frank Rolph, who financed the making of bowls on a really commercial scale. So the machine, in due time, found its way to Penshurst, where it is guarded today with as much care as when it was first invented.

But to return to that square of lignum vitae, which, with its corners cut off, went into the Star Chamber. You see it next as the finished bowl on a green baize table, rather like a double-size billiards-table, whither it comes for testing before going on its travels.

A fascinating game this testing of bowls. You send the master bowl down a chute at one end and mark the spot where it finishes its journey. Then you release the new bowls, hoping probably that they will disprove some of the stories of accuracy with which you have been regaled while waiting for the new bowls to appear. Alas for your hopes. The new bowl follows the exact line of the master, and soon you have a platoon dressed with an accuracy not even the Brigade of Guards could improve on.

G. C. Lawrence, *The Observer*, 1951

In the old tilting-yard of Lewes Castle, where once the knights of the castle disported themselves, they play a strange kind of bowls which, to the initiated, is the only true and authentic form of the national game which Drake knew and loved and which kept him late, so it is said, for his historic appointment with the Spanish Armada. This is undulating bowls, so called because the ground on which it is played is in its original, natural undulating shape. The green, in fact, is a pleasing piece of hillside meadow, trodden smooth by the feet of ages and now shaved with a mechanical mower, which is the only concession to the passing of time.

Lewes has the only surviving undulating green in the country, and very proud they are of it. Real-tennis players look down their noses at lawn tennis, English skaters view with scarcely concealed contempt the now all but universal 'Continental' style. So it is with bowls. Lewes regards its way as the only true way in which to play the ancient game.

At Lewes they make provision for the age and possible infirmity of the players. 'He who casts the jack,' say the rules, 'should consider the physical abilities of his partners and opponents.' A reasonable warning enough when it is remembered that the green covers three roods, seventeen perches, and 'the boundaries of the green are the only limits to the length of a cast'. The players then tramp uphill and down as their captains decide and as the luck of the green dictates. The game at Lewes may have one player against one or two, two against two or three, or three against three.

They have played bowls for three centuries uninterrupted and, thanks to a perpetual lease granted to their Society – the Lewes Castle Bowling Green Society, to give it its official title – by the Marquess of Abergavenny at a peppercorn rent, they propose to go on for another three centuries. Even the bowls they use are old, some dating back for a couple of centuries. And when a new pair, copied from the old as an experiment by an enterprising firm of manufacturers with an eye to business appeared in play this year, they were regarded as new-fangled freaks, though beautiful withal – and ignored.

You can play bowls at Lewes in almost any weather, and only in a downpour do the devotees adjourn to their headquarters at the White Hart – that ancient hostelry which was the scene of the famous secret meeting between the Foreign Secretary and the Soviet Minister after the 'Arcos' raid in the twenties, and of which the late Stanley Baldwin once said in the House of Commons, 'You get the best ale there' – and tell sad stories of the death of kings and bowlers long ago. Was not Tom Paine one of their regulars before he emigrated to America?

G. C. Lawrence, *The Observer*, 1950

Roy Downing of Worthing, who pioneered professional coaching in Britain, is advocating that the use of the word 'wood' to describe a bowl should be dropped. I know Mr Downing is not alone in preferring the use of the word 'bowl' to describe the object half-a-million people in the British Isles propel towards a 'jack', 'cot' or 'kitty'; but I see no reason why 'wood' should be discarded.

The 'wood' is part of the lore of our historic game. Sometimes a bowl is not a bowl at all! It can be an object in which water and roses are placed, or puddings are made. It is also used by Americans to describe a stadium. A bowler is not always a bowler. He may be a cricketer.

All sorts of words in our language have more than one meaning. A bat is a flying rodent, an instrument Mr Boycott uses (sometimes 'dead') to play against Indians, Australians and West Indians, and an object wielded effectively by the Chinese to dominate the game of table tennis. Nor does a change in technology necessarily mean a change of words is necessary. A football is still a football whether one of the variety fondly described in our youth as the 'leather sphere' or one of the lighter modern type our overpaid professional soccer players have used to so little effect recently.

Bowls abounds with paradox. A fast green is one on which Mr Bruce Hensell's moulded mass of phenolformaldehyde travels slowly. An end is not necessarily the end. Similarly a bowl is not a wood. So what?

Donald Newby (*World Bowls* magazine), 1982

Greens

Tidy suburban greens, squeezed between the privet and the 8.30 railroad to Town; flousy greens as untidy as a theatricals' landlady's parlour, greens apparently full of spivs and pin-tables; seaside greens where you get sprinkled with salt spray when the wind is in the wrong direction; sleepy, good-natured village greens where nobody cares if you dent the council's woods and you help with the roller; old school-tie greens, with the Western Brothers and other prefects standing aloofly around and where you feel still and awkward as the new boy; and, oh, yes, those collar-constricting greens on which you feel like some new candidate for an appointment visiting the prospective employer, all dolled up in your most impressive suit . . .

How I hate those collar-constricting greens, indeed all greens where I experience a sense of compression and suffocation. Perhaps it is because I am a citizen of the open spaces.

'J.F.', *pre-war bowls magazine*

The vast marshes in front of the writer's window are broken here and there by large, bare patches lying stark and baked in the sunlight like muddy pools in the surrounding green. All winter the turf-cutters have been busy, peeling choice stretches of level marsh to provide new surfaces for bowling greens all over the country. This is the home of the noted Silloth turf, much sought after because of its comparative freedom from weeds, an immunity perhaps derived in some measure from the silty nature of the soil and the periodic inundation of the high tides.

To one who has known the cutters at their work here, the sight of a bowling green will always call up a vision of miles of windswept sea-pinks rippling and glistening in the May sunshine, or of the gaggles of grey-lag geese which have fed on the surface of this turf through the keen winter months.

Illustrated Sporting and Dramatic News, 1921

The oak tree had stood in Windsor Park for over 250 years – five feet in diameter, 70 feet in height. It was a fine specimen, standing only a few yards from the edge of the bowling green. It threw a heavy shade on rink six. Sometimes bowlers wished it wasn't there.

On the evening of Wednesday, May 5th, a friendly triples was in progress between Windsor Great Park and British Airways' 'Concorde' club. It was overcast but fine, though several bowlers cast glances at an accumulating and ominous black cloud.

At 7.10 p.m. the world came to an end – or so the competing bowlers thought – as a thunderbolt struck the tree with devastating force. To the bowlers, some within ten yards and none more than 50 from the impact, the effect was almost indescribable. An eye-witness seated in the pavilion described the scene as from a slow-motion film, the bowlers leaving the green by a few inches simultaneously, then returning to earth either in a low crouch or on their backs. The scene remained static for several seconds.

First realisation was of a peculiar feeling in feet and legs; then that what was left of the Oak tree was on fire; finally that the greater part of the tree was liberally dispersed over the green and a radius of 80 yards. Later discussion disclosed that not one member had been aware of the arrival of the debris. The pieces varied from one piece five feet in length and as thick as a man's arm to shredded bark and large chunks and splinters, some embedded in the ground like native spears.

Not one person was injured, which was a miracle. The cars in the car park, were not so lucky: two were write-offs, one was badly damaged, and many had dents.

Although members did not particularly like the tree, neither did they want it dispersed by the forces of nature around their ears during a friendly game.

World Bowls magazine, July 1982

A bowling green is the place *par excellence,* where the motto of the French Republic – Liberty, Equality and Fraternity – can be most readily realized. Social distinctions are for the time being dropped and all are on perfect equality – with the exception of the greenkeeper. He, of course, is an autocrat and as superior to the others as the Headmaster of Rugby was to the King of England.

Daniel Leslie (Glasgow green-layer), 1907

Despite its many disappointments, there should be few occupations more attractive to an intelligent, conscientious man than that of greenkeeper. What makes ordinary labour often so repulsive under modern conditions is that the workman has nothing to show for his labour that he can definitely call his own except his wages – and his wife, if he has one, collars *them.* He feels a mere cog in the wheel of the industrial machine – lucky, indeed, if, some time or other, he doesn't feel his fingers there, too. This is particularly so in factory life. The pride of craftsmanship, which always means something to the genuine worker, is entirely lacking.

With the greenkeeper it is just the reverse. Everything that is good he can reasonably claim for his own, and, what is more, have his claim generously allowed.

But not one requisite for a good green will Nature, for all her wonderful bounty, give the bowler, unless he pays her assiduous court. Grass? Yes, galore, where it suits her. Rain? Alike on the just and unjust, but not always just when wanted. A level sward? Miles of it, but not a yard fit to bowl on. No, everything is dependent on the skill, industry and vigilance – he wants all these qualities – of the greenkeeper.

In the mining world many a manager has won a good reputation because he had a good mine to work on; and many a better man has failed because his mine has been a duffer from the start. Full many a successful skip, too, has made his name because he had the shrewdness or good fortune to get good men bowling for him; and many a might-have-been-better one has never been heard of because he lacked the requisite skilful, loyal support. Perhaps you won't mind my observing that full many a gent of a greenkeeper has been sickened of his job because he had in the first place a vile, intractable green to work on and, what made matters worse, an unreasonable, inconsiderate body of bowlers to work for? Bad greens are rarely due solely to bad greenkeeping; the causes are deeper, more serious and more obscure.

John May, *Our Game*, Australia 1937

Captaincy

My next door neighbour's wife was buttering a teatime scone when, without warning, her husband rapped the table with a teaspoon, rose to his feet and, with a glazed look in his eyes, welcomed her to the table and thanked her for being present. His wise wife clapped twice, and said 'That was fine dear – pass your cup and have some more tea.' All over the country, AGMs have been held and newly elected captains are about to find out what lies in store for them.

Not every man is stricken with the palsy at the thought of speaking in public: some *do* dread it, others, alas, love it. Most captains follow a pattern: welcome to our club, our green is playing well, the weather is good/bad, our ladies are wonderful and we don't care who wins so long as we don't lose.

Please, jokes are out. Don't drag in the one you heard last night: your audience also watches television. Remember, too, the ladies have heard it all before and, though you may love them all dearly, you are to them, at that moment, just a pile of dirty dishes. Keep it short.

The captain will always consult the ladies about the timing of tea. Some like it halfway through the game so that they can wash up and go home. Others prefer the meal to be at the end. It is a matter for consultation.

Be wary when visiting a club with a strong ladies' playing membership. There, sitting in the sun, sometimes knitting, sometimes just watching, is an angelic lady, apparently passing a pleasant hour. Look more closely and you will observe, round her hat, a collection of club badges and, if she is wearing a blazer, more than likely a county emblem. So long as her team is winning she knits on, but should a run of shots pile up against her side, she will, even at ten ends, ring the bell for tea. Watch out – don't lose your concentration.

Scottish visitors and tours to Scotland must be treated with great caution. When you are the host, the visiting captain will clasp your hand and warmly assure you that, on this tour, he has had to select from the members who, out of their weekly pensions, have been paying into a fund for this, their only holiday. As a result, he will add, today's side is really the club's geriatric team.

Don't be fooled. Every man is a Bryant. Each toucher is greeted with tribal cries, and if a winning shot occurs on the last end any ladies present will look anxiously for the emergency exits.

Be especially wary if you ever have the great pleasure of leading your own team on to a Scottish green. Your host, and indeed his whole team, will greet you warmly – and press a glass into every visitor's hand. As soon as you step on to the green you will find that a constant greenside bar service is in operation; and don't restart the battle of Bannockburn by trying to pay.

In Scotland, teatime for you as visiting captain is easy. The meal provided could feed half of Hampden Park. The Scots captain's speech will, so far as you are concerned, be in Greek and you will hear strange words such as pibroch, haggis and single malt.

While speaking, his eye will be anxiously watching the weather, and if one solitary drop of rain appears his hand – the one without the glass – will come down on your shoulder as he expresses deep concern lest his Sassenach friends catch a chill. For your sake he will then declare the game an honourable draw and suggest an immediate adjournment to the bar. Your reply should be confined to saying, 'Hear Hear.'

Your biggest hurdle as an arbitrator in your club may come when you have to settle a point raised by, or against, the Oldest Member. This much loved chap has never read a rule book in his life and has never foot-faulted in 50 years. With each delivery he manages to send the mat flying backwards into the ditch, while his wood lands with a hole-making thump ten yards from his front foot.

What to do? Ban him for what remains of his life? Confine him to an end rink? Put up with it and find a new greenkeeper? One club had a splendid idea. They coopted the old boy on to the greens committee and appointed him assistant green ranger, with the special duty of advising the committee whenever he came across a mark made by some careless member's wood. He never thumped another wood and the greenkeeper withdrew his resignation.

You will, as captain, take the chair at selection meetings, and discover that you do not do any selecting! You will also learn the following law: once a skip, always a skip. Should a particular rink lose 40 shots in two games, you will quickly realize that it is nothing to do with the skip's ability. Sometimes he has to carry a lead whose woods were always short; or he has a second who couldn't even keep the score correct on the card; or a third who couldn't measure. Sometimes he has had all three.

Take heart, you are not expected to select. Just sit back as each skip produces *his* rink for the next game; separate the combatants if things get too hot; sign the team sheet and buy the beer. Good luck, new captains all.

Robert Watson, *World Bowls* magazine, April 1981

Temperament

To be afflicted with the 'yellow streak' to a degree that makes the difference between a good win and a bad loss is a tragedy in the lives of sportsmen. In bowls it is more prevalent than in any sport we know.

Inability to stand up to the strain of things is nothing against a man. It is something difficult to define, for, whereas many of our best players unflinchingly and with amazing courage faced death a score of times in the war, a large percentage of them would fail with the strain of a big game at bowls, billiards, golf and other sports. Every man is a problem unto himself and must depend upon himself to eradicate any tendency to funk.

No man is entirely free from this trait. I can recall times in my earlier career when that creepy feeling about the region of the abdomen, the short breath during the first few ends and the consequent loss of control had a marked effect on my game. I soon learned that, if not eradicated, all my knowledge, practice and efficiency would be discounted by that something that asserted itself immediately the real strain was on. It gave me much thought and worry after a defeat to know that I could have done much better had it not been for a tendency to 'chuck it' at times.

Just as I beat it, so can the average player, although there will remain those who will never do so because they accept the inferiority complex as something beyond their control. Much better for a man to sit down and ask himself: 'I wonder if I *am* yellow?' This trait might apply only in a sporting sense. The same man would be stronger in other directions, where the man who is never affected in sport would be weak.

It is necessary that a player carries a big heart into the game. The streak can almost wholly be got rid of: strong will-power is all that is necessary. Beginners must acquire determination early and never look on any proposition as beyond them. Once rid of that want of confidence in one's self, the cancer is beaten if not really killed.

Many an early break is obtained on an opponent from the fact that he has not 'settled down' early. Such failure means a nervous approach; that chin-in-the-air, bigger-they-are-the-heavier-they-fall demeanour is missing . . . and all the time the other fellow either knows or assumes it. Such contests represent a first-class tragedy and the survival of the fittest.

My experience is that the alleged 'temperamentals' invariably make the best players in all sport: Crawford and Anderson in tennis; McConachy and even Lindrum in billiards; Waxman, Dobbie, Denniston and scores of others high up in our game. If I were a selector I would plump for the man with the fighting temperament, whose outstanding characteristic is: 'Yes, I can do it!' This trait is sufficient to cover a multitude of weaknesses.

R. H. Harrison (Australian bowls star), 1950

'Bowling looks so simple: you only throw one thing at another, that's all, isn't it?' I wonder how many men and women have said that much to me when I have tried to make converts of them to the game.

Let the novice step on to the green and find how difficult it is to assure himself of even 15-per-cent accuracy of aim and direction and he will immediately go home and set about thinking how skill is to be obtained, and will further ruminate upon what playful and wilful things are eyesight, strength of arm, nicety of touch, and . . . well, liver!

Bowls would lose all its flavour if every man had no 'liverish' feeling, or no day when he can see black objects squatting up on the white jack or dancing Irish jigs before his eyes at about 18 yards' distance! Of course, there are real livers and also whisky livers, but I am referring to those normal livers which have their 'off days' – as professional footballers put it when they wish to excuse a bad performance.

Broadly, bowlers can be classified into two types – the 'Strychnines' and the 'Bromides'. The 'Strychnines' require stimulating to give of their best; at school they probably needed the birch. They start sleepily and go from strength to strength. The bunting, the plaudits, even the hissings, are stepping-stones. They are the tournament winners, and if you want to put them down for the count you must catch them off their guard in the first round.

The 'Bromides' are the temperamental, taut people who beat themselves some way on in the tournament. They leap off with a flying start, put everything they have into the early rounds and then, walking as on a tightrope, pass out against some second-rater because they have exhausted their store of nervous energy. A dose of Bromide half an hour before an important match would do them a world of good. These explosively expanding Japanese water flowers must be taught to conserve their energy. No worse advice can be given than to tell them to 'buck up' or to be 'on their mettle'. They must be told to *relax* – and shown how.

Dr John W. Fisher, 1948

The strain is sometimes severe; you will see it in men's eyes at the critical stage. I remember the first occasion I played in the final of my club championship. After it was over I sat down to write a letter and could not write. My hand kept twitching involuntarily. The experience was not so much disquieting as revealing. I had never thought of myself as a nervous person and during the match had been unconscious of any nervous strain. And now this was the reaction. I was amazed.

W. Stevenson, 1949

Technique

When I tell you that Pinty Frazer had played bowls for thirty-five years and never won a competition you will doubtless recall members of your own acquaintance with similar records. Not only had he kept a clean sheet so far as victories were concerned, he had never even entered a club competition . . . that is, until the day last summer when his name appeared as a late entry for the Veterans Cup.

It was one of those times at Trundlers Park when, from insignificant beginnings, there comes an outburst of activity, particularly among the afternoon members, that causes otherwise normal men to discard lifelong bowling habits and adopt new and strange postures.

'I'm convinced,' said a member, 'that the only way to read a green is to get down on one knee when delivering a wood.' It was a wet afternoon and, as he had a captive audience, he went on. 'The nearer

one gets to the ground the easier it is to pick a true line to the jack –
and, you can't foot-fault when down on one knee.'

What causes a chance remark to change a usually placid band of
bowlers into a bunch of seekers-after-a-new-formula is difficult to
pinpoint, but the following day they were all at it. Some went down on
one knee before picking out a green. Others waited until the point of
delivery before sinking to the mat. One school swore it worked on the
back hand, while others said they'd never had it so good on the fore.

The solitary upright figure was Pinty Frazer. Having left one of his
legs on the outskirts of Tobruk, he found it inconvenient to carry a tool
kit which would have enabled him, while on the mat, to modify his
artificial replacement.

It was the ladies who called a halt to the new styles. They didn't
object too strongly to the damp patches on the knees of their menfolks'
trousers, and over the years they had become accustomed to rendering
first aid to the odd player whose years had caught up with him. But six
locked knees plus two near slipped discs in one afternoon was a bit
much. They made it known that afternoon tea would not be provided
until the pavilion resumed a normal appearance and looked less like a
casualty clearing station.

The thirst for perfection refused to die down. A retired teacher said
it was obvious that mathematics was the key. 'Take a known distance
between the front of the mat and the jack, bisect that distance and then
describe a parabola from the front of the mat to a point halfway
beyond the bisecting line.'

Another member had for long been an advocate for the need to
study grass: what caused it to grow, how it always, whatever the
height of the cut, had its shoots leaning towards the west bank of the
green. 'It's the worms,' he said. 'Worms always travel from west to
east, and the movement of their bodies in a constant direction causes
the blades on the surface to have a permanent list to the west.' He
looked round the room. 'Watch the way the grass leans and allow an
extra inch for its resistance – got it?' 'What happens when the worms
reach the ditch?' asked a member. 'Do they turn round and move the
other way – and does the grass follow?'

From a corner seat Pinty Frazer listened as all the theories got an air-
ing. Hitherto he had thought his handicap was too great for him to enter
competitions. His mind went back to his army training. 'Never,' his
instructor had said, 'never try anything fancy in the middle of a battle.

Stick to basic training, and go for the fellow with his mouth open.'
Pinty rose, adjusted his leg, moved to the notice-board and put his
name down for the Veterans Cup.

It was a two-wood scratch affair and his first-round opponent was
going through a knee-on-the-mat phase. Pinty, always upright, consulted a little notebook before he played any shot and won without too
much trouble. His next opponent was the mathematics man and spent
too much time on the mat confusing himself; Pinty, notebook at the
ready, won again. In the semi-final he came up against a member who
had spent too much time watching TV and who failed to master the
David Bryant twist-of-the-hand-behind-the-back technique. He, too,
went down to Pinty and his little notebook.

Came the final and the club turned out in strength – they
were anxious to find out Pinty's secret. Had he, after years of
watching others, found the philosopher's stone? Pinty was saying
nothing. He was up against a worm's disciple; but the worms must
have had a day off because Pinty and his notebook won by six
shots.

Pinty refused to reveal his secret and never again entered a competition. Alas, he played his last end a few months later and it fell to the
secretary to clear out his locker. At the back was the little book. All the
pages were blank except one, on which Pinty had written, '*Keep the
small disc to the inside.*'

Robert Watson, *World Bowls* magazine, March 1982

Gamesmanship

There are a variety of odd local games, and games developed in the
home, like 'roof-games' and 'tishy-toshy', and unorthodox games like
billiards fives or *boule* – the game of bowls played with metal balls. All
these need careful gamesmanship and are admirably adapted to a wide
variety of ploys. The player on the home court stands at a tremendous
advantage, specially if he has invented the rules of the game. He must
rub this advantage in by every method at his command.

To counteract any suggestions that the game is silly he should create
an atmosphere of historical importance round it. He should suggest its
universality, the honour in which it is held abroad. He should enlarge
on the ancient pageantry in which the origin of the game is vested,
speak of curious old methods of scoring, etc. Meynell uses the word

'terminologics' to describe the very complete language we have built around the game of *boule* (which in our game consists of rolling old bits of brass into a cracked gutter).

Note to teachers. It is more important that the student should develop methods of his own. Encourage originality. But perhaps teachers may be helped by seeing this specimen of a 'correspondence' which 'passed' between Meynell and myself. This we incorporated in a privately printed pamphlet, *English Boule*, which we leave about in the bathrooms, etc., of the boule-court house. The specimen may suggest, at any rate, a general approach:

Dear Meynell,

I forgot, when I was writing, to advise you on the financial matter, to say that I had checked up on the point you mentioned, and it is not uninteresting to note that the expression '*bowels* (i.e., boules) *of compassion*', first used in 1374, has no connexion with the ancient etiquette, recently revived as we know, according to which the *gouttie-etranger* (the gut-stranger, or guest player new to the *boule* 'carpet') is supposed to allow his host to win the 'bully-up' or first rubber sequence. The term, of course, acquired its modern use much later in connexion with the *boule* game which the Duke of Rutland played for a wager against Henry, son of Shakespeare's 'old Gaunt, time-honoured Lancaster' at Hove Castle in 1381, beating him on the last throw with a half-pansy and dubbing his victim 'Bouling-broke', an amusing nickname which, spoken in jest, became as we know the patronymic of the Dukes of Lancaster.

Yours

Stephen Potter, *Gamesmanship*

In the Hastings Tournament I was once drawn against an opponent who, as soon as he saw me lower my body to deliver, clapped his hands. I stood the annoyance for a few ends until I could bear the strain no longer and, pretending to deliver, caught the bowl quickly with my left hand, turned round and saw him cupping his hands and grinning. When I demanded to know what it all meant, his excuse was that he had rheumatics badly in his hands and that was the only way he had of exercising his fingers. Naturally, we did not speak for the rest of the game.

George T. Burrows

Noise

The world championships at Worthing suggest something should be done about noise and play-acting such as that in which Harry Reston indulged. A campaign (such as was so successfully undertaken against slow play in South Africa a few years ago) seems a better way of dealing with it than the introduction of any law.

Bowls (South Africa), 1972

When the word 'noisy' is mentioned English players instinctively associate it with Scotsmen. This conveys a compliment to the sons of the north, although meant to be otherwise.

What is it that causes a noise? Before a noise can be produced there must be pressure from somewhere. When a bowler reaches full pressure the safety-valve is thrown into action and steam is released. Result – noise! When the so-called noisy skip is taking part in a battle he enters it with as much vim and determination as if a kingdom depended on the result. He is fighting under high pressure, the pressure of intense enthusiasm, and if he had to remain silent he would burst! But it is noise to a purpose, the noise of a skip cheerily and vigorously telling his men what he wants them to do, applauding them when successful and encouraging them when they fail:

> 'Chap and lie, Sandy, and we'll dae them oot
>   o' a four!'
> 'Draw the jack to my feet, McKie, and sure
>   as a gun we'll get three!'
> 'A dead draw to the jack, Geordie, and
>   touch nothing!'
> 'Can you see the jack, Macpherson? Into the
>   ditch with it, and we'll bag a bundle!'
> 'Man, what a fine shot for an auld yin! Here,
>   gae us a shake o' your hand!'

Everything is susceptible to encouragement. Watch your dog. After an encouraging clap on the back, how proudly he cocks his tail and trots down the road, ready to face and fight anything on four legs.

My dear English brothers, you have no conception of the intense enthusiasm some so-called noisy skips can infuse into the game unless you have seen it played across the Border. In the Scottish finals I witnessed a few years ago there was one skip who looked quite seventy and who rushed up the green after every wood he delivered. His white hair streaking in the wind, eyes flashing and face lit with eagerness, he was oblivious to everything but the result of his shot. For the time being he was not a bowler but a warrior. Centuries had been rolled back, and for the moment he had become the living embodiment of some old Scottish ancestor leading his clan to victory. I envied every man in the old chap's rink.

Oh, for more of the eagerness, the breeziness, the enthusiasm, the self-abandonment, the good-natured banter, the spontaneous humour, the light-heartedness and boyish enjoyment which can be infused into the game by men who are not afraid to let themselves go! When I hear some noise on greens south of the Tweed I shall know that English bowlers are beginning to learn *something* of the real pleasures and possibilities of this 'noble old game', as Lord Rosebery has been pleased to call it.

D. B. Macbride (early Scottish bowler)

The law states: 'Spectators shall preserve an attitude of strict neutrality and neither by word nor act disturb or advise the players.' It is difficult, even impossible when a member of one's own club is playing. In my early days I was watching one of my friends in a game and after a really good shot I said, 'Well done!' His opponent turned to me and said, 'If you find yourself unable to refrain from making audible comments, will you please move away!'

Cecil Hall, *The Bowls News*, 1952

Runners and dawdlers

Following-up a wood is of no use to its direction or destiny and is annoying to an opponent. It is no legitimate part of bowls and should be discouraged by the authorities.

James Hartley, 1922

Within recent years, through the accession of young players, the tempo of the game has quickened, except in one respect which is an abomination. Formerly running-up after a bowl was exceptional and tolerated as an eccentricity. Nowadays the practice is so prevalent as to be a nuisance.

J. L. Stewart

What is the case in indoor bowls for restraining this natural instinct? First, there is the law on possession of the rink and obstructing an opponent. But more important, at international level, conduct of this kind is a gross breach of hospitality. It is akin to children when guests jumping on the furniture. Every time players misbehave in this way there is a strain on the seams which will lessen the carpet's life – and when the authorities accept the hospitality of a club for an international series they undertake to return the green in the condition in which they found it.

The Bowls News, 1972

In my earlier days one could estimate a rink game of 21 ends at two-and-a-half hours, but today it is common to see them dragging on from between three-and-a-half to four hours through the 'techniques' of studying and consultation. I understand from a player who went to Australia that players there are forbidden even to follow-up woods and their competitions run smoothly to time. I suggest to the IBB that steps be taken to discourage this creeping paralysis.

Jack Jones, *The Bowls News*

Firing

I played a few years ago in the Weston tournament against an old trialist from the Midlands. On the second end, although I had bowled three close woods there were still four against me in a tight little bunch when I went on to bowl my last wood. I decided to chance my arm; I let go a thunderbolt that smashed into the air and landed two rinks away, whilst my opponent's lignums scattered in every direction. I trotted up, feeling pleased to have saved four shots, but my opponent did not share my pleasure. With a scowl he muttered in a thick Midlands accent: 'What's thees, a bluddy skeetle alley?'

International bowler, 1965

Playing with great force for the purpose of striking out an opponent's bowl or running the jack in the ditch is occasionally necessary but is generally a haphazard game, for if the object be missed the bowl is lost or it may carry off one of the best bowls of one's own side, leaving the opponents stronger than ever.

Bohn's Library of Sports and Games, nineteenth century

It is an alternative to drawing very much patronized by 'flukers'. In an ordinary way it should be studiously avoided as dangerous.

Handbook of Quoits and Bowls, 1868

The objections in the eastern and southern counties are, first it is dangerous to players, second it damages bowls, third it is not sport – all of which objections may at once be described both as inaccurate and even ridiculous.

James Hartley, 1922

It is wide of the ethics of the science of bowling. The jack ought to possess a kind of sacred nature and rules made to prevent its being recklessly displaced.

W. J. Emmett (prominent bowler), 1914

The man who fires in and out of season is a weakness to any team; but if all fast shots were legislated out it would limit the game's possibilities and prove a calamity.

D. Irvine Watson (EBA singles champion, 1914)

A bowler whose club has recently joined a league told me the skittle shot is put into use very ruthlessly. . . . In response to his question whether the club should leave the league I say 'yes'; because bowls was never meant to be such a cut-throat game.

George T. Burrows, 1948

Driving is rarely necessary to a singles game and if a man can draw well he should have no fear of this shot. In other games, however, there are numbers of occasions for a player who can drive accurately.

Percy Baker, 1964

Reactions to the firing shot vary. During the Kodak Masters tournament at Worthing I overhead: 'It's not bowls,' 'It ought to be banned,' 'They should be penalized if they fire too often' . . .

What did not vary was the excitement the shot caused. Every time David Bryant, John Snell or Peter Belliss prepared to play it, the crowd hugged themselves and made noises of pleasurable anticipation. And the crowd, whatever their private feelings about it may have been, were right. The firing shot is the only violent element in the game and should be enjoyed and admired, for contrast as well as for tactical reasons. It is good theatre. If nobody in the play raised his voice occasionally the audience might nod off.

When people say the firing shot is alien to bowls they have a point. It *is* alien, if you do not like the game's leisurely tempo being disturbed. Alien or not, though, the firing shot exists, and you can either like it or lump it.

Another widespread notion is that the firing shot calls for little or no skill. That is rubbish. To use it deliberately and successfully, not just as a wild last resort, you need as much skill as for any other shot. You have to ponder and practise it as much as the draw. Players like Bryant, Snell and Belliss ponder and practise it.

I think particularly of Snell. His preparations for it during a match are rapt and meticulous. First, he adjusts his grip and positions himself comfortably on the mat. Second, he swings his right arm several times, in a longer pendulum than usual. Third, he stands to attention and holds his wood at full arms' length, like a duelling pistol, with his left arm steadying his right and his eye trained on the target. Then he sweeps his arm down, back and forward – and he rarely misses, if what we saw at Worthing is reliable evidence.

Sometimes he chose to fire with his first wood after his opponent had put *his* first by the jack – a feat roughly equivalent to trying to throw down the wicket from deep-square-leg with one stump to aim at. I am told this is habitual enough in bowls in Australia and New Zealand, where conditions are different; but it never fails to make British spectators goggle.

Bryant is less military than Snell but equally methodical. His right arm is bent as he settles himself, and bent as, with head slightly lowered, he lines up the jack or wood in his sights. His left heel is off the ground. His pause before delivery is as long as Snell's, and the bowl goes on its way with scarcely a bump or wobble. Of how many firing shots by ordinary mortals can that be said?

Belliss, with the physique of an All Blacks second-row forward, is less obviously scientific, more immediately explosive. There is no ritual. He swings his bowling arm with menace four or five times before bringing it down from the sky behind his head and releasing not so much a wood as a ballistic missile. More than with Snell and Bryant, you feel with Belliss's firing shots that they would pierce armour-plate. You can see he loves playing them and also loves following them with exemplary draw shots, as if to prove to the doubters on the bank, when he seems to be overdoing the drive, that he has a light touch, too.

The firing shot is as much a part of bowls as the bumper is of cricket, a legitimate and effective weapon if used sparingly and with skill.

Gordon Allan, *World Bowls* magazine, 1982

Indoors and outdoors

As a learner indoor player I took part in a singles championship at the Temple club in South London and met a star of the club, an international and expert singles player, Fred Biggin. A real lesson he gave me, and incidentally demonstrated to me an essential difference between indoor and outdoor play which I did not then appreciate. Following my usual drawing game I tried to bowl every wood close to the jack only to find that end after end I did not score. Biggin just used my woods, and by drawing them off as often as I put them there prevented me from using my accuracy of draw to my final advantage. I know better now.

After the game Fred, chatting about earlier triumphs (including the captaincy of England), surprised me by saying, 'Yes, when I was at my best, I could beat anyone.' Then he quickly added, 'And anyone could beat me!'

Arthur Sweeney, 1966

It is easier for the average player to bowl well indoors comparable with the success he may have on grass.

R. B. Lawford (English outdoor and indoor international), 1959

Protected from the disagreeable variations of the open, indoor play is simplified to an extent seldom possible outdoors; so the critics say that through the stability and simplicity of the conditions indoor play is of little value as training for summer bowling. They prefer the more exacting demands of outdoor play, a sterner fight to attain excellence.

The physical action necessary in both realms is identical in kind if not in vigour. The calls upon acumen and concentration are identical in nature if not in variety. For the best play indoors or outdoors all the qualities, if not the force, of the player's powers can be brought into use. The same technique and art are required: differences are of degree, not of essence. Efforts towards competence form a rehearsal for play anywhere.

The indoor bowler begins the outdoor season with a flying start, in full training of mind and body. He has not developed the stiffness consequent on a long vacation and he need not have become stale by impudent over-playing. It may be claimed, in all reason, that the identity of indoor play and outdoor play and the fruits of indoor practice on suitable areas ensure the transference of competence to the summer arena.

James Hamilton, *Bowls Review*, May 1949

Home advantage is greater on carpets than on grass. Outdoors, a home player often thinks he has a knowledge of the green. Living turf, however, changes so frequently with the time of year, time of day, weather and the greenkeeper's work-rate that the local's confidence is often ill-founded and he finds himself cruelly deceived. Indoors, although temperature and humidity can account for subtle changes, speed rarely varies, tricks are dependably constant and the homester can exercise local knowledge to real advantage.

David Rhys Jones, 1985

Fact

Nature was so generous with the primitive Hawaiians that it left them time for sports. One of the most popular games was played on a perfectly level greensward prepared for the purpose. Two upright stakes were driven into the earth a few inches apart. The contestants, taking position some thirty or forty yards distant, attempted to roll discs of lava stone between the stakes without touching them.

These stones were carefully shaped for the purpose. They were three or four inches in diameter, about an inch through at the edges but thicker at the centre and rounded exactly. Carefully polished and oiled after they had been used, they were wrapped in native cloth and laid away among the cherished possessions until needed again.

So fond were the Hawaiians of this game that in the early days the champions of one island would challenge those of another island. Thousands of natives would assemble to witness the contest and gambling was indulged in, many natives hazarding everything they possessed on the throw of the '*uru*', as the stone disc was called.

F. F. Bunker, *Hawaii and the Philippines*

Fiction

It would seem to be an inexorable law of Nature that no man shall shine at both ends. If he has a high forehead and a thirst for wisdom, his fox-trotting (if any) shall be as the staggerings of the drunken; while, if he is a good dancer, he is nearly always petrified from the ears upward. No better examples of this law could have been found than Henry Mills and his fellow-cashier, Sidney Mercer. In New York banks paying-cashiers, like bears, tigers, lions and other fauna, are always shut up in a cage in pairs and are consequently dependent on each other for entertainment and social intercourse when business is slack. Henry Mills and Sidney simply could not find a subject in common. Sidney knew absolutely nothing of even such elementary things as Abana, Aberration, Abraham or Acrogenae; while Henry, on his side, was scarcely aware that there had been any developments in the dance since the polka. It was a relief to Henry when Sidney threw up his job to join the chorus of a musical comedy and was succeeded by a man who, though full of limitations, could at least converse intelligently on bowls.

P. G. Wodehouse, from *The Man With Two Left Feet*

Reportage

You can recognize minority sports by the bland, uncritical way they are reported. All is for the best in the best of possible worlds – in contrast to majority sports, in which it often seems that all is for the worst.

The only minority sport of which I have first-hand knowledge is bowls and that is not, in the real sense, a minority sport at all, since it is played by hundreds of thousands of people in many countries. It is only a minority sport on the spectating side, which is enough to damn it in the eyes of the media, who grovel to the masses and love dead things like 'gates' and audience ratings. But never mind. Let us allow, for the nonce, that bowls is a minority sport. What must it do to become a majority sport?

Well, it must, as a matter of urgency, develop an image. It cannot get itself taken seriously without an image. It must 'come across' like an unctuous politician on television. It must 'put itself over'. The image must be 'macho'. Out with white-clad figures in the parks. Out

with sunshine and summer and cream teas. Out with sport and skill –
and in with players hurling woods at each other and abusing officials,
spectators burning deck-chairs and digging up the greens, and
compulsory drug tests on competitors at Worthing and Bournemouth.

Allegations of 'fixed' matches and a few suspensions for life would
also help. So would sex scandals and personality clashes – bed and
board. No sport worth the name is complete now without adultery
and boardroom disagreements. The adultery must always be written
up as if it had never happened before in the history of the world, and
the disagreements as if the directors had wrestled on the boardroom
carpet, when in fact hardly a voice had been raised in anger.

Given that image, bowls, or any minority sport, would be followed
as fanatically as football, and the apologetic air about the way it is
reported – when it is reported at all – would vanish. And one day in the
far future, the post-Bryant age, it would receive the ultimate tribute.
People would start saying they were sick of the mindless hooligans on
and off the green, that alcohol should be banned at big events, that
they were frightened to take their families to matches, that the
Government should act, and that the game was finished.

Gordon Allan, *The Times*, 1985

Final Ends

A young lady to whom I had introduced bowls a couple of summers
back exclaimed, 'Well, I am agreeably surprised; I always heard it was
so terribly vulgar.' And I am afraid that as regards not a few of the
public-house greens that still exist the remark would be perfectly
justified.

Sidney Daryl, *Handbook of Quoits and Games*, 1868

The bolstering up of courage by excessive use of alcohol should be
avoided, if only for the tendency it has on some people to blur the
vision.

Jack Jones, 1954

Here, within Gloucester gaol, is a fair bowling green and hither the
townsmen come to divert themselves. . . . If I were forced to go to
prison and make my choice I would come hither.

Thomas Baskerville, nineteenth century

An experienced curler and bowler was skipping a rink in which his old father was the third man. The son instructed him to play a dead draw to the jack; the father had other ideas and threw up a fast one which missed the head. The son slowly and deliberately made his way to the other end where his father was standing and solemnly addressed him in these words (he always spoke in the Doric): 'Ye're ma faither, Ah ken ye're a better man than Ah am, and Ah respect ye. But when ye're playin' bools wi' me and A'm the skip, ye'll dae whit Ah tell ye, or ye'll hiv to lift yer bools aff the green.' After which solemn objurgation, he betook himself methodically back to the head.

W. Stevenson

At 49–17 in a 51-up crown-green money match at Stalybridge before the war it looked odds-on the favourite scoring another two for game. The man who was trailing decided to play a 'through' wood and followed it as fast as he could go in what, to the crowd, seemed a last-ditch effort. But he didn't stop at the block; he ran straight off the green and through the gate.

John D. Vose

'What are they doing?' asked the lady. 'Playing bowls,' said her host. 'The idea is to get the black balls close to the white one.' 'Why don't they do so, then?' asked the lady.

Anon

About a skull: 'There's nae reason for ca'in apon't for a sang, true as its ear ance was and its tongue like silver . . . ony mair than there is for playin' bowls wi't on the green.'

Noctes Ambrosiance, 1928

Bowls are built with a bias, and so for that matter are many of the players.

A skip is the captain. He directs his men most minutely, carefully and conscientiously what they are to do – but they do not do it.

Canadian handbook, early twentieth century

Last End of All

'To the memory of Mr Alderman Nynn. An honest man and an excellent bowler.'

Gravesend gravestone

Selected Chronology

1588 Legendary game on Plymouth Hoe supposedly played by Sir Francis Drake when Armada sighted

1670 Rules laid down by Charles II and colleagues

1844 Bowls first recorded in Australia. Frederick Lipscombe, a British player, advertised a green at his Beach Tavern, Sandy Bay, Hobart, Tasmania

1845 Henry VIII's Statutes re banning bowls officially repealed

1849 W. W. Mitchell's Laws in Scotland

1861 Bowls first recorded in New Zealand. Green in Auckland laid by British settlers

1873 First Talbot Handicap at Talbot Hotel, Blackpool. Winner: Josh Fielding

1880 Formation of New South Wales BA, world's first bowling association

1882 First green in South Africa: St George's Park, Port Elizabeth

1892 Scottish Bowling Association formed

1894 First Scottish Championships. Winner: Singles – G. Sprot

1899 Imperial Bowling Association formed

1901 First official match between England and Australia in London. England won

1903 English Bowling Association formed. Dr W. G. Grace, president

1903 First Home International Championship, London. England won

1904 Irish BA formed

1904 Welsh BA formed

1905 English Bowling Association succeeded Imperial Bowling Association

1905 International Bowling Board formed

1905 First EBA Championships. Winners: Singles – J. G. Carruthers (Muswell Hill); Fours – Carlisle Subscription (Cumberland)

1907 Formation of British Crown Green Amateur BA

1907 Waterloo Handicap founded, at Waterloo Hotel, Blackpool. Winner – Jas. Rothwell (West Leigh)

1907 Formation of Victorian Ladies BA of Australia, oldest women's bowling association

1908 First Irish BA Championships. Winners: Singles – R. Archer (Ormeau); Fours – Kenilworth

1910 Formation of Kingston Canbury Ladies BC, probably England's first women's club

1919 First Welsh BA Championships. Winners: Singles – J. P. Williams (Grange); Pairs – W. R. Evans, T. Taylor (Penarth); Fours – H. G. Hill, A. E. Fiddes, F. W. Alty, A. H. Emery (Windsor)

1930 W. F. Wade (Hinckley, Leicester) first man to win EBA singles twice

1930 First official British Empire Games in Hamilton, Ontario, Canada. Winners: Singles – R. Colquhoun (England); Pairs – T. Hills, G. Wright (England); Fours – E. Gudgeon, J. Edney, A. Hough, G. Frith (England)

1931 English Women's BA formed

1932 First EWBA Championships. Winners: Singles – Mrs Tigg (Wadden Residents, Surrey); Pairs – Mrs Roberts, Mrs Craxford (Southgate)

1932 Welsh Women's BA formed

1933 First WWBA Championships. Winners: Singles – Mrs Insell (Newport); Fours – Thomastown

1933 Indoor section of EBA formed

1934 Second British Empire Games, London. Winners: Singles – R. Sprot (Scotland); Pairs – T. Hills, G. Wright (England); Fours – R. Slater, E. Gudgeon, P. Tomlinson, F. Biggin (England)

1935 First Denny Cup Tournament. Winners – Crystal Palace

1936 Scottish Women's BA formed

1936 First SWBA Championships. Winners: Singles – Mrs Paton (Wallace & Weir); Pairs – Blackhall; Fours – Bearsdon

1938 Third Empire Games, Sydney, Australia. Winners: Singles – H. Harvey (South Africa); Pairs – L. Macey, W. Denison (New Zealand); Fours – W. Whitaker, H. Robertson, E. Jury, E. Bremner (New Zealand)

1947 Irish Women's BA formed

1947   First IWBA Championships. Winners: Pairs – Alexandra; Fours – Cavehill

1950   Fourth British Empire Games, Auckland, New Zealand. Winners: Singles – J. Pirrett (New Zealand); Pairs – R. Henry, E. Exelby (New Zealand); Fours – H. Atkinson, H. Currer, A. Blumberg, N. S. Walker (South Africa)

1954   Fifth British Empire Games, Vancouver, Canada. Winners: Singles – R. Hodges (S. Rhodesia); Pairs – W. Rosbotham, P. T. Watson (N. Ireland); Fours – G. Wilson, J. Anderson, F. Mitchell, W. Randall (South Africa)

1955   Percy Baker (Poole Park, Dorset) sets record of 4 EBA singles wins

1956   EBA rules only competitors over age of 18 could compete in national championships

1958   Sixth British Empire Games, Cardiff, Wales. Winners: Singles – P. Danilowitz (South Africa); Pairs – J. Morris, R. Pilkington (New Zealand); Fours – J. Bettles, N. King, W. Phillips, G. Scadgell (England)

1960   First British Isles Championships. Winners: Singles – K. Coulson (England); Pairs – F. J. Harris, M. J. Brayley (England); Fours – A. Stewart, J. Laing, D. Kirk, R. Whitehead (Scotland)

1962   Seventh British Empire Games, Perth, Australia. Winners: Singles – D. J. Bryant (England); Pairs – R. McDonald, H. Robson (New Zealand); Fours – G. Fleming, D. Bryant, J. Watson, S. Drysdale (England)

1966   Eighth British Empire Games, Kingston, Jamaica. Bowls not included

1966   First World Championships, Sydney, Australia. Winners: Singles – D. Bryant (England); Pairs – A. Palm, G. Kelly (Australia); Triples – D. Collins, A. Johnston, J. M. Dobbie (Australia); Fours – N. Lash, R. Buchan, G. Jolly, W. P. O'Brien (New Zealand)

1966   Age limit for competitors in English championships lowered to 16

1967   First British Isles Indoor Championships. Winners: Singles – D. Bryant (England); Pairs – A. Knowling, A. Spooner (England); Fours – Wales (Skip, G. Humphries)

1969   First Women's World Championships, Sydney, Australia. Winners: Singles – G. Doyle (Papua New Guinea); Pairs – E. McDonald, M. Cridlan (South Africa); Triples – S. Sundelowitz, Y. Emanuel, C. Bidwell (South Africa); Fours – S. Sundelowitz, Y. Emanuel, C. Bidwell, M. Cridlan (South Africa)

1970 Ninth British Commonwealth Games, Edinburgh, Scotland Winners: Singles – D. Bryant (England); Pairs – N. King, P. Line (England); Fours – C. Delgado, A. Kitchell, R. da Silva, G. Souza (Hong Kong)

1971 English Indoor Bowling Association formed

1972 Second World Championships, Worthing, England. Winners: Singles – M. Evans (Wales); Pairs – C. C. Delgado, E. J. Liddell (Hong Kong); Triples – W. M. Miller, C. Forrester, R. Folkins (USA); Fours – N. King, C. Stroud, E. H. Hayward, P. Line (England)

1973 Second Women's World Championships, Wellington, New Zealand. Winners: Singles – E. Wilkie (New Zealand); Pairs – L. Lucas, D. Jenkinson (Australia); Triples – New Zealand; Fours – New Zealand

1973 Percy Baker's record of 4 EBA singles wins broken by David Bryant with his 5th win

1974 Tenth British Commonwealth Games, Christchurch, New Zealand. Winners: Singles – D. Bryant (England); Pairs – J. Christie, A. McIntosh (Scotland); Fours – K. Clark, D. Baldwin, J. Somerville, G. Jolly (New Zealand)

1975 David Bryant takes 6th EBA singles title

1976 Third World Championships, Johannesburg, South Africa. Winners: Singles – D. Watson (South Africa); Pairs – W. Moseley, D. Watson (South Africa); Triples – K. Campbell, N. Gatti, K. Lightfoot (South Africa); Fours – K. Campbell, N. Gatti, K. Lightfoot, W. Moseley (South Africa)

1977 Third Women's World Championships, Worthing, England. Winners: Singles – E. Wilkie (New Zealand); Pairs – H. Wong, E. Chok (Hong Kong); Triples – J. Osborne, M. Pomeroy, E. Morgan (Wales); Fours – L. Lucas, C. Hicks, M. Richardson, D. Jenkinson (Australia)

1978 Eleventh British Commonwealth Games, Edmonton, Canada. Winners: Singles – D. Bryant (England); Pairs – C. C. Delgado, E. J. Liddell (Hong Kong); Fours – K. F. P. Chok, M. Hassan Jr., R. E. da Silva, O. K. Dallah (Hong Kong)

1978 First Kodak Masters, Worthing, England. Winner: D. Bryant (England)

1980 'Open' Bowls accepted in England

1980 Fourth World Championships, Frankston, Australia. Winners:

Singles – D. Bryant (England); Pairs – A. Sandercock, P. Rheuben (Australia); Triples – J. Hobday, A. Allcock, D. Bryant (England); Fours – P. Chok, G. Souza, E. Liddell, O. K. Dallah (Hong Kong)

1981 Fourth Women's World Championships, Toronto, Canada. Winners: Singles – N. Shaw (England); Pairs – E. Bell, N. Allely (Ireland); Triples – L. King, R. O'Donnell, L. Sadick (Hong Kong); Fours – E. Fletcher, B. Stubbings, G. Thomas, M. Steele (England)

1982 Twelfth British Commonwealth Games, Brisbane, Australia. Winners: Singles – Willie Wood (Scotland); Pairs – J. Watson, D. Gourlay (Scotland); Triples – F. Kennedy, A. Bates, M. Mills (Zimbabwe); Fours – R. Dobbins, B. Sharp, D. Sherman, K. Poole (Australia)

1982 Women first included in Commonwealth Games

1982 International Bowling Board allowed the introduction of open bowls (endorsing the decision taken by a number of its member bodies two years previously)

1984 Fifth World Championships, Aberdeen, Scotland. Winners: Singles – P. Belliss (New Zealand); Pairs – S. Arculli, J. Candelet (USA); Triples – S. Espie, S. Allen, J. Baker (Ireland); Fours – G. Turley, J. Haines, J. Bell, A. Allcock (England)

1984 First Granada Superbowl. Winner: D. Bryant (England)

1984 Gateway took over Masters. Winner: D. Bryant (England)

1985 Liverpool Victoria Insurance took over sponsorship of Superbowl. Winner: N. Burrows

1985 Fifth Women's World Championships, Melbourne, Australia. Winners: Singles – M. Richardson (Australia); Pairs – F. Craig, M. Richardson (Australia); Triples – D. Roche, N. Massey, M. Meadowcroft (Australia); Fours – S. Gourlay, E. Christie, Annette Evans, F. White (Scotland)

1986 Thirteenth British Commonwealth Games, Edinburgh, Scotland. Winners: Men's Singles – I. Dickison (New Zealand); Men's Pairs – G. Adrain, G. Knox (Scotland); Men's Fours – R. Weale, W. Thomas, H. Thomas, J. Morgan (Wales). Women's Singles – W. Line (England); Women's Pairs – M. Johnston, F. Elliot (Ireland); Women's Fours – L. Evans, J. Ricketts, R. Jones, L. Barker (Wales)

Appendix I

_____ King Charles II's Laws of the Game, 1670 _____

Rules for Game of Bowls, as settled by His Most Excellent Majesty King Charles II, His Royal Highness James, Duke of York, and His Grace George, Duke of Buckingham, in the year 1670: the game to consist of five or more points as may be agreed upon by the party engaged. Four or six bowlers constitute a set.

1. The party who hath the highest die shall lead the jack, keeping his foot on the trig, which must be placed at least one yard from the verge of the green. No cast shall be less than thirty yards.

2. Whoever shall once throw the jack off the green shall lose the leading of the jack to their opponents, and shall be obliged to follow the jack so led by their opponents or adverse party.

3. At the commencement of every end the trig shall be placed where the jack was taken up, or three strides wide of it in any direction before the jack be thrown; provided that by so doing the cast be not less than thirty yards.

4. If the jack be bowled off the green, there shall be a fresh cast, and the same party again lead.

5. If a bowl whilst running be stopped by the adverse party, it shall be laid closely behind the jack.

6. If any bowler do take up the jack before the cast or casts won be granted, he shall lose the cast to the adverse party.

7. If any bowler who lieth all, i.e., who is nearest the jack, do take the jack up, or cause the same to be taken up, before his opponent has thrown the last bowl, his side shall lose the cast and the lead shall begin again.

8. If any bowler who lieth all do take up the jack or cause the same to be taken up, before his own partner hath thrown his last bowl, he shall lose the benefit of that bowl.

9. If any bowl do lie between the jack, and the bowl that is to be measured, or the jack leaneth upon the bowl, or the bowl upon the jack, it shall be lawful to bolster up the bowl or jack, and to take away that which hindered the measuring, provided it does not prejudice the adverse party in so doing. If it shall appear to the spectators (being no bettors) the adverse party was prejudiced thereby, although the bowl did win, yet the benefit thereof shall be lost.

10. If in measuring it shall appear that the bowl or jack was removed or made worse by the measure, the cast so measured shall be allowed to the adverse party.

11. If any bowler bowl out of turn, his bowl may be stopped by the adverse party, but not by him who delivered the same.

12. If any bowl be stopped whilst running or touched by its own party, it shall then be taken away.

13. If any bowler do deliver his bowl or bowls not touching the trig with his foot, it shall be lawful for the adverse party to stop same whilst running and make him bowl it again, but it shall not be lawful for him that bowls to stop it.

14. If any bowler who lieth all do take up a bowl or bowls before the adverse party hath granted them, the cast shall be lost and the jack shall be thrown away.

15. Bowlers nor bettors shall do nothing to prejudice or favour a bowl by wind, hat, foot or otherwise, and if done the cast shall be lost.

16. No cast shall be measured before all the bowls are bowled.

17. If he that is to throw the last bowl do take up the trig, or cause it to be taken up, supposing the game to be won, or that he may do some hurt, the same bowls shall not be bowled that cast or end, for the trig once taken up shall not be set again.

18. If any running bowl be stopped or touched by a spectator, not being a bettor, whether it be to the benefit or hindrance to the caster, the same bowl shall take its chance and lie.

19. If a bowl be moved out of its place by the party that bowled the same at any time before the cast is ended, the same may be cleared away by the adverse party.

20. Keep your temper and remember that he who plays at bowls must take rubbers.

Appendix II

Scottish Laws of the Game

W. W. Mitchell drew up the Laws in 1849. They were published as follows in his *Manual* in 1864.

I.
A RINK.

When two, three, four, or any number of players, not exceeding eight, form sides and commence a game, they make what is called a rink. Eight players, that is four on each side, make a complete rink, and are classed as leaders, second and third players, and drivers. Each player plays two bowls, so that when a rink is complete, sixteen bowls are played in all. In the absence of one player, his side is permitted to play his bowls, which are called 'odd'. A toss-up decides which party is to play first. One bowl of each side is played alternately. The space or division of the Green is also commonly called a rink.

II.
FORMING THE FIRST RINK.

1. As soon as two or more Members enter the Green, they may commence playing, it being understood that others as they arrive, may, if they wish it, be admitted into the rink, until it is complete.   2. The number of players in a rink not to exceed eight.   3. When there are four players in a side, the last party admitted to play second, or third, as his driver may direct, but the leaders and drivers retain their positions until the game is finished.

III.
FORMING A SECOND AND ADDITIONAL RINKS.

1. At the termination of a game, when there are more unengaged players present than eight, and less than twelve, the last four who came upon the green to form a separate party.   2. In like manner, a third, or any additional number of rinks, may be made up.   3. Members on arriving have the privilege of joining any party which is not complete, except when the game is single-handed, and either player has scored four.

IV.
FORMING SIDES, AND CLASSING PLAYERS.

1. The Sides to be formed by ballot, each party naming its own driver, who

shall arrange the players into classes of first, second, and third.   2. The order not to be changed after the first end has been played.

V.
LEADERS.

1. The first player, or leader, to place the cloth and throw the jack.   2. Before throwing the jack, he shall announce to the driver the result of the last end, or state of the game, as instructed, and shall also be guided by him as to where to throw the jack.

VI.
SECOND AND THIRD PLAYERS.

1. When playing Club Matches, and other extraordinary games, the second player to write upon a card the names of the players on both sides of the rink, arranged in the order in which they are to play in it.   2. Also, to mark on the other side of the card the result of each end, or state of the game as announced by the leader.   3. When the driver is about to play, the third player to act as his substitute, unless otherwise instructed.   4. No direction to be given, unless required by the driver, or when it is absolutely necessary on account of some change in the position of the bowls.

VII.
SKIPS OR DRIVERS.

1. The drivers, or last players, to have sole charge of their respective sides, and their instructions to be implicitly obeyed by the other players.   2. They may appoint substitutes to direct when it is their own turn to play.   3. They are to be judges of all disputed points, and if agreeing, their decision to be final; if not, the matter to be decided by an umpire appointed by them.   4. No person to direct, except the party in charge; but any player on the same side may advise what, under the circumstances, he deems best to be done.   5. As soon as a bowl is greened, the director must retire two yards, at least, from the jack, in order that the opposing party may, like himself, witness the play and its effects.   6. The last player to remove the cloth to the bank.

VIII.
SPACES, RINKS, OR DIVISIONS OF THE GREEN.

1. The spaces or divisions of the Green ought to be numbered 1, 2, 3, 4, 5, &c., and when about to play a Club Match, or a match with another club, the Nos. to be put into a bag and drawn out in the presence of both parties by those who have been appointed to drive, or by their substitutes.   2. Previous to beginning a Single-handed Match, the numbers of each unoccupied space to be put into a bag and one to be drawn out, within the limits of which the play of the party must be confined, unless otherwise agreed upon.

3. Promiscuous games may be played without having recourse to drawing – but the play, in like manner, must be limited to the space.

IX.
SHOTS, OR POINTS IN A GAME.

1. A promiscuous game to consist of nine points; and a Match game of twenty-one, thirty-one, or any other number previously fixed upon for each rink; or it may consist of any number of heads, or be played for two hours, or any other length of time, as may be agreed on.   2. When more than one rink is engaged in the same Match, the result of each to be added together, and the gross numbers to decide the contest.

X.
THE CLOTH.

1. The party playing to have one foot on the cloth, or at the jack, if playing from one.   2. The cloth to be properly placed before being played from, and not afterwards moved.   3. If moved by accident, to be placed as near the original spot as possible.

XI.
THE JACK.

The jack is a white, globular ball, from six to nine inches in circumference, and is made of potter's clay, hardened and enamelled. It is the object played to, and, being moveable, is subject to many changes of position, all of which diversify the game, and not unfrequently render the situation and play extremely interesting.

XII.
THROWING THE JACK.

1. The throwing of the jack, and playing first, to be decided by ballot, or a toss-up.   2. If it run into the ditch at the first throw of a game, it is to be placed about two yards from it.   3. If it run into it at any subsequent throw, the other party to have the option of throwing it anew, but not of playing first.   4. If it run within a yard of the ditch, it may be moved a yard farther from it by either party.   5. If it run too near the side of the space, it must be moved to a sufficient distance from it to allow both fore and back hand play.   6. When an end terminates near the middle of the Green, the jack may be thrown either back or forward, as the party playing first may determine.

XIII.
THE JACK NOT TO BE INTERFERED WITH.

1. If none of the previous Rules have been transgressed, the jack to remain

wherever it is thrown; or, if moved, it must be by mutual consent.   2. After being once played to, except when in the ditch, it is not to be touched or interfered with, in any manner, otherwise than by the effects of the play, until the end is counted and both parties satisfied.   3. If driven so far to the side as to interfere with the play of the next rink, the end to be begun anew.

XIV.
THE JACK IN THE DITCH – REBOUNDING.

1. When the jack is run into the ditch by a bowl, the place where it rests to be marked, the jack placed on the Green at the edge of the ditch, opposite where it lay, and replaced when the end is played out.   2. Should it run against the bank and rebound on to the Green, it is to be played to in the same manner as if it had never been moved.

XV.
THE JACK BURNED.

When the jack or bowls are interfered with or displaced otherwise than by the effects of the play, they are said to be burned.   1. When the jack is burned by a neutral party, the end must be begun afresh.   2. If burned by any of the players, the opposing party to have the option of playing out the end, or beginning it anew.

XVI.
BOWLS.

Bowls, generally, are made of *Lignumvitæ*, a dark, dense, and heavy wood. In shape, they are less or more oval, according to taste; and for a similar reason they vary in size. But bowls which exceed 16½ inches in circumference are not permitted to be played in any of the National or Club Matches.

XVII.
BIAS.

A bias is given to them by the inner half of the bowl being made less, or leaner, than the outer half; and a greater or less bias is of course given to them by extending or restricting this principle. At one time the bowls were made equal in this respect, a bias being given to them by loading the inside centre with lead; but this practice has been departed from long ago, and has now become obsolete; as has also that of each player regularly playing three bowls.

XVIII.
TOUCHERS.

1. A bowl which touches the jack at any time during its course on the Green is called a toucher, and counts the same as any other bowl, wherever it

rests.   2. Should a bowl, after it has stopped, fall over and touch the jack, it is not to be regarded as a toucher, if another bowl has been played.   3. A toucher must be distinguished by a chalk mark, and not interfered with except when in the ditch, when the place where it rests must be marked, the bowl removed, and replaced when the end is played out.   4. If moved outwards while being chalked, it must remain so; but if moved towards the jack, it must be restored to its original position.   5. Unless marked before the second succeeding bowl be played, it is no longer to be regarded as a toucher.

XIX.
DITCHERS.

1. A bowl which does not touch the jack during its course on the Green, and runs against the bank, or into the ditch, or is afterwards driven into it by the effects of the play, is called a ditcher, and does not count in the game, and ought to be removed to the bank.   2. If not removed, and a bowl, afterwards played, should rest partly on it, and partly on the Green, it must then be removed by the party to whom the bowl so resting belongs.   3. Should a ditcher, under any circumstances, return to the Green, it must be removed.

XX.
BURNED BOWLS.

1. If a bowl, while running, is accidentally burned by a neutral party, or by an opponent, it shall be in the option of the party playing to let it rest, or play it over again.   2. If burned by his own party, it may be put off the Green.   3. When a bowl, while at rest, is burned by the party to which it belongs, it may be removed from the Green.   4. If burned by a neutral party, or by an opponent, it is to be replaced as near its original position as possible.

XXI.
PLAYING BEFORE A BOWL STOPS.

1. No party to play until his opponent's bowl has ceased to run.   2. A bowl so played may be stopped, and caused to be played over again.

XXII.
BOWL COMING TO REST.

After the last played bowl of an end stops running, a half minute to be allowed, if required, before counting the game.

XXIII.
PLAYED BY MISTAKE.

1. When a bowl has been played by mistake, if belonging to the opposite

party, it is to be replaced by the player's own bowl.　2. If belonging to the player's party it must remain.

XXIV.
PLAYED OUT OF TURN OR ORDER.

1. When a bowl has been played before its time or turn, the opponents may stop it, or allow it to remain where it comes to rest, or they may cause it to be played over again in its proper order.　2. If it has moved either jack or bowls, the opponents to have power to cause the end to be begun anew.　3. A bowl, which has not been played in order, cannot afterwards be played, if the second succeeding bowl has been greened.

XXV.
CHANGING BOWLS.

No player permited to change his bowls during the game except by consent of the opposite party.

XXVI.
ODD BOWLS.

1. When the sides of a rink are unequal in number, they are balanced by the deficient party playing odd bowls.　2. When the party playing them consists of two or more, no player to play more than one of them.　3. The first and last players only to play the odd bowls.

XXVII.
END, OR HEAD.

End, or Head, are synonymous terms in use to denote the termination and result of the whole bowls played after each throw of the jack.

XXVIII.
RESULT OF EACH END.

1. After an end is played, neither jack nor bowls to be touched until both parties are satisfied.　2. When two or more bowls are resting on each other, they are not to be disturbed or removed, until the result of the end is declared.　3. When apart, each bowl may be removed and counted, as soon as it is admitted to be a shot by the opposing party.

XXIX.
KEEPING ORDER – CONTROL OF THE RINK.

1. As soon as the last played bowl stops, the party who played it to lose control of the rink, while their opponents obtain possession of it, and must not be interrupted by remarks, or otherwise, while deliberating as to the best

play, or when giving directions.   2. The preceding Rule not to be in force from the time the bowl is greened until it stops.

XXX.
FORE AND BACK HAND.

Although some bowlers, in playing, make use of their left arm and hand, they are the exception, and the terms *fore* and *back* hand do not apply to them, but to all other players. The fore, or open hand, is on the player's right, with its bias to the left towards the jack; and the back, or cross hand, is played across the body to the left of the jack, with its inside, or bias, towards it.

XXXI.
PLAYING IN THE DUSK.

Under no circumstances is a cap, or other object, to be laid on the Green, or placed on a bowl, or the jack; but a cap, or any other object, may be held over one or other, or in front of either, for the guidance of the player.

XXXII.
ON-LOOKERS.

1. All players, while looking on, to stand *jack high*, at least, and, unless acting as directors, not within three yards of the jack.   2. Parties not engaged in the game must confine themselves to the banks.

XXXIII.
MATCHES.

Matches are of various kinds, but, generally, are classed under the heads of Promiscuous, Club, and Single-handed. Promiscuous matches are those which are played between the members of a club as they arrive on the green, for which see Laws II. and III. of this Section. Club matches are of four kinds, viz.: – 1, Those which are, or have been, arranged to take place among the members of the club; 2, Those which are played by one club against another, on the green of either; 3, Those which are played on a neutral green; and 4, Those which are played by the united clubs of one district against those of another. Single-handed matches are those which are played for the *Championship*, &c. [For farther particulars regarding matches, and other explanatory matter, see Section V.]

As Champion Matches were instituted for the purpose of increasing the skill of individual members of the Clubs, we would suggest the propriety of causing successful competitors to remain ineligible to enter the contest again, for two successive years after they have attained the championship.

XXXIV.
CHAMPIONSHIP OF THE CLUB.

1. The whole of the Champion Matches must be played off within dates specified.   2. If any of the matches have not been played, parties must agree before specified dates as to which name is to be retained for the next drawing, and give due notice thereof to the Secretary or Green-keeper; otherwise, both names will be scored off.   3. The parties whose names are entered on the left side of the drawings are held to be the Challengers, and if they neglect this duty, their opponents will be entitled to score them off.   4. As neither absence from town, nor any other cause, will be held as an excuse for not playing the champion matches, all parties are recommended to avail them-selves of the first fine weather to play them. (For mode of drawing, &c., see Section V.)

XXXV.
SINGLE-HANDED MATCHES.

1. Single-handed Matches for the Championship, and other club games, are not to be stopped by any one, unless all the other spaces of the Green are occupied.   2. When so occupied, not more than one single-handed match to be played at a time.   3. The last match begun to be the first stopped, and the score, as it then stands, to be marked, and the match played out on a future occasion.

XXXVI.
MATCH AMONG THE MEMBERS.

When the Members are about to play a Match among themselves, the players to be divided as equally as possible by two of their number, agreed upon at the time, who shall toss for the first choice.

XXXVII.
MATCH WITH ANOTHER CLUB – APPOINTING OF DRIVERS AND OTHER PLAYERS.

1. When about to engage in a Match with another Club, the office-bearers to appoint the drivers.   2. The drivers, afterwards, to meet and make choice of their associates, arrange them in the order of play, and intimate to the parties so chosen, their appointment and position in the rink.

In some Clubs the directors, when preparing to play matches, select the whole players, and arrange them in the order they are to play. By this operation, the driver has no choice either in the selection or classing of the players. As the social well-being and prosperity of a Club depends in a great degree on the manner and practice in which members are selected to play at important matches, great care, and a nice discrimination, is at all times necessary to be used in their selection. Almost all players desire to take a part in them, but, as the object is to win, the best players only ought to be selected, and generally are so, but there is perhaps a tendency to abide by the same players on every occasion, particularly if they have once been successful. This, however, is an error, and gives rise to dissatisfaction amongst those members who can, perhaps, play equally as well, and yet, are seldom or never selected to play at matches. Their best mode, under such circumstances, is to challenge to combat the selected parties; when, if the challengers prove successful, they thereby establish a claim to be selected on the next occasion.

XXXVIII.
PRIZE MATCHES – LOCAL COMPETITION – CLUB *versus* CLUB – ON NEUTRAL GREENS.

1. The game shall consist of 31 heads.   2. The whole of the matches must be played by each Club on a neutral green.   3. No Club to play more than one rink on the same green.   4. As soon as the game is finished, each driver shall return a note of the score of his rink to the general Secretary.   5. When the whole of the returns have been received, the general Secretary shall sum them up, and read the result to the parties assembled.   6. He shall afterwards declare the name of the winning club, and present the Prize to the President of it, if present, or if absent, to his accredited substitute.

XXXIX.
ARRANGEMENT OF LOCAL CLUB MATCHES FOR THE SEASON.

At the general meetings held in March by the various Clubs, delegates shall be appointed for the purpose of considering and agreeing upon the time and place that the various Matches for the season shall take place. The delegates to meet on the first Thursday of May; and the arrangements, when completed, to be printed, and a copy of them to be posted in a conspicuous part of the Bowl-house of each Club.

XL.
GENERAL RULE.

1. Many of the preceding Rules have no penalties attached to them, and all are framed on the understanding that none of them will be wilfully violated.   2. When any of them are violated that have penalties annexed, the penalty cannot be enforced after the next played bowl has stopped.   3. When the bowls or jack are displaced, contrary to rule, the opposite party to have the right of replacing them.   4. Parties who have occasion to use the measuring tapes, are requested to be careful of them, as when roughly dealt with, they are easily put out of order.

XLI.
INJURING THE GREEN.

Players are strictly prohibited from riding bowls up and down the Green after a game is finished. They are also particularly requested not to play long jacks when the Green is soft, or to deface or injure it in any manner.

Index